The Brazilians

Their Character and Aspirations

The Texas Pan American Series

The Brazilians

Their Character and Aspirations

BY JOSÉ HONÓRIO RODRIGUES

Translated by Ralph Edward Dimmick
Foreword and Additional Notes by E. Bradford Burns

UNIVERSITY OF TEXAS PRESS, AUSTIN AND LONDON

The Texas Pan American Series is published with the assistance of a revolving fund established by the Pan American Sulphur Company and other friends of Latin America in Texas. Publication of this book was also assisted by a grant from the Rockefeller Foundation through the Latin American translation program of the Association of American University Presses.

Printed in the United States of America
by the Printing Division of The University of Texas, Austin
Bound by Universal Bookbindery, Inc., San Antonio

Foreword

"No one knows for certain what Brazil is. Rip apart the interior, scruti-
nize all the physical secrets. Close the frontiers and count the inhabitants.
Examine thus the body of Brazil. But what of the soul? Who knows
Brazil's soul? When was it that Brazil revealed itself?"* These are the
statements and questions of a Brazilian intellectual attempting to define
and to understand his enormous and complex land. Brazil has long been
a country in search of its own meaning and mission.

Early in their history Brazilians began to puzzle over their surround-
ings and their relation to them. The literati studied, analyzed, and
debated those subjects. Ambrósio Fernandes Brandão in 1618 made
probably the first effort to interpret Brazil in his informative *Diálogos das
Grandezas do Brazil* ("Dialogues concerning the Grandeurs of Brazil"),
a praise of his adopted land set in the form of a series of refutations of
commonly repeated criticisms of Brazil in the early seventeenth century.
His carefully written and convincingly argued study was the culmination
of a century of works written to laud and to describe the new land, its
lush vegetation, exotic fauna, mysterious Indians, lucrative resources,
and—above all else—its limitless potential.

In the centuries which followed, other Brazilians contributed their
interpretations. The eighteenth century produced an entire school of
nativistic writers—André João Antonil (pseudonym for Giovanni Antonio Andreoni), Sebastião da Rocha Pitta, José de Santa Rita Durão,
Gaspar da Madre de Deus, to mention only a few—who pondered the
meaning and the mission of Brazil. Independence in 1822 so exhilarated
that school that the bucolic nativists became fiery nationalists. Still, of
all the introspective studies of their homeland made by Brazilians in the
nineteenth century, none surpassed in perception and clarity the single
essay of a Bavarian botanist, Karl Friedrich Philipp von Martius, who
spent the years 1817–1820 journeying throughout Brazil. Much later, in
1843, he wrote his provocative essay "Como se deve escrever a história

* Afonso Arinos de Melo Franco, *Preparação ao Nacionalismo* (Rio de Janeiro:
Civilização Brasileira, 1934), p. 179.

do Brasil" ("How the History of Brazil Should Be Written"). Martius
was the first to appreciate the fact that Brazil's unique quality derived
from the cultural fusion—still in process—of the aboriginal Indian inhabitant, the imported African slave, and the European settler. Each
contributed to the formation of a distinctly Brazilian civilization. In that
amalgamation of races, Martius saw the key to understanding Brazil.

Nationalism waxed during the last decades of the nineteenth century.
As the new century opened, the intellectuals determined to define their
nation, its character, and its aspirations. Afonso Celso heralded the new
search with his blatantly optimistic *Porque me Ufano do meu País*
("Why I Am Proud of My Country"). The antithesis of Afonso Celso's
florid catalog of national virtues and blessings was Paulo Prado's *Retrato
do Brasil* ("Portrait of Brazil") written in the late 1920's. Its opening
sentence sets the depressingly pessimistic tone: "In a radiant land lives a
sad people." His exposure of Brazilian weaknesses was intended to be
the first step toward rectifying them. The works of Afonso Celso and
Paulo Prado represent the two extremes in the intensified effort in the
twentieth century toward national psychoanalysis. Between those two
extremes stand a variety of other worthy studies, all products of the first
half of the twentieth century: Plínio Salgado, *Psicologia da Revolução*
("Psychology of the Revolution"); Sérgio Buarque de Holanda, *Raízes
do Brasil* ("The Roots of Brazil"); Afonso Arinos de Melo Franco,
Introdução à Realidade Brasileira ("Introduction to the Reality of
Brazil") and *Conceito da Civilização Brasileira* ("An Understanding
of Brazilian Civilization"); and Gilberto Freyre, *Brazil: An Interpretation*, later published in Portuguese under the title *Interpretação do
Brasil*, and still later expanded into *New World in the Tropics*. Freyre
has made a number of other interpretive studies, the most significant of
which is *The Masters and the Slaves*; the first Portuguese-language edition, bearing the title *Casa Grande e Senzala*, dates from 1934 and the
first English translation appeared in 1946. In *The Masters and the Slaves*
Freyre perfects the idea first advanced by Martius: Brazil's unique
civilization results from the biological and cultural fusion of three races.

It is to this school of interpretive studies of Brazil that the present
work of José Honório Rodrigues belongs. In a now well-established tradition, Rodrigues confronts the questions of who and what the Brazilian
is, what Brazil stands for, where it has been, and where it is going. He
seeks to understand and to explain his nation. In order to do so, he poses
two questions: what are the national characteristics and what are the

national aspirations? Both questions are complex; yet, in the pages
which follow, the reader will find well-reasoned answers. Professor Rodrigues reveals how the Brazilians define themselves and how outsiders
define them, what they aspire to be, the way in which they want to develop. A wealth of information on growth and development and abundant statistics substantiate these answers. The answers are, I believe,
quite realistic. The author avoids the weaknesses of Afonso Celso and
his followers, and the reader will detect notes of pride and optimism
which eschew the dreary extremism of Paulo Prado. Rodrigues succeeds
in skirting Scylla as well as Charybdis.

   This book quite obviously is about Brazil. Yet, on one level, it has a
much broader approach, as it is also about an underdeveloped country
which shares much in common with other underdeveloped countries in
Latin America, Africa, and Asia. According to the author, the aspirations of the Brazilian people are independence and sovereignty; territorial integrity; effective occupation of the entire national territory; national unity; a balance between centralism and regionalism; improved
communications and transportation; the psychosocial integration of all
inhabitants through miscegenation, racial tolerance, and acculturation
of immigrants; social justice; democratic, representative government;
diminution of the powers of the oligarchy; economic development; universal education; and improved health care. These might well be the
aspirations of the people of Burundi or Burma, Tanzania or Thailand,
Ecuador or Ethiopia. On the broadest level, then, we have a case study
of the aspirations of underdeveloped peoples. Professor Rodrigues ap-
preciates this larger application of his ideas but chooses to apply them
to his more specific topic. He makes these aspirations particularly Brazilian by placing them within the context of Brazilian history, for above
all else he is a historian. Intimately familiar with the Brazilian past, he
has drawn freely from it in his analysis. And Brazil has had, as Rodrigues' comments and allusions reveal, a fascinating history.

   Brazil was discovered in 1500 by a Portuguese fleet, under the command of Pedro Álvares Cabral, while it was en route to India from
Lisbon. Trade with the East took precedence over the newly found land
in the West until other Europeans began to poach on that territory in
search of brazilwood and by their presence threatened Portuguese sea
lanes in the South Atlantic. In 1534, to encourage colonization, the Portuguese monarch divided his lands in the New World into fifteen
captaincies and distributed them among twelve of his courtiers. Because

they proved to be ineffective settlers the crown centralized control under a governor general in 1549, the date when the colonization of Brazil began in earnest.

The first task was to wrest the long coast from hostile Indians and clear it of European interlopers. Having accomplished that by 1616, the Luso-Brazilians next turned their attention to the conquest of the interior, their second major task. The intrepid *bandeirante*, that explorer in search of Indian slaves or precious metals, set out for the hinterland and eventually carried the Portuguese flag to the foothills of the towering Andes. Too late Spain realized what was happening in South America and the Spanish monarch was forced to concede to Portugal the lands which the Luso-Brazilians had explored and scantily populated. The Treaty of Madrid (1750) demarcated Brazil's frontiers along lines surprisingly similar to those of today.

From the interior the *bandeirantes* sent back Indian slaves, always too few in number and reluctant to adapt themselves to forced labor on the sugar plantations and in the mines. A more adaptable work force was found in Africa. Ships brought increasing numbers of slaves to bear the burden of Brazil's development. Gold, discovered in 1695, infused a new prosperity into Brazil, whose once lucrative sugar trade had encountered increasing competition from the Caribbean colonies for the European market.

Consolidation was the final phase of the colonial period, 1750–1822. Sebastião José de Carvalho e Mello, better known as the Marquis of Pombal, dominated the reign of José I, King of Portugal from 1750 to 1777, first as foreign minister and then as prime minister. Pombal unified and centralized Brazil by amalgamating the states of Maranhão and Brazil, abolishing all remaining hereditary captaincies, and restricting the authority of the municipalities. Brazilian unity in the national period owes much to the centralization imposed by Pombal. At the same time the ideas of the European Enlightenment began to penetrate Brazil. The elite in the small but growing urban centers imbibed those heady doctrines and expressed its dissatisfaction with the metropolis, turning soon to plotting against Portugal—as shown by the *inconfidências* in Minas Gerais (1789) and Bahia (1798) and by the revolution in Pernambuco (1817).

Brazilian history took a novel turn in 1807 when the Portuguese royal family fled Lisbon for Rio de Janeiro barely in advance of the French occupation. Enjoying life in Rio de Janeiro, King João VI lingered there until 1821, long after Napoleon's armies had been expelled from Portugal. At last, he reluctantly returned to Libson, leaving the Bragança heir, Prince Pedro, in Rio de Janeiro as regent of the Kingdom of Brazil, the former colony having been raised to equality with Portugal in 1815. The Côrtes (parliament) in Lisbon exerted every effort to reduce Brazil to its previous colonial condition, but the Brazilians refused to allow their status to be lowered. Won over to the Brazilian side by the patriot and savant José Bonifácio, Prince Pedro declared Brazil's independence on September 7, 1822. Brazil became independent in name only, however; the colonial structures and institutions remained. When Emperor Pedro I was deposed in 1831 he left the New World with his Portuguese retinue. The Brazilians for the first time began to govern themselves. As the Brazilian-born heir to the throne, Pedro II, was too young to rule, regents governed in the name of the child emperor. Without the control of a firm and respected authority, centrifugal forces, numerous in such an immense and varied land, tore the nation asunder. Permanent disunion threatened. Politicians of all hues looked to the crown to save the nation. As a consequence Pedro II assumed the exercise of his sovereignty in 1840, some four years before his legal majority. The hoped-for result took place: peace and stability returned. The unity of the nation was preserved.

During the long rule of Pedro II (1840–1889) the Empire progressed materially, coffee earned high returns as the principal export, and the cities grew in size and importance. The new urban class and the powerful coffee planters began to challenge the traditional control of the sugar-plantation aristocrats—the chief supporters of the monarchy. Unlike the once-affluent but now-impoverished sugar-planter class of the Northeast, the emerging urban-coffee alliance favored change. Cities in particular became centers of agitation. After 1870 new ideas aiming at the disestablishment of the church, manumission of the slaves, and proclamation of a federal republic radiated from the urban centers. When the monarchy had alienated the three groups that traditionally supported it —the sugar-plantation owners, the church, and the military—it fell, being totally unable to mount any resistance and finding no defenders.

The Republic proclaimed in 1889 represented principally the powerful coffee interests and the new urban classes. The economic center of the nation had shifted from the sugar-producing Northeast to the coffee-producing Southeast. Political power shifted accordingly. São Paulo and its coffee-growing allies, Minas Gerais and Rio de Janeiro, dominated the Old Republic (1889–1930), a political control broken only by the revolution of the Liberal Alliance, which brought Getúlio Vargas to power. Brazil was already in the process of industrialization—a process to which both world wars and even the depression of the 1930's gave a powerful impetus.

When the Brazilians resolved to industralize they also—knowingly or unknowingly—resolved to destroy much of their colonial heritage with its feudal characteristics. Industrialization and feudalism obviously were incompatible. Since 1930 an ever more intense struggle has been waged between those who want to preserve the old Brazil and those who desire to create a new system and modern structures. The struggle is traumatic. Since World War II, as Professor Rodrigues amply illustrates, the urbanization and the industrialization of Brazil have been rapid. Both developments inevitably threaten the archaic elements of Brazilian society with change and reform. A third tendency notable in Brazilian development from 1945 until 1964 also threatens the traditionalists: increased democratization.

For the moment, that laudable tendency to strengthen democracy has been halted if not reversed. Democracy in Brazil—in all Latin America —suffered a severe blow on April 1, 1964, when the military, usually well behaved in Brazil, overthrew the President and seized power. This time, contrary to all precedent, the officers kept power. They refused to retire to the barracks. In rapid succession the military government disbanded all political parties, imposed censorship, packed the Supreme Court, deprived over 400 citizens of their political rights for ten years —including such internationally respected figures as Juscelino Kubitschek and Celso Furtado—intervened in the state governments, and dismissed legally elected governors, senators, and representatives. In short, the military interrupted the progress and continuity of Brazilian history.

The imposition of this unfortunate military dictatorship occurred after José Honório Rodrigues wrote this book. Consequently, the reader will find references in the text to some institutions which ceased to exist in 1964. For example, the author discusses political parties, which were disbanded forcibly in 1965. He also refers to public-opinion polls, which, in the context of events from 1964 to the present, would doubtless reflect different results than they did during the heyday of democratic growth, 1945–1964. Still, I do not believe that the events after April 1, 1964, invalidate Rodrigues' conclusions respecting the Brazilian character and national aspirations. Professor Rodrigues is speaking of the vast majority of Brazilians and of their hopes. This present aberration is but a pause in Brazil's development, brought about by a military minority in alliance with the most reactionary elements of Brazilian society and with the approval of myopic foreign governments. If it does anything, the military dictatorship will strengthen the Brazilian character and aspirations discussed in this book.

The American public is indebted to José Honório Rodrigues for his interpretation of the fifth largest and eighth most populous nation in the world, a nation which Arnold Toynbee predicted will be among the great powers of the next century, a prediction Brazilians enjoy making too, as evidenced by Pimentel Gomes' recent book, *O Brasil entre as Cinco Maiores Potências ao Fim dêste Século* ("Brazil among the Five Major Powers by the End of This Century"). The first work of Rodrigues' to appear in English was an essay on a nineteenth-century Brazilian historiographer, "Alfredo do Vale Cabral, 1851–1894," *Inter-American Review of Bibliography*, VIII (1958), 3–30. Several other essays and articles followed: "The Influence of Africa on Brazil and Brazil on Africa," *Journal of African History*, III (1962), 49–67; "The Foundations of Brazil's Foreign Policy," *International Affairs*, XXXVIII (1962), 324–338; "Webb's Great Frontier and the Interpretation of Modern History" in *The New World Looks at Its History*, edited by Archibald R. Lewis and Thomas F. McCann (Austin: University of Texas Press, 1963); "Brazil and China: The Varying Fortunes of Independent Policy," in *Policies toward China. Views from Six Continents*, edited by A. M. Halpern (New York: Council on Foreign Relations, 1965); and three historiographical essays in *Perspectives on Brazilian History*, edited by E. Bradford Burns (New York: Columbia University Press, 1967). In 1965 his book on Afro-Brazilian relations was translated into English and published by the University of California as *Brazil and Africa*. This book is his second to be translated into English.

A knowledge of Portuguese would allow the reader to become much better acquainted with Professor Rodrigues. His bibliography is extensive and space does not permit me to present it here. I do feel, however, that mention should be made of some of his outstanding books: *Civilização Holandesa no Brasil* (São Paulo: Companhia Editôra Nacional, 1940); *Teoria de História do Brasil* (São Paulo: Instituto Progresso Editorial, 1949), 2d ed., 2 vols. (Rio de Janeiro: Civilização Brasileira, 1957); *Brasil, Período Colonial* (Mexico: Instituto Panamericano de Geografía e Historia, 1953); *Brasil e Africa* (Rio de Janeiro: Civilização Brasileira, 1961), 2d ed. rev. (Rio de Janeiro: Civilização Brasileira, 1964), translated by Richard A. Mazzara and Sam Hileman as *Brazil and Africa* (Berkeley: University of California Press, 1965); *Conciliação e Reforma* (Rio de Janeiro: Civilização

Brasileira, 1965); and, of course, this present work, first published in São Paulo by the Editôra Fulgor in 1963 and reprinted in 1965. In addition Rodrigues has contributed profusely to scholarly journals both in Brazil and abroad. He has been one of the most prolific, perceptive, and competent of contemporary Brazilian historians.

In Brazil, where history is generally the avocation of the dilettante, the study and writing of history have been the vocation of this author. He has held with distinction a series of research appointments which put him into constant contact with the Brazilian past: technical assistant at the National Book Institute, professor of Brazilian history and diplomatic history at the Rio Branco Institute of Itamaraty (the Ministry of Foreign Affairs), chief of the Research Division of the Rio Branco Institute, professor in the School of Sociology and Politics of the Catholic University in Rio de Janeiro, director of the Rare Book Collection of the National Library, and director of the National Archives. Presently he is executive director of the Brazilian Institute of International Relations and professor of the economic history of Brazil at the University of Guanabara.

Like many other historians in Brazil, José Honório Rodrigues entered the domain of Clio from the broader realm of law and the social sciences. When he received his degree from the University of Brazil in 1937, the study of Brazilian history was just beginning in the universities. In 1933 the Catholic University in São Paulo was the first to establish such a course. The following year the University of São Paulo added a similar chair. From its founding in 1935, the University of the Federal District (then Rio de Janeiro) offered courses in Brazilian civilization. The alma mater of Senhor Rodrigues did not offer a course in Brazilian history until 1939. Rodrigues, therefore, was obliged to initiate himself in the study of Brazilian history. He began with a broad reading program which emphasized European thinkers and historians—Georg Wilhelm Friedrich Hegel, Karl Marx, Wilhelm Dilthey, Gustav Radbruch, Heinrich Rickert, Max Weber, Ernst Troeltsch, Ernst Cassirer, and Jakob Burckhardt. The European historians who exerted the strongest influence on his formation were Henri Pirenne, Johan Huizinga, George Macaulay Trevelyan, and Arnold Toynbee. He became acquainted with the works of American historians as well, among whom he has shown a preference for Charles A. Beard and Frederick Jackson Turner, the former for his economic interpretations of history and the latter for his geographic interpretations. On more than one occasion Rodrigues has compared Turner's concept of the frontier with João Capistrano de

Abreu's theory of the influence of the interior on Brazilian development.

It is not surprising that Capistrano de Abreu was the Brazilian historian who most affected Rodrigues. Capistrano was the first who could look beyond the facts to their meaning and significance. Like some of the European and American models whom Rodrigues revered most, Capistrano knew how to analyze, synthesize, and criticize. When as a student Rodrigues read the impressive *Capítulos de História Colonial*, he became at once an admirer of Capistrano de Abreu and has been a devoted disciple ever since. As a tribute to that influential book and its author, he made a definitive edition, the fourth, of *Capítulos*. He served as both secretary and president of the Sociedade Capistrano de Abreu and edited the three-volume *Correspondência de Capistrano de Abreu*, the introduction to which contains Rodrigues' masterful essay "Capistrano de Abreu e a Historiografia Brasileira," the best study yet written on that great scholar.

Two Brazilian social historians, Oliveira Viana and Gilberto Freyre, likewise influenced Rodrigues. As a student, he knew the former and was an assistant to the latter. He admired both men for their philosophical insight and their interpretive analysis.

Professor Rodrigues is himself a critical, analytical, and interpretive historian. He disdains the lifeless factual exposition so characteristic of Brazilian historiography and laments the absence of a general history of Brazil which is meaningful and well written. There are good histories of the colonial period or of the Empire or of one or another aspect of Brazilian development. However, there is no sweeping and meaningful study from the discovery to the present. Rodrigues sets the writing of such an interpretive synthesis as his major goal. Certainly he has been preparing himself well to undertake such an assignment. His books and articles on Brazilian historiography reveal a keen insight into and an appreciation of the past. Other works—of which this book is representative—display his ability to interpret and to synthesize.

The contributions of José Honório Rodrigues in this book are many: he analyzes his country's contemporary politics, characterizes his compatriots, supplies a historical interpretation of Brazil, and codifies Brazil's motivating aspirations. It is fortunate that the book has been translated into English. Americans—who only now are realizing that they must reckon with Brazil—will find José Honório Rodrigues a sure guide to understanding this emergent nation manifestly destined to achieve world importance.

E. Bradford Burns

Note: Footnotes marked by numerals appeared in the original work, with the exception of about a half dozen that were added by the author for this edition. Those marked by other symbols were supplied by E. Bradford Burns.

Preface

Under the influence of its leading factfinder, the highly Germanic, highly authoritative, intransigent defender of reason of state Francisco Adolfo de Varnhagen, Brazilian historiography has, as Capistrano de Abreu said, been molded with an iron hand.* Everything that failed to come up to officially approved standards, every failure to conform, every evidence of radicalism was rejected or reproved. For the professionals and for the elite, Varnhagen's *História Geral do Brasil*[1] ("General History of Brazil") represents a remarkable effort, an extraordinary service from the viewpoint of research, of the accumulation of data, and of the establishment of dates, names, and facts. It is a milestone in Brazilian historical writing, but it attributes only marginal importance to the common people, who, however, were the true forgers of the country's material development and of Brazilian national character. Varnhagen's view served the purposes of the dominant elite and became incorporated into its ideology. His view set a seal of approval on Portuguese colonial policy in Brazil; it reinforced the thesis favoring the survival of obsolete, archaic institutions; it rejected every radical concept or idea of reform that appeared in the colonial period and that had a role in the struggle for independence or in the various rebellions that shook the country.

Ever since, this conservative line of thought has predominated in the interpretation of Brazilian history, despite the attempts of a few—such as Capistrano de Abreu, João Ribeiro, and Euclides da Cunha—to provide a new orientation in the years from 1900 to 1907. As their work was not of a general nature, being of the essay type or dealing with periods or episodes, it lacked the bulk required, if not to overcome, at least to counterbalance the conservative influence of Varnhagen. These three writers began what Francisco de Assis Barbosa has called "a Mod-

---

* Francisco Adolfo de Varnhagen (1816–1878) was the first Brazilian national historian of importance. João Capistrano de Abreu (1853–1927) was doubtless the most important of Brazil's historians. He achieved a brilliant synthesis in his writings, most notable in his *Caminhos Antigos e Povoamento do Brasil, Capítulos de História Colonial, 1500–1800,* and *Ensaios e Estudos.*

[1] Francisco Adolfo de Varnhagen, *História Geral do Brasil.*

ernist revolution in history," owing either to their choice of topics or to their manner of interpretation. Since, according to the conservative theory, the populace has no part in the historical process, the privileges and benefits which the state can confer belong by right to the real or titular holders of power. This myth has contributed still further to rendering the elite sterile and lacking in creativity; it has brought about a leadership vacuum which has greatly harmed the country and would have done so to a further extent were it not for the sterling qualities of the common people.

In a country which has been living in a state of volatility, the problem of overcoming the crises of growth has been aggravated by this vacuum and, simultaneously, by the presence of false leaders of the agitator type, restless and dominated by feelings of shame and guilt. It is those feelings which are responsible for the long-winded outbursts in which they defend their own honor and attack that of others. They forget that the only honor important in history is national or public honor. In conformity with Varnhagen's view of reason of state, however, no history has taken the common people into account or expressed a belief in the value of their services. Some historians took fright at what the consequences might be if their studies of the past were carried forward to more recent periods. Some drew back and, turning from their initial attempts at renovation, subjected themselves completely to the dominant view, as established by Varnhagen, of the benefits of the quasi-feudal Portuguese colonial structure, praising it as he had done. Still others attributed the evils of Brazil to the populace, which they transformed into the villain of the country's history: The nation's capital defects derived from the covetousness of the Portuguese, the sensuality of the Negro, and the indolence of the Indian. Nothing could be done about it: Brazil was all wrong, for that reason and for that reason alone. A dominant minority had created all that was good and civilized in the country; consequently, it was the sole personage worthy of emphasis in the pages of history. Since the populace was to be deplored and since history had been made by the minority, just as government was conceived as government by the elite, so also history was conceived as the history of the elite.

There has always been a profound disdain in Brazil for national reality, especially on the part of the dominating minority, whose successive generations have held power ever since the winning of independence. Tradition is the sacred name invoked in the battle against innovations and changes proposed by rationalists and radicals. Brazil has always been the prey of an antipolitical sentiment which, viewing political ideals and principles as abstractions and distortions, has concealed national reality or conjured it out of sight. National reality is a sum of regional realities, of contrasts and similarities. Only rarely has it been captured. It was a Frenchman, Jacques Lambert,* who had a vision of "the two Brazils." There are many realities. There is an official reality, better expressed by the national budget than in the constitution or in presidential messages; there is a practical-theoretical reality, which many writers in the fields of fiction and of the social and historical sciences seize upon, to the displeasure or suspicion of the political opportunist; and there is a marginal reality, which is not foreign to the course of history, but which is ignored by official history and policy. In a country in which the sphere of the possible greatly exceeds that of the real, as José Bonifácio said, people rub their eyes and do not believe what they see. Reality or realism is a myth to the minority. The problem consists in knowing whether the confusion of the real with the possible or of myth with reality is the result of insuperable difficulties or of a generalization of the ineptness that is characteristic of the elite.

Reality has been captured in fragments, in segments of life, by some writers, through intuition or study; it has been discerned in certain phases by creative leaders who were exiled or expelled from participation in the nation's historical development, or who gave up, or committed suicide, or compromised themselves by acts of conformity or conciliation; and, finally, it has been perceived by the common people, whose role, though unappreciated, represents the great success story in Brazilian history, just as the role played by the dominant minority is a disappointment.

The time for change has come, however, and the giant will arise and move forward under the direction of creative minorities inspired in the interest of the common people and the nation. In view of its size† and great expectations, Brazil does not wish to run the risk of a major explosion. Excitement over growth, with an increased hope for more educated people, better housing, larger salaries, and better standards of living, is no mere hullabaloo raised for the benefit of political orators. It expresses concern for more civilized ways of life and for an end to

---

* The fascinating study of Brazil made by Jacques Lambert is *Le Brésil: Structure sociale et Institutions politiques.*

† Brazil in 1967 boasts a population of over eighty million, a fraction of what this nation, the fifth largest in the world, with 3,286,169 square miles, could support. About two thirds of the population is concentrated in the one third of the territory fronting on the Atlantic Ocean.

the archaic feudal relics of colonial times which have remained imbedded in national existence.

There is, in fact, a general desire for structural change, for new forms of administration that satisfy national interests and popular aspirations. I realize that the expression "national interest" is used in a vague, abstract sense. Nevertheless, it has an objective, practical sense, as the constitution itself recognizes. National interest is what serves the interests of the common people and the federal union, in whose name the nation was constituted.

Consequently, a new view must be taken of history, a view that recognizes the virtues and the achievements of the common people and sees that the populace is assigned its due place in the body politic. Fortunately, this has been done recently in a few pioneering works in the social sciences and in fiction, the last-mentioned being the farthest in the van. The heart and the hands of the common people have made Brazil what it is and not what the elite would like it to be. For this reason it is necessary to eliminate the pseudo happening or pseudo fact—a piece of information which is true, but which is silly, insignificant, and empty, and which conveys a false view of historical development. Hence the false legends and the depressive effects created by certain works of elite tendencies which seek merely to uphold outworn privileges and ensure the persistence of traditional patterns, or to explain away failures of leadership and justify the condemnations pronounced by certain groups, the basis for which is nothing but intolerance.

Brazilian history has neglected the common people and concentrated on the role played by leaders, praising them without passing judgment on their responsibilities. The populace has always been presented as a fearsome specter—fatalistic, subservient, gloomy, vegetating in indifference to pseudo happenings. Leaders have always been made to appear capable, gallant, efficient, brilliant, roseate, hindered from advancing by *hoi polloi*. But past history, like the future, represents a hope if it uncovers errors, reveals what is sound, and clears the way for the development of positive values by removing the inhibitions occasioned by a falsely roseate presentation of the past.

It would be neither desirable nor right to deny the greatness of figures who struggled in the past to create the future. In the case of a historiography dominated by attention to personalities and biography, however, it is good not to forget that the ways of elder generations—what is termed tradition, as opposed to truth—can result in inertia and have regressive effects.

This book was born of a desire to see contemporary events in their historical perspective. It is suggestive rather than exhaustive; it seeks to arrive at understanding rather than judgment. Briefly, I believe that it presents a few new viewpoints—which may be the object of controversy —without any attempt at sweeping the past under the carpet. It makes no pretense at building up anyone's hopes, but its optimistic tone (indicative of a belief in salvation rather than in the damnation in which certain indignant political leaders place their trust) represents a position taken in opposition to the antipopular theses of certain currents of Brazilian historical and biographical writing. The Brazilian people suffer from economic and cultural deficiencies, as their history plainly indicates, but they have shown themselves capable of singular deeds and undertakings.

The Brazilians: Their Character and Aspirations was written under the incitement of a moment of great creative hopes in the nation's life and of the enthusiasm generated by recent decades of development. Despite the attendant inflation, the creation of Brasília brought a faith in the future such as had rarely been known in Brazil. But the truth is that the course of Brazilian history does not follow a straight line of development but a cyclical path, with phases of advance and phases of retreat, in view of the formidable resistance offered by certain economic groups and reactionary leaders. Periods of progress are followed by times of stagnation, depending on leaders, economic conditions, and international situations.

The dispute dates from the revolution of 1930,* regarded by some as a creative movement, characterized by industrialization, nationalism, and development, and considered by others as a chaotic eruption of the forces of destruction, corruption, and subversion. In the first case the spirit of optimism prevails; in the second, that of indignation. As no one can escape from history, and as the present cannot be held of secondary importance, these stages of acceleration and retardation ill conceal the final victory of national aspirations. Following their line of evolution, they will eventually break the chains of reaction which bar their way and put an end to the policy of advancing only by short, deliberate steps.

The policy of retreat initiated by the *coup d'état* of April, 1964,† which interrupted democratic legality and the great political and civic debate on the subject of national reforms, was not an unforeseen eventu-

* The revolution of 1930 brought Getúlio Vargas to power.
† A military *coup d'état* overthrew President João Goulart and put the military in control of Brazil's destiny on April 1, 1964.

ality, as can be discerned from passages of this essay. The false road taken by the National Democratic Union and other parties of the right, the deformed view of the evils of corruption (present in Brazilian history, as in that of other countries, ever since colonial days), the struggle against Communism (the dangers of which were exaggerated with a view to silencing inconformity and crushing less radical aspirations), the blockade raised against popular and labor-union leadership (despite the fact that it is demagogic and incompetent), the trust in popular respect for authority—all breed today as in the past the tendencies to *coups d'état* and conspiracies, which unfortunately characterize the political history of the country to a greater extent than is supposed.

As can be seen from this essay, if revolutions are not characteristic of Brazilian history, as is supposed by some American and European scholars who are wont to present a false view of the Brazilians, this does not mean that the nation's evolution was always a peaceful one. More characteristic of Brazil than revolution, whether bloody or peaceful, is conspiracy. One year after gaining its independence Brazil suffered its first *coup d'état* with the dissolution of the constitutional assembly on November 12, 1823.*

"Today rascals are having their day," José Bonifácio said to General José Manuel de Morais, the officer sent to arrest him. And from that time on, such days have succeeded one another with so great frequency in Brazilian history that the French minister to Brazil, Count Alexis de Saint-Priest, observed that, since no one was capable of governing, everyone engaged in intrigue, and the relation of the government to the opposition was not one of combat but of conspiracy.

He wrote in 1831, on the eve of another coup, of another conspiracy, the head of which, a confirmed conspirator, was to become regent of the Empire. The well-known reports of the French and Austrian ministers at the court show how the Lima e Silva family conspired under the leadership of Francisco the regent,† the father of Luís, the future Duke of Caxias.

The Swedish minister, M. de Ankarloo, whose diplomatic reports remain unpublished in the Royal Swedish Archives, declared flatly that

* Emperor Pedro I dissolved that assembly because of its vehement criticism of the Portuguese (Pedro had been born in Portugal) and because it sought to limit his powers, privileges, and prerogatives. Pedro then, in 1824, promulgated his own constitution, which lasted until the overthrow of the monarchy in 1889.

† When Pedro I abdicated in 1831 his son, Pedro II, was too young to exercise authority. Regents ruled in the name of the young emperor until 1840. Francisco de Lima e Silva was one of the early regents.

the general "was viewed as the demagog in chief, for which reason doubtless he was made regent." Thus are confirmed previously known reports, including that of John Armitage, concerning the discontent, the intrigues, and the conspiracies of the Lima e Silvas. Already at that early date the sole exception was the future Duke of Caxias, the only member of the family who loyally proposed legal means of reacting to Dom Pedro I, as Capistrano de Abreu, Monsignor Pinto de Campos, and Alberto Rangel have reported.

From that time on, conspirators sought support from the army, and conspiracy à la Lima e Silva flourished therein. The conspirators profited while feigning to sacrifice themselves: "It was not to see Brazil ruined," said Francisco de Lima e Silva on the occasion of another little conspiracy aimed at preventing Araújo Lima, the future Marquis of Olinda, from taking office as sole regent, "that I and my family sacrificed ourselves on the seventh of April."

Lack of military discipline was so general and the conspiratory mentality so dominant that it was necessary to dissolve the army, reducing it to a merely symbolic fraction, and to create the National Guard, trained and directed by Major Luís Alves de Lima e Silva, the future Duke of Caxias, who found himself obliged to deny his father, the regent Francisco, and to devote all his efforts and all his force of discipline to the ends of peace in order that throughout the later history of the Empire the army might serve the constitution and legality alone.

From that time on, these two tendencies have alternated in Brazilian history. Predominance of one or the other among those in posts of command has determined in the constantly recurring crises the position of the army and, in consequence, whether constitutional order was to be maintained or to suffer chaotic interruption.

The crises of the Regency period, like those of the early days of the Republic, closely resemble the crises of the present day, both formally and structurally, though there has been an increase in the number of participating elements and in the degree of intensity. For some time the country has been subject to the army's varying inclination to support legality or intervention. This disturbs the nation's rhythm of growth and renders its path difficult; it represents tutelage over the people, who now number more than 85,000,000. These citizens have the right to make decisions at the ballot box independent of the opinion of a few generals, who must answer to history for discrediting the nation, for interrupting the course of democracy, and for provoking the economic costs and damages of their interventions.

The return to democratic legality, with the calling of elections, has at this moment become the most legitimate of national aspirations. The heirs of Caxias should ensure that it is achieved, guaranteeing to the people their rights and imposing on conspirators the triumph of discipline.*

JOSÉ HONÓRIO RODRIGUES

* The Duke of Caxias was a faithful servant of Emperor Pedro II, and, thanks to his powerful position in the army, he guaranteed the subservience of the military to the civilian government of the second emperor, 1840–1889. Subsequent leaders of Brazil's military have been less scrupulous in keeping the military outside politics.

Contents

Illustrations

The Brazilians

Their Character and Aspirations

INTRODUCTION

Political Psychology and the Brazilians

1. National Characteristics

I have brought together in this book two essays which have a close relationship one to another, although they were written at different times. The first was delivered as a lecture in 1957 and later developed for presentation at the Third International Colloquium on Luso-Brazilian Studies (Lisbon, 1957). In that year and during those which preceded, I had been reading a number of studies of a theoretical nature on the topic of national character, a subject which had come to the fore again as a result of World War II, under a guiding inspiration quite different from that which had marked the studies of collective psychology initiated by Wundt and Tarde. Particularly interesting to me among the works published by UNESCO, which had already begun its "Way of Life" series on different peoples, was the study by William Buchanan and Hadley Cantril, *How Nations See Each Other*.[1] The subject gradually gained consistency; theory, particularly in the anthropological field, was developed and found support; sociology and psychology made their contributions to a bibliography which is today quite extensive. A whole body of theories and methods lay ready for use in monographs. At the same time, there was a systematic opposition, led by those who saw in the examination of national character a return to social prejudices that were either outmoded or in the process of becoming so. In nearly all instances this opposition had in mind hereditary character, rather than character as developed within a historic context, and hence subject to change. This was the case of Hamilton Fyfe, in his *The Illusion of National Character*.[2]

If the studies of Geoffrey Gorer[3] and Margaret Mead,[4] owing to their facile generalizations, represent unsatisfactory applications, the sociological work of David Riesman[5] signifies a great advance from both the

[1] UNESCO, *How Nations See Each Other*, by William Buchanan and Hadley Cantril.

[2] Hamilton Fyfe, *The Illusion of National Character*.

[3] Geoffrey Gorer, *The American People: A Study in National Character*.

[4] Margaret Mead, "The Study of National Character," *The Policy Sciences*, edited by D. Lerner and H. D. Lasswell.

[5] David Riesman, *The Lonely Crowd: A Study of Changing American Character*.

theoretical and the practical viewpoints. Character was considered as a product of social patterns which varied with the vicissitudes of history, and which were to be correlated with demographic tendencies. In Riesman's view, the individual benefits by living more or less confined within the uniform of national character imposed upon him by tradition and necessity. Since character is socially conditioned, there is logically a relationship between a given society and the kind or kinds of social character that it produces.

Maurice L. Farber,[6] one of the first to develop methods for research into national character, linked it with history. Social and national character are meshed with history, and history, as a study of change, aids understanding not only of the constant or permanent but also of variations.

The determination of national character cannot, then, be divorced from history. It is impossible to arrive at an understanding of society or politics in themselves alone; they can be understood only in their historical developments. The most important contribution of Riesman, analyzed in an extensive critical study,[7] consists in his having observed, with regard to character, the tendency toward change. This cannot be seen without recourse to history, without the historical variations produced by the dynamic interplay between the permanent and the variable. The historian must face the question, and not abandon it to the anthropologists and sociologists, who, if they have advanced understanding of the problem, have not resolved it.

The path followed in the present presentation, tentative though it may be, is totally different from any taken before. I believe that in order to depict characteristic traits it is necessary to see them from a number of angles. In the case of Brazil, this means seeking, first, the view foreigners have had and currently have of the Brazilians; second, the view the Brazilians have taken and currently take of themselves; and, finally, the relation of these views or images to social and economic structures. For I believe that economic abundance and underdevelopment are the marks, in the course of historic evolution, of Brazilian sufficiencies or insufficiencies.

Once the first part of the essay was written, on a tentative rather than exhaustive basis, since the accounts of only a few of the more representative travelers were examined, the study was laid aside, though I did not

    [6] Maurice L. Farber, "The Problem of National Character: A Methodological Analysis," *The Study of Personality*, edited by Howard Brand, pp. 387–397.

    [7] Seymour M. Lipset and Leo Lowenthal (eds.), *Culture and Social Character*.

put it out of mind. Other tasks and other enthusiasms prevented its completion. Indeed, when I could give thought to the matter, it was to add some other aspect which should be considered. Interesting points occurred to me, and, while I was unable to carry out the necessary research, they still merit mention. As for the second and more difficult part of the study, I could not limit myself to the bibliography of Brazilian character: I would have to establish on the basis of direct knowledge, and not of interpretations, the images which reflected the various currents and periods; I would have to reread the whole body of Brazilian fiction, seeking the true image of Brazilian types and of the social manifestations of Brazilian character. Álvaro Lins recently wrote that "it will be possible to reconstruct and write the whole of Brazilian history on the basis of our literature in prose and verse."[8] If literature can and must be a source of direct knowledge for historians, in the sense that sermons constituted the basis for Bernard Groethuysen's portrait of the moral conscience of the French middle class, it is true that not only literature but also other sources must be examined. Literature, moreover, like history, has in many cases been written from an un-Brazilian viewpoint, on themes utterly foreign to national life. Graça Aranha, one of the leaders of the Modernist movement, wrote in his novel *Canaan*[9] a work which is anti-Brazilian, the literary expression of the colonial complex.

A history of the image of Brazil as seen by the Brazilians—the official image, that of the opposition, that of the political thinkers, that of the different sets, and the popular image—would require a reading of other sources: the annals of the Congress, ministerial reports, speeches from the throne, presidential messages, newspapers and other periodicals, and the whole of folk and popular literature. (Cavalcanti Proença is preparing with care and devotion a bibliography and anthology of the last-mentioned.[10]) How is one to accept merely the naive view of Brazilian stereotypes offered by the present moment, and not seek to learn their origins and the changes through which they have gone? To link character with demographic tendencies, and to relate social changes to economic evolution would require so vast an amount of research that in time my courage or my enthusiasm would flag, since, as I see the matter today, it would be a lifetime task for any one man. Teamwork would be out of the question. Brazilian institutions for studies in the social and

[8] Álvaro Lins, "Sugestão para uma História Literária do Brasil," *Diário de Notícias* (Rio de Janeiro), 22 abril 1962.

[9] José Pereira da Graça Aranha, *Canaan.*

[10] M. Cavalcanti Proença, *Literatura Popular em Verso, Antologia.*

political fields evidence an undisguisable aversion to historical research. Their direction is legalistic; their present interest is exclusively socio-logical; and they suffer from a quasi-imperialism exercised by sociology and anthropology.

I realize, therefore, that this essay leaves much to be desired in many respects, beginning with the material on which it is based, namely, travelers' impressions. One can hardly take sufficient precautions in dealing therewith, in view of the haste with which visitors leap at con-clusions and their lack of understanding; nonetheless, a certain amount can be deduced from their very distortions. As Max Scheller observed, liking is not the only source of comprehension. Dislike is another.

I resolved, however, to publish the essay as it was written in 1957, with merely stylistic corrections. I hope that it may suggest new paths for historical research, whose status in Brazil is currently archaic, owing in part to the medieval dominion exercised by university professors, in part to the nostalgic seduction of the colonial period, and, very par-ticularly, to the survival of an agrarian economic structure and to the outmoded domination of culturally expatriated minorities.

Still other observations should be made with regard to this little essay. In a cultural continent such as Brazil, which shows signs of both develop-ment and underdevelopment, of Africanization and Westernization, of varying levels of historical progress, of both haste and sluggishness in economic and social evolution, time sequences exhibit varying types of conformity and rebellion. Patterns vary in the different Brazils. In one, dominated by tenacious social custom and structure, people learn to live by adaptation rather than by innovation. In another, ceremony and etiquette are of little significance, but there is great sensitivity to expec-tations and to new situations that have presented themselves. In still another, formal etiquette exists alongside rustic crudeness, ceremony alongside offhandedness, custom alongside inexperience. Breaks in his-torical continuity and economic and social incongruities make it even more difficult to express social forms of character. The tendencies, the negative and positive aspects here presented are offered as provisional hypotheses. It would be a denial of reality to view the matter otherwise. There is no single type of Brazilian character, nor is there a series of categories according to which it can be classified. On the other hand, to assert that every Brazilian is in himself a battlefield in which social forces are joined in combat would be the ultimate in individualism; it would defy all scientific treatment. The unity of Brazilian history does not exclude diversity of social forms or variety in the roads taken by social development.

Those who believe that studies on national character imply a static concept should note these two points: first, the desired aim is to behold forms of social conduct as they appear in history, in the course of change, as the obsolete is discarded and as realization comes of what is indispensable; second, a variety of types of social character develop and undergo transformation in a given society, particularly one such as Brazilian society which is in a process of change, seeking to arrive at a synthesis.

For the reasons set forth above, no attempt has been made to define these types. Neither has any attempt been made to determine the essential features of a basic personality, since this, as David Riesman wrote recently,[11] appears to exist only in comic books, not in history books. The attempt has been made, in a one-sided, provisional sketch, to delineate a few general features or characteristics of different types and classes existing in Brazilian society, in the course of its history, according to the picture which foreigners have formed thereof.

An oversimplified formula—the Brazilian is or is not sad, is or is not cordial or hospitable—will not suffice. The key is not to be found in the Indian, or in the Negro, since crossbreeding has resulted in the dissolution of their cultures. Neither is the key supplied by the Portuguese, from whom, since the earliest years of their history, the Brazilians have been drawing increasingly far apart. It does not lie in the frontier, in the backlands, or in the littoral. It is not supplied by the bandit, by the Franco-Europeanized man of culture, by the voodoo cult leader, by the religious fanatic, by the country "colonel,"* by the farm laborer, by the sugar-mill owner, by the plantation master, by the tradesman, by the industrialist. It is not provided by the bigwig, the snob, the slicker, the cultural expatriate, or the *caiado*.[12] The attempt here is made to cover

---

[11] David Riesman, "The Lonely Crowd: A Reconsideration in 1960," Lipset and Lowenthal (eds.), *Culture and Social Character*, p. 426.

* The word "colonel" refers to one of the landed and moneyed country gentlemen, who often held a rank in the militia, frequently that of colonel. By extension the term "colonel" came to identify all of that class. They were not entirely dissimilar to our Kentucky "colonels" of yesteryear.

[12] *Caiado* derives from the verb *caiar*, meaning "to whitewash." It has been applied in Brazil to those persons of dark skin who powder their faces in an attempt to pass for white, less with a view to avoiding racial discrimination, as in the United States, than with the aim of being taken for members of the upper classes, which are predominantly white in composition.

all this and something more, and it calls for broader and more serious research.

"We are what came over in Columbus' caravel," Machado de Assis wrote in 1876. This is a moot question. A classic orthodox view holds that the Brazilians are neo-Europeans.[13] "Let us ask ourselves, rather," Professor J. L. Faure wrote in 1936, "what will become of Europe, the mother of civilizations, the mother of the Americas, when she sees her overseas children growing in the light of glory, while she herself perhaps is bending her brow to the earth in despair."[14] The Europe-centered concept, so strongly defended by the Brazilian elite and the dominant minorities, was still better defined by Troeltsch,[15] when he inquired as to the position of America with respect to Europeanism. For him America had always been a colony, completely impregnated with the spirit of old Europe; it was bound to follow more and more closely the inner logic of European spiritual development. Its period of colonial provincialism had come to an end; it would advance toward an un- foreseeable future, carrying with it all the forces of Europeanism.

European influence has not remained unshaken, as the persons just mentioned and those who today speak—in a political rather than in a cultural sense—of a Western civilization of American peoples, would seem to believe. Certainly they accept the cultural transformations which have quietly come about as a result of internal change or in consequence of influence actively exerted by immigrant groups, by *caiados*, and by cultural expatriates. They seem to forget, however, that the current cultural situation is the joint product of a variety of factors —of old things forgotten or transformed, of new things absorbed, adapted, or eliminated. The study of history is the study of these changes and of their effects on man and the community. Contact with the Western world has brought about the death of several cultures and has resulted in appalling caricatures, but it is gradually opening the way to synthesis. For even where a Western institution is supposedly accepted without alteration, it does not remain as it was but adapts itself to the general structure of the people who have adopted it. Whatever the reasons therefor—economic, social, or spiritual—the dissolution or decay of a variety of cultures (Indian, Negro, Arabic) tends to bring about a synthesis of such a nature as to forbid speaking of the Brazilians merely in terms of the imitation of Western Europe represented by the

[13] J. Halcro Ferguson, *Latin America: The Balance of Race Redressed.*
[14] J. L. Faure, *O que é e o que será o Brasil.*
[15] Ernst Troeltsch, *Der Historismus und Seine Probleme*, pp. 729–730.

dominant minorities, in terms of the exaggerated caricature represented by other ethnic groups, cut off from their roots in the past, or in terms of cultural transition, void of values, in which magic and witchcraft are dominant forces.

In February, 1819, Bolívar said at Angostura, with remarkable intuition, "We are neither Europeans nor Indians, but an intermediate species between the aborigines and the Spaniards." It is a question of a synthesis in which each succeeding generation seems to be living in a new world, censurable and even incomprehensible in the eyes of its predecessor. "We are Occidentals," declared a rebel against voodoo superstition, the fanaticism of the backlanders, banditry, and present-day hesitation in regard to total alignment with the interests of the so-called Western powers. This takes no account of the tensions represented by the War against the Indians,* the Palmares War,† and the struggles of the backlanders; it takes no account of the marks left by slavery and the Law of Free Birth;[16] it takes no account of blind incomprehension and cruelty, and of the compensations and transitions that were required in order that something new might result from the synthesis of these encounters. In 1915 João José Maria, the leader of the fanatics of the region contested by the states of Paraná and Santa Catarina, gave voice to these tensions, writing: "We've got no land rights; people from Europe can have everything for the asking."[17]

Periods of relative calm alternate with revolutions—attempts to leap forward in history—the effects of which extend and deepen contrasts or shorten phases for arriving at a more advanced synthesis. Interpretative analyses vary in accordance with the background—political as well as cultural—of the researcher. Viana Moog, a son of São Leopoldo, the oldest colony of European settlers in Brazil, of necessity thinks differently from Dias Gomes, a son of Salvador. The former's *Bandeirantes and Pioneers* and the latter's *Journey to Bahia* give brutally contrasting

---

* The War against the Indians (1683–1713) was a particularly bitter struggle between the Luso-Brazilians and the Indians of Ceará and Rio Grande do Norte. It took nearly a generation of intermittent warfare to subdue the Indians.

† Palmares, which existed from 1630 to 1697, was a confederation of settlements of fugitive Negro slaves in the heart of Alagoas. At its maximum Palmares boasted of twenty thousand inhabitants. The Luso-Brazilians made repeated efforts to recapture the Negroes and to destroy their settlements. The final campaign to eradicate Palmares began in 1690, but the last remnants of the runaways held out until 1697.

[16] This law provided that children born to slave mothers after September 28, 1871, were to be free.

[17] Herculano Assunção, *A Campanha do Contestado*, Vol. 1, p. 245.

views of the image of Brazil.[18] The one, purely Occidental, does not carry its rationalization beyond the limits of European comprehension. It is valid but limited in its understanding of the Brazilian cultural synthesis. The other opens a breach between the world of Western values and the supernatural world of Afro-Brazilian society. It portrays conflict and tension. In particular it shows that imposition of totally different standards on popular cultures is mere veneering. Such standards are not organically assimilated: either they provide the culture no strength for growth or they destroy it.

European civilization was not implanted in Brazil without great changes, due to elements both native and foreign—Indian, Negro, Oriental, and Arabic in origin—or without the survival, at the same time, of popular cultures of a mixed type in the backlands—cultures which arose when primitive cultures perished on contact with European civilization, recently reinforced by Euro-American civilization, with its new positive and negative values.

A society of this type, which changes and yet resists change, which seeks a synthesis but encounters so many antithetical elements, presents both essential and marginal differences in the features of its various types of social character. This hypothetical, provisional sketch is merely suggestive and meets only its prime objective: to determine how foreigners have viewed Brazilians.

[18] Clodomir Viana Moog, *Bandeirantes and Pioneers*, translated by L. L. Barrett. Alfredo Dias Gomes, *Journey to Bahia*, adapted from *O Pagador de Promessas* and translated by Stanley Richards.

2. National Aspirations and Political Parties

The second essay, which was written in 1960 and has been revised and enlarged, does not call for many explanations. It is a synthesis of great national aspirations—of permanent objectives that have been achieved once and for all, and of present-day objectives in the process of appearance, achievement, or extinction. The introductory section seeks to show the meaning of those objectives and how they have interacted. Here I wish merely to emphasize that I do not believe that Brazilian history is as "bloodless" as it is currently the fashion to say. In the first place, in the Marxian sense of the word, Brazilian revolutions have not been real revolutions, because they have not aimed at a structural modification of the economy or at a change in social relationships. The traditional landed aristocracy has always had a final veto, with the result that radical changes of the type produced by social revolutions have never occurred. Struggles disturbing the traditional balance of power have taken place between the formally constituted government, representing dominant economic forces, and informal groups desirous of partaking of power and of representing those forces. Attachment to an individual personality is the expression of this social relationship—in the last analysis a holdover from the colonial period.[1]

Open class struggle is more characteristic of societies in a state of growth, in a phase of transition, whereas in societies that are stagnant or slow in evolution, struggles take place between persons of the same standing and of identical situation or interests. It has frequently been said, in scornful tones, that Latin America was conceived in revolution: the very discoverer, Columbus, knew rebellion on the part of Roldán. As I shall emphasize later, revolutions are peculiar to no people or continent, and the personal character of seizures of power without any change in the social relation between classes is not original with Latin America but is characteristic of so-called Western civilization. The only exceptions are represented by Great Britain and the United States, each of which has had but one great revolution in its history. I believe that the role of personality was merely carried to more exaggerated lengths in the semicolonial societies of America, in which, after independence, the same economic structure and the same class and caste relations prevailed as before. The United States is the only society in America in which the break with the past and the colonial structure was complete: the people expected and received land, assistance, roads, and many improvements from the government. In Spanish America and in Brazil, semicolonial governments, poor in resources, had little to offer the people and were dominated by the rural oligarchies.

It is impossible to deny the social characteristics of the War against the Indians (1683–1713), when the natives resisted the take-over of their lands; of the Palmares War (1687–1697); or of innumerable Negro insurrections or social movements, such as that which took place in Bahia in 1798.* Prior to independence, the revolt of 1817 had its

[1] José Honório Rodrigues, "Personalismo e Caráter Nacional," *Jornal do Brasil* (Rio de Janeiro), 23 abril 1957.
* The Revolt of the Alfaiates (Tailors) was one in a series of *inconfidências* against Portugal. This revolt at Bahia in 1798 was significant because it demonstrated that some knowledge of the French Revolution as well as of the French philosophers had penetrated the humbler classes in Brazil. The curious name of this *inconfidência* comes from the fact that a large number of tailors participated in the plotting.

social aspect,* as did the 1833–1836 revolt in Pará known as the "Cabanagem," the rebellion of the "Cabanos" in Pernambuco (1834–1835), the "Balaiada" Revolt in Maranhão (1838–1841), and the "Praieira" Rebellion in Pernambuco (1848–1849).† As Capistrano de Abreu observed, all of these manifestations voiced protest against the age-old wrongs of the oppressed and, one might also add, social and nationalistic demands. Later movements by backlanders or fanatics, involving struggles for land or against social oppression—such as the Canudos War (1893–1897), the revolt which took place from 1912 to 1916 in the area contested by the states of Paraná and Santa Catarina, the Juàzeiro sedition (1913–1914), and the activities of the bandit Lampião—show the bloody side of Brazilian history.‡ The sailors' revolt of 1910, directed against the use of the cat-o'-nine-tails, was not "stupid," as Pedro Calmon described it. The revolts of 1842 in Minas Gerais and São Paulo, the Farrapos (Ragamuffin) Rebellion in Rio Grande do Sul (1835–1845), the Federalist revolt in the South and the revolt of the fleet in the Bay of Rio de Janeiro (1892–1895), the seditions of 1924 and 1926, the rebellions of 1930 and 1932, the coups of 1937 and 1938 were armed uprisings, political movements, attempts at a change of command, the reflections of economic crisis.§ They were not, however, social revolutions; they did not seek to bring about structural reforms, even when victorious. The revolt of 1935, although led by a coalition established on the initiative of the Brazilian Communist Party and under predominantly Communist influence, was not a class struggle, but a military insurrection. In the increasingly difficult economic situation that arose after 1929, a struggle was waged between groups of the same class—the coffee oligarchy, the great landowners, bankers, and industrialists—enjoying limited and varying popular sup-

* A revolt led by the liberals of Recife, Pernambuco, called for the establishment of an independent republic in the Northeast in 1817.

† During the Regency period (1831–1840) revolts occurred throughout Brazil as the central authority declined. The last revolt during the rule of the second emperor was the Praieira Rebellion in Pernambuco, 1848–1849.

‡ The references here are to the definance of state and/or church authority by Antônio Conselheiro in the backlands of Bahia; João Maria, "the monk," in the backlands of the South; Padre Cícero in the backlands of Ceará; and Lampião in the backlands of the Northeast.

§ The seditions of 1924 and 1926 were isolated military uprisings; the rebellion of 1930 opposed to traditional hold of São Paulo over the presidency and brought the southerner Getúlio Vargas to power; the rebellion of 1932 was the reaction of São Paulo against the rebellion of 1930; the coup of 1937 enabled Vargas to extend his administration and to decree the Estado Nôvo; the conflict of 1938 was an effort of the outlawed Integralist Party to seize power.

port. All aspired to power, but in simple terms they can be divided into liberals and conservatives. The rural and urban workers making up the majority of the population did not participate in these movements, which were confined to the middle class and the so-called petty bourgeoisie of the cities. Struggles between different sectors of the oligarchy, between liberals and conservatives, left no bloodstains on Brazilian history: all were settled by compromise, save those of 1935 and 1938.

A bloodless history? Perhaps it can be called so in comparison with the history of the Spanish- and Anglo-American peoples. In any case it is certainly not a bloody history. The reason for this lies not only in the fact that class struggles have never reached bitter proportions but also in the capacity for shrewd compromise which has distinguished the political leaders of the oligarchy—the so-called art of conciliation, which Honório Hermeto Carneiro Leão, Marquis of Paraná, perfected in 1853, but which I believe was born of contact with, and the need for control of, great masses of illiterate, unsatisfied Negroes.[2] Particularly accomplished at this art were the men of Minas Gerais and Bahia—those obliged to deal with the most cruelly exploited populaces in Brazil. A large share of power, or of the delegation of power, always lay in their hands. Anyone with a taste for statistics will soon see that the lion's share always fell to them in exercising command and in representing the nation. Little or nothing was ever done without them. It is not to be forgotten, moreover, that the illiterate were not excluded from the electoral colleges and the ranks of voters during the years from the end of the colonial period to 1881, when the influence of Rui Barbosa succeeded in having them removed from the rolls.[3]

The entrance of the working classes into the political arena, with their organization as a political force, is changing the face of things, and the real struggle between conformity and nonconformity is now beginning. Since 1930 the historical importance of this struggle, with all its implications and complications, cannot be underestimated. The appearance of various urban minorities, the growth of labor organizations, the despair of the middle classes, the populist offensive, the struggles between the various economic, social, and even regional interests, the rise of nationalistic forces, the intolerance exhibited by the oligarchy and the group with international financial connections, the decline of the country

---

[2] See José Honório Rodrigues, *Conciliação e Reforma no Brasil: Um Desafio Histórico-Político*, in which the author develops the theory of political conciliation.

[3] José Honório Rodrigues, "O Voto do Analfabeto e a Tradição Política Brasileira," *Conciliação e Reforma no Brasil: Um Desafio Histórico-Político*, pp. 135–163.

"colonel," the evolution of farm workers' demands—all these show that it is no longer possible to govern after a fashion which has become outmoded and that a stalemate has been reached.

The persistent irresolution of the principal political parties, and the bold indecision of the politicians—of whom some glow with serene confidence, others are attacked by feeling of inferiority, while still others snooze away after the old fashion—make one think that their objective is no more than the gaining of time. Indecision, however, even more than compromise, is the psychological essence of Brazilian politics, the result of centuries of inertia. Indecision is the product of standing at dead center and of the nonexistence of an effective majority. In election after election the achievement of such a majority is sought, always under threat of annulment by the group exercising domination. The dominant minorities have found in the power of veto their prime arm. Vetoes are imposed on everyone and everything, from the chosen candidate to the elected official. If the veto does not become effective, owing to the reinforcement of majority opposition by support from the military (almost always democratic in inspiration), a compromise solution is sought in delay. This has made many an Indian a chief, and many are they who think only in terms of compromise. They forget that this offers only two prospects: putting off a hopeless deadlock, which would prevent a deal between representatives of unreconcilable views, or a resort to irreconcilable extremes and hence to radical revolution.

The significant fact is that virtually all political, economic, and social problems are bound together with a Gordian knot. Nevertheless, in a period in which it is highly important that decisions be reached, indecision appears to be the principal means by which some person or party retains power. It is no longer political conflict which divides the nation, but economic and social problems. While compromise is a party function, it degenerates into mutual frustration when the aim is mere bargaining for political concessions. In reality, on the rare occasions when the parties compete with one another (and one can speak of their achieving majorities only after discounting the 50 percent of the population which is illiterate), the similarities between them and their links with the past or their lack of modernity render them incapable of formulating and taking decisions. The PSD (Social Democratic Party) has always been a party of the oligarchy, with strong rural connections, and the UDN (National Democratic Union) has instinctively looked to the past. Both have taken alarm at the extent and rapidity of Brazilian growth, over which they exercise no control. The PTB (Brazilian Labor

Party),* essentially urban in character, seems to want to change the labor movement into a conservative, bureaucratic force, and, thanks to the presence in its ranks of government-sponsored labor leaders,† it fights as an element of discipline and stabilization. Populism is of importance for the political destiny of Brazil; its principal allies are radio and television, which, unfortunately, have been commercialized and are dedicated to barbarizing the great masses of illiterates. Those who are acquainted with the past and the present of the movement have noted that it vacillates between deviations into radicalism—though not of the most extreme type—and concern with turning politics into a profitable business enterprise.

Of the large parties, one is interested in preserving the current state of stalemate; the second cannot adjust itself to new situations and thereby likewise favors indecision; while the third betrays the historic tradition of the labor movement by allying itself to the dominant party of the oligarchy. All seek to delude; they do not want basic reforms; they take on the most varied of coloring, mingling the grossest of conservatism with the most revolutionary of proposals. The political behavior of their leaders is characterized by indecision, their instrument of political action being compromise.

Of the three, the PTB is the most progressive. Its basic ideology today is nationalism; its socialism is less doctrinaire than opportunistic, more a matter of circumstance than of substance. The PTB's nationalism represents a fusion of patriotism, the struggle for economic freedom, and the fight against imperialism. The form of economic exploitation that the PTB advocates is a mixture of the defense of national interests and aspirations, the tendency toward neutralism, and the reaction to international tutelage. The extremist views of the party are closely linked to anti-Americanism. The other parties are chance coalitions formed to wage election campaigns, without particular political significance. Exceptions are represented by the PSP (Social Progressive Party), in which populism is predominant; the PSB (Brazilian Socialist Party), a small group made up of an elite of intellectuals and labor leaders, of no special influence; and, finally, the PCB (Brazilian Communist Party). This last-mentioned has been outlawed and rendered ineffective in

* The PSD, UDN, and PTB were the three major political parties in Brazil. They were formed after Vargas fell in 1945 and lasted until the military government disbanded all political parties in 1965.

† Labor leaders very often are beholden to the government, upon whose favor they depend.

action; it has been transformed into a sect, divorced from the working classes, bereft of any special influence, owing particularly to popular antipathy for inflexibly doctrinaire dogmatism.

Nationalism is not a party matter: its defenders and assailants are to be found in all parties. In 1960 and 1961 a survey promoted and directed by Americans[4] showed that 84 percent of legislators thought the government should encourage foreign capital investment in Brazil and only 4 percent thought it should not. About 49 percent thought that the remittance of profits abroad should be regulated; 18 percent felt that some investments should be permitted and others not; 16 percent were of the view that foreign investors should not be allowed to drain the Brazilian economy; 13 percent held that a large portion of profits should be reinvested in Brazil. Of the one hundred legislators interviewed, the members of the Brazilian Labor Party expressed themselves in favor of foreign investments. As for public opinion in general, the indices are lower: 33 percent of urban dwellers and 17 percent of those in rural areas favor foreign investments; 24 percent and 11 percent, respectively, are against them; 43 percent of the former and 72 percent of the latter have no opinion on the matter, which shows that here nationalism is not a significant issue. The survey pointed out that only 19 percent of urban dwellers and 6 percent of those in rural areas had heard or read anything concerning nationalism and Brazilian nationalists. Professed nationalists, who know what nationalism is, make up only 7 percent of the urban and 1 percent of the rural population. The majority of nationalists are men, and are to be found in university circles in the cities.

The Social Democratic Party, which has been more rural than urban, maintains ties with the past, and has found its strength and influence in the illiterate and semi-illiterate inhabitants of rural areas, poor and under the domination of the large landowners and political bosses. As the sector of society which it represents is guided by tradition, its interest has lain in preserving the *status quo* and in defending the state of stalemate which leads to indecision and compromise. Its sole aim is to be the government, to be with the government, or to adhere to the government. As a rule its politicians exhibit sentiments of guilt, since they—especially those representative of the more backward sectors of this party—together with the politicians of the UDN are responsible

[4] Lloyd A. Free and Hadley Cantril, *Some International Implications of the Political Psychology of Brazilians.*

for the most obstinate resistance, in the area of decision, to any sort of change.

The National Democratic Union, an urban rather than a rural party, finds its strength and influence in the middle class. Its solutions are always of a moral nature; it attacks corruption, but shows little concern for social justice and welfare. Moral indignation and logorrhea are its arms of political action. It is losing strength daily, because urban congestion, industrialization, the coming of new generations, and demographic change—the influx of poverty-stricken people from rural areas —are swelling the ranks of the proletariat and shantytown dwellers, who resist aggressive, moral preaching that fills the lower classes with hatred that the party then exploits for its own advantage.

Neither by the sensual pleasure afforded by rhetoric nor by the visceral satisfaction provided by brute aggression will the urban masses be led to accept the leadership of the middle class, so scant in numbers, so respectable in a populist era, but so incapable of bringing its interests into harmony with those of the working classes. The contribution between its respectability and the gross personal attacks in which its leaders indulge is not to be marveled at, nor is the malevolence of its followers, who are attracted by verbal acerbity. The culmination of the middle class's moral indignation in 1954,* with the vetoes it sought to impose and the intense pressure it exerted against nationalism, caused the urban majority to turn against it and gave impulse to progressive tendencies.

A feeling of humiliation, then, is the social penalty imposed on those who, in defeat, see their standards of conduct constantly set aside by the majority. Immobilism and incapacity to find adequate solutions express the contradictions of the two great parties. Connections are becoming ever closer among the great industrialists, bankers—with thirty-five representatives in the Congress—big businessmen, and even big landowners, who seek to oppose, via one party or the other, populist demagogy and laborite nationalism. Their effort has intensified the state of stalemate and contributed to indecision and temporary compromises. The influence of economic power, exercised in various ways, has not been able to resolve indecision. First, because the classes exerting that power are themselves divided as to whether solutions should be of

---

* Reference is made here to the charges of corruption leveled against the government of Getúlio Vargas, elected to the presidency in 1950. The demands for Vargas' resignation led to his suicide, August 25, 1954.

a progressive or conservative nature; second, because they have not been able to bring their interests into harmony with those of the working classes; and, third, because the parties of the center are more or less alike, operating in the same area of agreement, appealing to the same people, and thereby increasing indecision.

If the Social Democratic Party is stupid, the National Democratic Union is still more so, as Sir Ivor Jennings said of the British Conservatives and Liberals. Neither believes in anything; their politicians defend neither principles nor programs. The objective of their members is preservation of the social injustice represented by the *status quo*. They neither wish, nor are able, to break the barriers of privilege. The thirteen existing parties show the need for reform in matters of elections and representation—reform which the larger parties have been putting off, fearing to stir up a hornet's nest.* Indeed, their ideological inconsistency is not the result of the high incidence of illiteracy and the consequent difficulty of giving expression to the interests and aspirations of the common people.

The American survey directed by Lloyd Free and Hadley Cantril showed that if the public, urban and rural, was hesitant in regard to, or ignorant of, international affairs and problems of nationalism, it was acutely aware of, and preoccupied with, personal aspirations and even national aspirations. Both are clearly defined and summed up in the so-called basic reforms. They are completely independent of the nation's geography, of the imbalance between the various regions, of the different degrees of progress or the varying social, economic, and political conditions. The various sectors of the public know and can define their permanent aspirations, for which they have fought throughout history. This much is independent of ideology. It is in the area of political action that variations present themselves with respect to practical means of achievement, for it is there that one finds reflections of the differences in the ranks of the governing elite and evidence of the areas in which ignorance prevails with regard to urban and rural public opinion.

With respect to the personal aspirations of 2,168 individuals, 1,026 urban and 1,142 rural, 44 percent of the former and 41 percent of the latter assigned first place among their aims to a decent or improved

---

* These remarks on the multiple political parties were made, of course, prior to the dissolution of all such parties by the military government in 1965. The military government of Castelo Branco then proceeded to create two official parties, one loyal to the government and the other the loyal opposition. As one wag noted, one party answers "Yes, Sir!" and the other just "Yes."

standard of living for themselves and their families; 43 percent of both gave second place to personal and family health; 29 percent of urban and 12 percent of rural dwellers aspired to own their own houses or apartments or to make improvements in the dwellings they already possessed; 28 percent of urban and 13 percent of rural individuals desired adequate opportunities, including education, for their children; and 16 percent and 7 percent, respectively, aspired to happiness (a happy marriage, a happy family life, children). Aspiration to an improved standard of living is more pronounced in the urban area of the Northeast (55%) than in the urban East (30%) and South (44%), and more in the rural Northeast (47%) than in the rural East (38%) and South (39%). Personal aspirations present very high indices of affirmation and expression, and it will not be for ignorance thereof that the political parties will fail to promote them. Only 5 percent of urban dwellers and 12 percent of rural dwellers failed to express themselves.[5]

Of great significance, also, was the response given to the question concerning personal progress in the last five years. (The survey was carried out at the end of 1960 and the beginning of 1961.) It is apparent that all city dwellers had a feeling of having made considerable personal progress, although the urban Northeasterner was less positive on the topic than his opposite number in the East or South, and 44 percent of rural dwellers considered themselves better off in 1960 and 1961 than previously. Although 24 percent of country dwellers felt they were worse off, no feeling of despair was evident. What is more important, 60 percent of the urban population and 40 percent of the rural population felt that personal improvement was possible and expected to achieve it.

In Lloyd Free's survey the persons interviewed were asked to identify on a scale ranging from good at the top to bad at the bottom the situation of Brazil at the current moment, five years previously, and five years thence. The final result showed notable agreement between legislators and the rural and urban public as to the situation of the country and its progress.[6] Confidence and a feeling of advance dominated the response. An eminently optimistic tone is predominant in the personal aspirations of the Brazilian people. This is not surprising, for optimism, as a philosophy of historic hopes, is a Brazilian characteristic.[7]

If the people are not hesitant in regard to their own aspirations,

[5] *Ibid.*, pp. 52–68.

[6] *Ibid.*, pp. 55–58, 64–67.

[7] José Honório Rodrigues, "The Foundations of Brazil's Foreign Policy," *International Affairs*, 38, No. 3 (July 1962), 338.

neither do they vacillate with respect to what is essential for Brazil. I made a point of stressing, at the beginning of the chapter on permanent national aspirations, that they are independent of regional differences, of classes, and of ethnic minorities, and also that the future of the nation will be determined by the balance between the permanent aspirations and those of the present day. Lloyd Free's survey shows the general or national character of certain interests, and, furthermore, that national prosperity and economic stability are popular objectives. The survey indicates that 42 percent of urban dwellers and 31 percent of those in rural areas were of the opinion that obtaining a better or more decent standard of living and greater national prosperity represented their desires and hopes for the future of the country. Of these, 20 percent and 12 percent, respectively, felt that such prosperity would be obtained through technological advance and greater productivity. The greatest desire of 35 percent of city dwellers and 25 percent of country dwellers was for economic stability and absence of inflation; for 21 percent and 9 percent, respectively, a good, honest, efficient government was the ideal. Of those interviewed, education ranked first with only 9 percent and 4 percent, respectively, full employment with 6 percent and 4 percent, and social justice with 5 percent and 6 percent. The low indices of these last-mentioned show the great popular intuition that other aspirations will be more readily attained when national prosperity and economic stability are achieved.[8]

The high percentage in favor of an honest and efficient government shows the extent to which the people are aware of the moral poverty of the prevailing leadership, the lack of administrative cadres, and the little that the minority parties have to offer. The values assigned to the objectives in themselves show the extraordinary political perception of the people: between national prosperity and economic stability, placed at the top of the scale, and education, full employment, and social justice, at the bottom, come good government and efficient, honest administration. The urban and rural masses, therefore, do not allow themselves to be sidetracked, like the petty bourgeoisie or the middle class, who take as their prime objective winning the struggle waged against

---

[8] National independence—as represented by freedom from interference or excessive influence on the part of other powers, by development of an independent foreign policy, or by economic self-sufficiency—was listed immediately after education and before full employment and social justice by 7 percent of urban dwellers and 1 percent of those in rural areas. Congressmen (38% as a whole) placed it immediately after an improved standard of living. This point will be treated in my forthcoming book *A Política Exterior do Brasil: Fundamentos e Flutuações.*

corruption or on behalf of morality. Improvement of the economic standard of living as a basic popular objective is both a personal and a national aspiration. The high rank assigned to it, especially when one considers that 64 percent of the legislators also listed it as the prime goal, means that the nation is conscious of its problems and morally and spiritually prepared for the tasks of development. There can be no development without the spirit of development, just as there has been no capitalism without the capitalistic spirit, or socialism without the socialist spirit. The people want and desire development.

On the other hand, war in general (for 23% of the urban and 17% of the rural public), economic instability and inflation (19% in both cases), disunion, political instability, and civil war (16% of the urban and 3% of the rural public), inadequate or lower standards of living (9% and 8%), Communism or internal Communist threats (8% and 6%), and bad, dishonest, inefficient government (8% and 3%) constitute, in this order, the principal preoccupations and fears of the people. Preoccupation with war is natural for a people that has made a permanent aspiration of peace and international arbitration. It shows that the governments have done right in directing foreign policy toward peaceful relations with all, toward the condemnation of war, toward nonintervention, and toward defense of the right to self-determination.* Disquietude in regard to economic instability and inadequate standards of living backs the popular aspiration to development, just as fear of the chaos of civil war shows the strength of the aspiration for national unity and territorial integrity. The relatively small fear of Communism shows not only that the people are little inclined to extremist ideologies but also that the leaders of the UDN and other right-wing parties have gone astray in taking the struggle against Communism for the main political problem facing Brazil.†

The limited preoccupation with bad government is not surprising. It reinforces the thesis of those who say that Brazil has progressed despite bad governments. These are a chronic ill in the country, provoked in part by party leadership and limitation of the area of political decision. Fortunately, the people of Brazil do not suffer from generalized or national frustrations which would result, as in the case of Germany

---

* Here again one sees the changes enforced by the military government since 1964. Brazilian intervention in the Dominican Republic in 1965—an action unanimously opposed by the people but imposed by the military government—counters the traditional policies of nonintervention and self-determination.

† The same statement could be made with regard to the present military government.

and Italy, in profound hatreds and acts of discrimination. The Brazilians trust in their future; they trust in their achievements—independence, territorial integrity, national unity—they trust in the balance of regional interests, in psychosocial integration, in racial tolerance; they are not frightened by political phantoms; they have hope for economic development, well-being, social justice, and the benefits of education. Popular discontent is also chronic in Brazil, because the common people have been defrauded of their vote by the dominant minorities. The latter are the direct heirs of the former colonial authorities, for whom the populace constituted an abstraction—a mere possession of the crown or of private individuals.

The Brazilian people were "castrated," to use an expression of Capistrano de Abreu which cannot be repeated too often. They had no voice; they were given no hearing; they were subjugated and bled—exploited, victimized, pumped dry, and tormented. For this reason, let it be said once again, it is wrong to say that the history of Brazil has been bloodless. If, in the collective sense, it does not have the bloody character of Spanish American and United States history, from the individual viewpoint it was a cruel history, as a result of the poverty in which the people were kept, infant mortality, poor health, lack of doctors and hospitals, low life expectancy (average life expectancy for a slave was only 15 years), and disregard for the people's most legitimate demands. Among these was the call for ownership of the land. This demand was occasioned by the semifeudal system of land grants, which the Land Law of 1850 failed to abolish, since this would have been contrary to the interests of the dominant minorities. Even today, agrarian reform continues to be delayed by chicanery, although the demand therefor enjoys unanimous national support.

Can the Brazilian people overcome their internal dissensions sufficiently to establish an effective political majority that will set reform in motion and thereby avoid revolution? One that will carry forward logically and rationally the movement toward progress and development begun by Getúlio Vargas and resumed by Juscelino Kubitschek?

If they are to do so, a weak presidency is out of the question. Equally inadmissible is the fragmentation of power represented by the parliamentary system—a lunatic tendency in a country as unstable as quicksilver.* Is the presidency to be the symbol of reform and the Congress that of counterreform? The Brazilians, with their attachment to personalities, have long had the habit of attributing to the presidents the

---

* The Brazilians had a parliamentary system *sui generis* during most of the rule of the second emperor. They tried parliamentary government again from September, 1961, to

qualities and defects of their administrations. Many of the presidents, however, have been less cause than effect. They have acted as transmissions rather than motors. Some have been motors—motors for development—and their functional disorders have resulted from lack of an effective majority or of a spiritual platform from which they could dominate the nation. Today spiritual conditions facilitate, support, and promote material growth.

The development movement must be less opportunistic and more realistic; less a matter of the moment and more one of structure. It must take advantage of the psychological opportunity offered by an awakening awareness of insufficiency among the Brazilians, to impose a decision and bring about structural reform, thereby helping to promote development. As the Brazilian people are not followers of ideologies, however, time and being are not to be gained by any sort of philosophical cha-cha-cha. Marx said of the young Hegelians that they fought for phrases and slogans. They simply forgot, he said, that those phrases can be met with other phrases, and that one cannot really fight the existing world if he fights only the phrases current in that world.

With or without phrases, with or without the classic, orthodox trichotomy of right, center, and left, with or without coalitions, inspired or not by philosophies, the march toward progress will be made—but never on the basis of improvisation. There are limits to indecision. How long will the Brazilians be able to pay the price of irresolution? How long will the people be able to support superficial conciliation or an endless search for solutions?

Time was squandered in the days of the Colony, the Empire, and the early Republic. Now time is at a premium. There is a rhythmic adjustment between time and opportunity. Previously time was lost because there was no opportunity. The Brazilians perhaps lost out on a number of occasions; they made false starts; they choked on their own oratorical excesses. The several booms in sugar, minerals, cotton, rubber, and coffee did not represent national advances but advances for the crown or certain individuals or groups. Big business deals did not cause the nation to grow; they merely fattened the minorities.

If lost time cannot be bought back or otherwise recouped, the Brazilians cannot permit irresolution, disunion, and compromise— which brings weariness and stagnation without real advantage for the people, who are the nation incarnate—to deprive them of still more of

---

January, 1963, when they overwhelmingly repudiated it in a plebiscite favoring a return to the presidential system.

the time needed for the gigantic tasks that confront the present generation.

Growth in the number of voters owing to the rising birth rate, the increased number of poor families, an awakened consciousness in the great urban and rural masses, who rise like human walls between the old politicians and their bygone domination, and participation on the part of the proletariat all call for real leadership—a leadership that will face those tasks and exploit all possibilities to the maximum, freeing the Brazilians from survivals of the colonial past and promoting material and cultural development. The Brazilians are engaged in a great re-examination of their destiny. There must be a nationwide response, enlisting the talent, ideas, energies, and devotion of all. A great future has long been predicted for Brazil—one characterized by great feats and accomplishments. These, however, must be the achievement of the rising generations, whose talents are being badly trained, or wasted.

3. Personalities and Power

Leadership is a fundamental problem during the period in which these new generations are being trained. (82% of the population is less than forty years old; 41.8% is fifteen years old or younger.[1]) As a mere matter of demographic structure, their entrance into the ranks of voters, of party members, of participants in political debates threatens the hold of conservative routine.

Relations between personalities and power are extremely complex as regards their historical significance. What personal qualities, aside from the common ones, attract power? In recent years the voter's preferences have undergone great changes. The attributes of aristocratic bearing, gravity, and rigidly moral conduct, inspired in the tradition and routine of a rural society—a society whose members sought in themselves the font of counsel and decision, and directed themselves toward fixed objectives determined by the economic structure, by their parents, by the group to which they belonged—have since 1930 lost all chance of bringing success at the polls, having ceased to appeal to the voters. The dramatic disappearance of São Paulo politicians from the national

[1] Conselho Nacional de Estatística, *Flagrantes Brasileiros*, Vol. 11, p. 7.

scene is attributable to this change in taste.* Even the youngest of the Paulistas seemed to suffer from premature decrepitude, and the oldest from protracted senility.

Getúlio Vargas introduced new elements, while preserving such traditional qualities as composure, dignity of office, and a serene demeanor. He did not belong to a privileged class nor was he nominated by any of the old party machines. His attraction consisted perhaps in his ideas of social justice—new at that time for Brazilian politicians—and in his direct popular appeal, particularly to the proletariat. He was not a demagog, but made use of plain language and common sense. Since his time the struggle among the various Brazils—best expressed by Jacques Lambert's simplification: old Brazil and new Brazil—has broken down the highly individual character of traditional society. The new phase has been represented by the emergence of new types of personality, of new forms of appeal, of new actors on the political scene.

A society in a stage of growth calls for new forms of adaptation by politicians to social needs and for new psychological methods of appealing to the public. Politicians can no longer seek inspiration in themselves or in tradition, routine, and the stable economic groups which have controlled history from the wings. It is "the other people"—those who have been appearing at the polls in ever greater numbers, representing ever-varying interests, divergent or otherwise—who are deciding whether power will be put in their hands. There are survivals of tradition; there are the forces of industrialization and urbanism which are altering social relations; there are new captains of industry and new consumer leaders. Society is no longer to be measured by the fixed standards of the past. Some people continue to eat up words, adoring loquacity. Others want facts, numbers, and concrete objectives. Formerly no great psychological resources were called for; today the human types created by bits of history and society are so numerous and varied that a politician must use different psychology in different areas in order to satisfy or inspire everyone. New middle classes, larger working classes, new industrialists have different images of power and expect different characteristics of their leaders. The politician finds in these "other people" who are entering upon the scene, if not a source of direction, at least a source of approbation. In addition, captains of industry and consumer leaders seem to dispute the preference in the

* The politicians from São Paulo dominated the Old Republic, 1889–1930. Vargas greatly decreased the political influence of the Paulistas.

struggle for power, seeing themselves as heroes, who by tenacious effort have achieved success. Some are comic-book heroes and hope to enter into history as political leaders; some are moralizers who seek a source of power in the middle classes; still others seek oligarchic power in the dredgings of history.

Fieriness, oratorical gifts, a sonorous voice, personal magnetism, and above all the moral-indignation routine are the principal resources of the political leader of the middle classes. Of one such—the most representative of all—it can be said that he believes, as no Brazilian has ever believed before, that violence is the fundamental element in history.* The impoverishment of the middle class, its emotional insecurity, its feelings of guilt and inferiority have led it to support the verbal violence, the threats of punishment, the moral aggression which that leader practices without any Christian indulgence whatever. However, not only does humaneness, which is an essential characteristic of the Brazilian people, repel violence—which has not been a common instrument for the acquisition of power—but also, as regards predestination, Christian sentiment rejects the idea that the prospect of damnation should prevail over the hope of salvation. As St. Augustine tells us, for the Christian, history is the product of sin, that is, the breaking of divine law out of an eagerness to know good and evil. For the middle class that the previously mentioned leader guides, there can be no forgiveness for error; there is only chastisement, insult, and calumny. In every word and thought, the leader seeks, by threat of terrorism, the source of power, so that he can punish those who disagree with him. Resentment, disguised as moral indignation, is a characteristic of the middle class, of those who live under conditions that oblige them to self-restriction and bring about the frustration of their natural desires. The leaders who nourish the resentment of the middle class tend constantly to falsify history, or at least to propose monstrous divisions and to render that class's participation in historical development of marginal importance. It is rendered still more marginal by the disassociation of the middle class not merely from popular aspirations of the day but also from such national characteristics as compromise, conciliation, liberalism, tolerance, and peaceful racial and social relations.

Another type of leader† also found his essential weakness in an

* The description of this political leader points to Carlos Lacerda, perennial critic of Brazilian governments, whether as a journalist or as governor of the state of Guanabara.
† The description which follows is of Jânio Quadros, a former governor of São Paulo, overwhelmingly elected president in January, 1961, only to resign suddenly in August of the same year.

inability to compromise and in recourse to authoritarianism. His leadership was inspired in broader sectors than the middle class, but it was owing to the defects of that class that he met with failure. Success for him was a tragedy. He gave out that he would fight to demolish the citadel of privilege, and he entered it in triumph. The citadel proved a prison, however, and the leader was forced to renounce the chieftainship and become as it were a renegade. His spontaneous withdrawal from the scene after several victories was one of the most humiliating spectacles in Brazilian history. Foreign policy dominated his administration, but the reason for his renunciation was not to be found therein. The tragedy stemmed from his inflexible will, which would not admit of compromise—the commonest form of political maneuver in Brazil. In the case of this man, who sought to appear as the incarnation of authoritarian virility, incapacity for compromise and frustrated audacity gave rise to an unresolvable conflict between potency and impotence. It is easier to retain than to regain, but even so the man is not out of the running and may find strength to recoup his loss, achieving a balance between the strong presidency that is indispensable for development and the capacity for transigence that is so necessary for political victory.

Neither of these two leaders shows signs of possessing that trace of optimism that appeals to Brazilians. The optimistic leader,* who sees development as the main problem, who confidently promises a quick alleviation of the troubles of the masses, who believes in salvation rather than damnation, who shows no hatred, who practices no discrimination, who nourishes neither frustrations nor resentments, continues to be the most authentically Brazilian and the most acceptable to his fellow countrymen. If the first-mentioned types stand for the most anti-Brazilian of political currents, the last type represents the most typically Brazilian of all. If in the soul of each there is an intense vitality, an untiring energy, and a magnetic influence, there is none like the last to give so true an incarnation of the Brazilian nature—tolerance, aversion to violence, human sympathy and understanding, faith, optimism. This type of leader promises peace and tranquility—always timely aspirations— although he knows that history is in truth dramatic, that it represents disquietude and restless living. He finds constant renewal, not in solitude and meditation, but in converse and contact with the public. He is always engaged in struggle, in campaigns of public interest; he seeks to keep up with the times. He is always modern. He finds truth in the

* For example, Juscelino Kubitschek.

overall picture, not in details. His method is intuitive, but he is logical in action. A leader of this type knows no hatred or discrimination; he makes no impositions. He tranquilizes, calms, convinces. When he is victorious he neither belittles nor persecutes the vanquished. He seeks alliance with still another kind of leader, who appeals in particular to the working classes.

The progressive convictions expressed by this last-mentioned type of leader make no concealment of their reform-oriented character. It is this type of leader's function to direct a measured advance, providing the necessary pauses, and, in case of unavoidable necessity, giving a false sense to history.* Contrary to what his fiercest enemies think— especially the leaders of the middle class, filled with indignation at his vulgar appeal to the masses—he acts as one of history's shock absorbers. The crises which have several times caused him to be threatened with expulsion, the conspiracies to eliminate him from the political process, and the attacks of the middle class have given him a sense of being under siege, which has sometimes caused him to assume a radical course, not in the direction of the Communist left, but in that of nationalism and socialism. At other times, after the bestowal of certain international blessings, the so-called traditional conservative classes have attempted a *rapprochement*, extolling peace, tranquility, and good business deals —which always call for assistance from the state. They entice the leader with promises of the confidence of the center; they declare themselves against demogogy; they pretend to have banished distrust. In reality they are exerting pressure from all sides, trying to get the leader to hoodwink the populace in regard to its needs. The leader of this type is marked by ambivalence between the libertarian and the liberticide, between the cowardly tyrant and his fearless henchman.[2]

In truth, what counts with the common people is what is happening now, not what happened long ago or what is going to happen in the future. As they have played a secondary role on the political stage and continue to be only semisovereign—owing especially to their illiteracy† —leadership does not express fully the relation between personality and power. As the political struggle becomes fiercer, as pressure groups dis-

---

* This last description applies best to Getúlio Vargas, president from 1930 to 1945 and from 1950 to 1954; but in a more limited aspect it could apply to João Goulart, president from 1961 to 1964.

[2] This type of leader has generally come from Rio Grande do Sul. Concerning the ambivalence mentioned above as manifested by citizens of that state, see José Honório Rodrigues, *O Continente do Rio Grande.*

† The illiterate cannot vote in Brazil.

pute the control of parties and the reins of command, the Congress is becoming a nest of representatives of groups, or, as Earl Latham has said, it is being transformed into an arbitrator, adjusting the balance of power between the groups in conflict. Only when there is real popular sovereignty will the government become representative of the nation and first priority be given to national interests. The survival of democracy in Brazil is not endangered unless defense of the selective interests of a small minority is continued.

It is becoming daily more impossible to keep up this defense. The current aspirations of the Brazilian people are growing more rapidly than the levels of satisfaction promoted by the dominant minorities. The difference between the standard of living which presently prevails and that to which the people aspire is ever greater. The people do not, however, seek for extremist solutions, for, as will bear repetition, they are hostile to ideologies. Their position is not fixed, doctrinaire, closed, and dogmatic, but flexible, open to conciliation, swayed by personalities. The people accept the most incredible of alliances promoted by political leaders, and reject discriminatory, fanatical, extremist, authoritarian attitudes on anyone's part.

The people's permanent aspirations constitute the hallowed substance of the Brazilian national heritage. Aspirations of the day, which are variable, may not conflict with permanent aspirations—which are the expression of the people rather than of their leaders—but merely serve to render them a greater stimulus to progress. Current aspirations should bring the nation up to date and make the people contemporaries of the age in which they live.

A clear consequence is immediately apparent: if underdevelopment is to be overcome, the presidency must be strengthened. Only effective presidential leadership, exercised through a unified command, can fight for the country's permanent objectives, mobilizing the resources of the nation for the tasks of the day. A plebiscite, a majority, a leadership that are truly representative of the nation will preserve the identity of present-day with permanent goals. The struggle now in process is not between conservatives and liberals, but between progressive reformers and counterreformers. The struggle is between accelerators and retarders of the course of historical development, between those who live on nostalgia for the past, whose conduct is determined by outmoded values, and those who draw strength from the fact that they are alive—very much alive—and involved with the problems of the people and the nation.

PART I

National Characteristics

You may be sure that it is a difficult thing for a man to remain at all times the same.

Francisco Otaviano de Almeida Rosa
Speech in the Chamber of Deputies,
February 11, 1864

4. National Characteristics

Studies of Brazilian character have both a philosophic and a literary tradition. From José Bonifácio, in the early days of Brazilian independence, to the most recent essayists, an increasing interest of the Brazilians in themselves and in their country has resulted in an environment favoring scholarly study of the topic.[1]

The bibliography of attempts at interpreting the constants in Brazilian character in the light of history is so extensive that it would take a more exhaustive study than this to indicate the origins of the studies made and the results achieved. Not all show the same qualities of observation, research methods, and capacity for interpretation. They vary to a disproportionate degree.

Impressionism predominates in almost all. However, merely because the authors did not make a rigorous examination of primary source material or proved unable to establish proper controls for their findings, these studies should not be set aside. Scientific impressionism, like literary fiction, represents an instrument of analysis and interpretation.

Though with almost a century's difference in time and dissimilarity of approach both José Bonifácio and Capistrano de Abreu dealt with "national character," the term has yet to find a precisely defined meaning. Study of the topic attained a stage of maturity during World War II, when it became a practical matter, both useful and necessary. Previously, at the end of World War I, Salvador de Madariaga had been commissioned to study Englishmen, Frenchmen, and Spaniards, because it was recognized that a comparison of the cultures of different peoples could be relevant to the problems of world organization and world peace.

Faced with total war — including psychological warfare — against little-known enemies, who were difficult of approach, the United States encouraged such study for practical purposes. Knowledge of the nature of one's enemies could be a powerful weapon in the arsenal of psychological warfare with respect to political maneuvering and even to the nature of military operations. The study had, moreover, another, still greater significance: the satisfactory planning of international relations

[1] The principal Brazilian studies are listed in the bibliography at the end of this volume.

after the war would be immeasurably aided by an understanding of the goals, motivations, and emotional complexes characterizing nations considered from an individual viewpoint.

Under the pressures of waging war and building for peace, research methods and techniques of analysis were developed for theories regarding national character, and conclusions were drawn. There were many, however, who were opposed to the direction taken in the search for national characteristics, especially those who took an internationalist viewpoint, since it was felt that the idea of the existence of national character was a product of nationalism. The various theories of national character, from those of Morris Ginsberg to those of David Riesman and David Potter, gradually gained the most disparate of adherents, and today in a number of countries, both European and American, study is being made of the distribution of certain traits typical of different human groups. Even in the Soviet Union it is recognized that, while the mainstream of world history is one, the existence is necessarily implied of tributary currents representing a diversity of historical forms and variety in social development, in accordance with the specific conditions of the peoples of different countries.

Since the time of the first studies by Otto Klineberg it has been recognized that a knowledge of history is an absolute prerequisite to development of a complete picture of national character. Gradually, through recourse to new methods of psychoanalysis and cultural anthropology, concepts were more sharply defined, techniques were improved, research was carried further. For Riesman, character, in the contemporary scientific sense, is the aggregate of standardized uniformities of learned response which distinguishes men of different regions, eras, and groups. The individual always benefits from living more or less confined in the uniform of national character imposed upon him by tradition and necessity, or, if you prefer, by history and society.

After individual studies came group surveys, some sponsored by UNESCO, with a view to establishing the national stereotypes or images which people have of themselves or of other nations.

If national character denotes the total behavior of a given people, the attempt should be made to establish first common traits of general distribution and then the patterns of conduct recognized in the group as a whole. National character is the point of tension in the study of relations between the individual, culture, society, and the state. Hence the importance and significance of the study thereof. Writers from Sílvio Romero, Capistrano de Abreu, João Ribeiro, and Afonso Celso to

Oliveira Viana, Monteiro Lobato, Paulo Prado, Sérgio Buarque de Holanda, Alcântara Machado, Afonso Arinos de Melo Franco, Gilberto Freyre, João Camilo de Oliveira Tôrres, Alceu Amoroso Lima, Eduardo Frieiro, and Viana Moog have sought to catalog the characteristic features of the Brazilian people, more from the viewpoint of qualities and defects than from that of expressions of historicosocial conformity.

It would not be difficult to sum up the qualities and defects which they have noted in such a fashion that the frequency of recurrence of certain attributes would provide a picture of Brazilian psychosocial traits. As a number of scholars have already pointed out, however, the culture of a given people does not derive from a summing together of regional groups or of individuals but from the integration of those elements in a new synthesis, whose spiritual content is revealed in society by traits that remain or vary through the course of history.

Consequently, in an attempt to capture changing characteristics and to establish the constancy or permanence of some of them, it would seem advisable to bring out their social function, that is, their function in the society of each period.

In the first phase of Brazilian history, so great are the contradictions between the thesis represented by the Portuguese and the antithesis represented by the environment, the Indians, and the Negroes, that the synthesis of old and new results in an entirely new and original creation, despite the dominance of European influence and the triumph of Lusitanianism in the outward appearance of social forms.*

As Capistrano de Abreu observed, the first settlers (deserters, convicts, and victims of shipwreck) fall into two diametrically opposed categories: some succumbed to the environment to the point that they pierced their lips and ears, practiced ritual killings of prisoners, and ate the flesh thereof; others resisted the environment and molded it to their will. There was, however, an intermediate type, represented by "Caramuru," Diogo Álvares,† who neither wore lip and ear plates nor came to a place of power, but who managed to live on good terms with the natives. He exercised little influence and suffered little in return. The force of nature is, then, decisive. If one adds to it the influence of the Indians with whom the land was in some places densely populated, in

---

* The classical study of this synthesis was made by Gilberto Freyre in his *The Masters and the Slaves.*

† A shipwrecked sailor who made it ashore in Bahia during the first half of the sixteenth century, he was saved by an Indian princess in a manner reminiscent of Captain John Smith's being saved by Pocahontas.

others sparsely—the total number along the coast and in the hinterland having been recently estimated to have totaled 1,500,000 in the sixteenth century—it is evident that from the beginning Brazil was not the same as Portugal.

Under the Europeanizing influence of the Portuguese, Indian culture began to decline, and the first settlers were taken as models, their political and social principles imitated. The vanquished Indians and the captive Negroes, aided by nature and time, were, however, to impart distinguishing traits to the society which the settlers endeavored to implant and develop along foreign lines. The complex which came into being was not wholly Luso-European, since the course of history is not determined by victors alone.

Society in the first centuries of the colonial period was summed up thus by Capistrano de Abreu: Social evolution, as regards the Brazilian family, consisted in a greater number of illegal unions and an increasing degree of parity among ethnic stocks. The first representatives of religion were dissolute priests, whose conduct was a cause of scandal. The moral improvement of the clergy was the work of the Jesuits.* Literature began with comedies and miracle or morality plays—literature for people who did not know how to read, literature identified with religion. Evolution consisted in the elimination of the religious element and the appearance of a literary form for people who did know how to read. Public manifestations were not limited to religious rites—processions, novenas, pilgrimages. Comedies were performed in the churches, as were religious plays in which quatrains were sung to guitar accompaniment. Gambling had a beneficent effect in a society in which religious matters were reserved for the clergy and in which the least word, however innocent, could be twisted so as to have the most serious of consequences. The less people thought and talked the better. Conciliation among the various human elements was impossible: even among the Portuguese hostility prevailed. The man from Portugal did not wish to be taken for a plebeian; there were gypsies and Moors. The colony already had pharmacies and bachelors of jurisprudence.

The family could be portrayed thus: a moody father, a submissive wife, and terrified children. The land was melancholy owing to the privations suffered there, internal dangers represented by Indians and animals, and dangers from without, which kept the inhabitants in a constant state of alarm.

* The Jesuits began to arrive in 1549 and exerted a great influence on the course of Brazilian history until their expulsion in 1759.

The Brazilian-born children of Portuguese were treated with disdain, as being "lacking in wit" and given to Indian ways. The lowest class of the population was made up of slaves, either native Indians or Africans and their descendants, people possessed of neither land nor personal liberty. Somewhat above them came individuals who were Portuguese by birth or descent, landless, but free. At the top of the hierarchy came the rural landowners, in particular the plantation master, "a title to which many aspire as it brings with it service, obedience, and respect from many," as Antonil said.* Forces of disintegration were dominant, and only differences were to be perceived: there was no consciousness of unity, only of multiplicity. Racial discrimination existed, crossbreeding with Negroes being looked on with aversion. Yes, forces of disintegration were dominant, and hostility was general.

This was the general picture from 1500 up to the war for the recovery of Pernambuco (1645–1654).† From that period up to the discovery of gold,‡ great material and economic changes—exploration of the interior by *bandeiras*,[2] the winning of the backlands, the spread of cattle raising—brought about changes in feeling, morality, and characteristics.

The aid that Pernambuco and the Northeast received from all Brazil revealed the first stirrings of a feeling of national unity, the beginnings of a bond between the various ethnic elements.

The feeling of disdain for the land and the people born therein gradually disappeared. Despite racial prejudice, which resulted in separate religious associations for colored people and which forbade the ordination of mulattoes, miscegenation gradually brought about a close companionship among the great ethnic groups, of which the Negroes proved to be the mainstay of the colonial economy. As a result of the great victory over the invaders from The Netherlands won by the colony's own forces, of the feats of the *bandeiras*, of the wealth derived from cattle raising, the feeling of inferiority was overcome. The native-born Brazilians felt themselves equal to the Portuguese of the mother country.

* André João Antonil (pseudonym for Giovanni Antonio Andreoni) was author of *Cultura e Opulência do Brasil*, published in Lisbon in 1711 but immediately confiscated by the Portuguese government for fear it would arouse the greed of other European states.

† Pernambuco and most of the Northeast had been seized by the Dutch. The Brazilians fought the hated Protestant Europeans in a protracted guerrilla war and finally expelled them in 1654.

‡ The date 1695 is usually given for the first major gold discovery.

[2] The *bandeira* was an armed expedition which, departing from the captaincy of São Vicente (later São Paulo), explored the backlands with a view to taking Indians captive or to the discovery of precious metals.

When the latter tried to reassert their superior, protective attitude, an irrepressible and irreparable feeling of separation arose between Brazilians and Portuguese. This resulted in struggles against the *emboabas* and *mascates*, as the Portuguese were scornfully called.[3]

The discovery of gold served only to increase the feeling that the Brazilians were equal to the Portuguese, but strife between Portuguese and Brazilians, Indians and Europeans, Negroes and whites indicate the difficulties of getting along together.[4]

Immigration from Portugal did not increase, because laws of 1667 and 1720 hindered freedom of movement by inhabitants of that kingdom. As a result of the premature nature of settlements and the scattering of the Portuguese over the empty lands opened up by the *bandeiras* or the cattle raisers, the dominant mass of the population was constituted by Indians, Negro slaves, and crossbreeds of primitive culture, hostile to the Portuguese, or at least to their attempts to reassert a superiority which was no longer recognized.

Although there still were some rudiments of culture and education to be found along the seaboard, the people of the interior regressed or even fell into barbarism, since they were incapable of maintaining the contacts required by advanced civilization. The great rural landowners were self-sufficient and exercised incontrollable authority. Only beginning to 1690 were judges created to serve the backlands, and even then they remained submissive to the power of the great landed proprietors.

Economic life suffered atrophy. No freedom of any sort existed, except to export raw materials to the market of the mother country. Government policy closed off foreign markets, while scattered holdings, distance, and difficulties of communication rendered the domestic market precarious. Group hostility continued to exist, though tempered by miscegenation, a practical effect of the lesson derived from life in common. The barbarous conditions in which the people of the hinterland lived, without schools, books, or press, continued to exert a negative influence.

The extension of the frontier at the beginning and the end of the seventeenth century meant new cultural contacts that were decisive in the development of national characteristics. The state of Maranhão,

---

[3] *Emboaba* derives from the Tupi *mboab*, descriptive of aggressiveness. It was applied by the Paulista to the Portuguese and other outsiders who flocked to the gold-mine area and were considered fortune hunters. *Mascates* were street peddlers.

[4] Particularly to be recalled in this regard are the War of the Emboabas (1708–1709), the War of the Mascates (1710–1711), the War against the Indians (1683–1713), and the runaway-slave refuge of Palmares (1687–1697).

created in 1621, like the captaincy of São Paulo, was wholly Indian: the Portuguese language did not become dominant in them till 1755 and 1758, respectively. Thus Tupi had a new impact on Brazilian cultural life.* Capistrano de Abreu has denied that indolence and idleness were the characteristics of the Indian, but a verse originating in Pará reflects those traits:

> Life in Pará
> Is a life of repose;
> You pretend to eat
> And in a hammock you doze.[5]

The "Continent of São Pedro do Rio Grande," as the present state of Rio Grande do Sul was known, was likewise an Indian province, but the triumph of Portuguese came about more rapidly, owing to the preceding action of the *bandeiras*, which brought areas occupied by Spaniards and Jesuits under Lusitanian domination. A characteristic feature marks this limitless region, broad, generous, rich, independent—freedom. Carried to an extreme, however, untrammeled by discipline or court authority, it leads to tyranny and the rule of the proud-willed man on horseback, sometimes confused with the *caudillo*. A popular verse also expresses this sentiment:

> The true son of Rio Grande,
> The gaucho in verity,
> Loves above all
> The warm sun of liberty.

Pombal's political plan of 1757, together with the creation of the viceroyalty and the transfer (1763) of its seat to Rio de Janeiro, reestablished in some measure the unity that had been threatened in 1621.† Lack of institutions of higher learning and of a press,‡ and slavery with its accompaniment of idleness, indolence, servility, and corruption, prevented, however, the formation of a real public consciousness. Hostility, friction, and ill will continued, and at times led to

---

* The Tupi Indian group is the largest and most widespread in Brazil. The Tupi language was regarded as the "general language" for the Indians.

[5] Pará was a very poor region, in which hunger was frequently prevalent. Indolence, as described in this quatrain, derived in part from undernourishment.

† In that year, Brazil was divided into two colonies: the state of Maranhão and the state of Brazil. The Marquis of Pombal, who dominated Portuguese politics from 1750 to 1777, took many steps to unify and centralize the control of Brazil. Among others, he abolished the state of Maranhão in 1774 and incorporated it into Brazil.

‡ A press was established in 1747 and immediately abolished.

insurrections: the revolts of the Negroes and the Minas conspiracy of 1789, known as the Inconfidência,* represent attempts to regain lost time in the social and cultural areas.[6]

The percentage charged by the crown on all mining production in time became the mainspring of the whole colonial mechanism. Never in Brazilian history was the tax collector so important as then. Hence the antirevenuer complex of the people of Minas, the incurable opposition to taxation. The Inconfidência, like other conspiracies, was inspired by idealism—more by ideas of non-Portuguese European origin than by Brazilian American realism. Education continued its work of terrorism, stifling vivacity and spontaneity in the pupils. Few persons learned to read. Preuniversity- and university-level courses (in commerce, military engineering, and economics) were instituted in the second half of the eighteenth century. The work of three centuries may be summarized in Capistrano de Abreu's admirable synthesis:

. . . five ethnographic groups bound actively by a common language and passively by a common religion, molded by the environments of five different geographical regions, filled with a noisy enthusiasm for the natural riches of the land, feeling aversion or scorn for the Portuguese, yet having no particular esteem for one another.[7]

The noisy enthusiasm for the land, the aversion to the Portuguese—which after independence was to turn to disparagement and indifference—and the separate characteristics which Brazil developed under the colonial system resulted in still further incompatibility with the mother country, and generated, in addition, not nativism but nationalism. The decree of 1785, prohibiting the manufacture of silk and cotton textiles, but not of coarse cloth for the common people, was the logical culmination of the discriminatory laws of the metropolitan government. At the end of the eighteenth century the scattered location of centers of production and the difficulties of communication between them rendered contact infrequent, favored distrust, awakened antipathy, and contributed to unsociability, subjectivism, and that lack of realism

---

* The famous although poorly planned Inconfidência of 1789 in Minas Gerais declared independence from Portugal. Tiradentes (Joaquim José da Silva Xavier), its martyred leader, emerged as a national hero.

[6] Note particularly in this regard the Revolt of the Alfaiates (Tailors) in Bahia (1798). See Afonso Rui, *A Primeira Revolução Social Brasileira, 1798*. As for Negro revolts, see José Honório Rodrigues, *Teoria da História do Brasil*, 2d ed., Vol. 1, p. 215, n. 64.

[7] João Capistrano de Abreu, *Capítulos de História Colonial*, rev. ed., pp. 337–338.

which causes people to prefer to speculate on goals rather than on the means of attaining them. The people, but slightly educated along the seaboard and living in ignorance in isolated pockets of the interior, were not in a position to develop a social ethic.

The decline of the colonial system began in 1808, suffering a severe blow with Dom João's decree opening the ports of Brazil to friendly nations.* Profound spiritual changes were to come about. Travelers of the period shortly afterward, such as Spix and Martius (1817–1820), asserted that the 24,000 Portuguese and the various foreigners who had come to the country would make changes in the characteristics of the inhabitants and of their society, the tone of which "evidenced little European influence."[8]

Once independence was gained, the feeling of equality in regard to Portugal was replaced by a sense of superiority. A reaction set in against all the evils stemming from three centuries marked by slavery, lack of education and freedom of expression, total submissiveness on the part of women, servility, economic oppression, and excessive discipline of children, who lived in terror and were severely chastised. Great land-holdings, idleness, a horror of work—the punishment of those who did not own slaves—continued to make for great deficiencies and insufficiencies in the Brazilian economy, and, in consequence, in the overall national culture. Unfortunately, many mistakes could not be corrected at once, for, instead of taking into consideration the germs of organization that were sprouting in juntas and local councils, statesmen read Benjamin Constant and the contemporary ideologists.† Already the Brazilians were—to use their own expression—"doing things to impress the English." They applied the political principles of the most advanced European countries to the new-born nation. Thus a new Europeanization of the superstructure took place, for feelings of subordination and inferiority were still prevalent, particularly with respect to the French and English.

The tendency to idealism, the habit of always wondering first and

---

* The royal family, fleeing Napoleon's armies, migrated to Brazil in 1808. The prince regent, later João VI, at once opened Brazil's ports to world commerce and then lifted the ban on manufacturing.

[8] In order to avoid repetitious footnotes, I have indicated in the bibliography at the end of this volume the works by foreign travelers of which I have made use.

† Two Constants are found in Brazilian history. Reference here is made to the first, Benjamin Constant de Rebecque (1767–1830), the French writer and politician. Later Brazilians would follow the republican ideas of Benjamin Constant Botelho de Magalhães (1836–1891), the Brazilian military-school instructor.

foremost what people in Europe would say about what was done in Brazil, could not fail to have bad results. Until abolished in 1888, slavery was the economic mainstay of the country. Miscegenation continued its work, and the various ethnic groups came increasingly to share in a common existence, developing a relationship that was ever richer in human meaning.

5. Brazil as Seen by Foreigners

A majority of travelers reported that the Brazilian of the nineteenth century abhorred manual labor—which was performed by slaves— and, as the Portuguese colonists of old, aspired to sudden, rapid enrichment. Slavery left deep marks: servilism on the part of the mulattoes, prejudices against active life on the part of the slaveholders, and a disinclination to serious endeavor in the areas of commerce and industry. The latter of these was nonexistent; the former was in the hands of foreigners, particularly the retail trade, which was dominated by the Portuguese. There was no specialization by trades; the journeyman, who also made use of slaves, exercised a variety of activities, even as in colonial times.

Between 1836 and 1842, according to Kidder and Fletcher, the most prominent men in Brazil were members of the learned professions. Anything like an important mechanic or tradesman's occupying a high official position was completely unheard of. The technical and commercial professions were scorned, the learned held in great repute. All—or almost all—those who wished to distinguish themselves turned to the priesthood, arms, law, or medicine. So-called social mobility, or movement from one class to another, continued to exist. Persons who had been the object of deference would lose their rank, whereas others, overcoming obstacles, would manage to escape from the lower classes and to rise in the social world. It had always been thus in Brazil. Brother Vicente do Salvador, writing in 1618, declared: "A man goes to Brazil a convict and returns full of riches and honors." This sentence, however, applied only to those born in Portugal in the colonial period, when race prejudice made it difficult for others to rise in the world. By the nineteenth century, it was possible for people of color also to rise. Of these the mulattoes showed themselves the cleverest, ablest, and most artful. Sociability was nonexistent, but little by little a society given to dreaminess and idle conversation, absent-minded, unrealistic, continuously under strong French influence as regarded styles and literary taste, took on more life.

Segregation of women was complete at first, in both town and country. Women completed their limited education at the age of thirteen or fourteen, by which time they were trained for domestic duties. At first these were restricted to supervising the work of the slaves; later, with the abolition of slavery, they were extended to care of the house and the children. In 1808 women were still reduced to domestic obscurity. Only after 1820 did they begin to appear—on rare occasions—in theaters and other public places. After 1863 such appearances became more frequent.

Education continued to be deficient—incomplete, impractical, based on memorization. Some parents, especially rich landowners in Minas Gerais, sent their sons to be educated in Europe. Others, particularly in Bahia, feared that they would fall into bad company or contract marriage with inferiors in Europe. The children of the plantation master were brought up by Negro mammies and were fully exposed to the harmful influence of slavery. Instruction, though limited (it was not extended to the masses), showed some signs of progress: by 1874 there were 4,563 private schools.

Children, disciplined to excess, had a grave and pensive air. They seemed in fact miniature adults rather than boys and girls. They did not run, roll hoops, or throw stones like children in Europe or the United States, Kidder and Fletcher noted. Contrary to what Gorer observed,[1] in Great Britain it was they who exhibited themselves to their parents. The terrified children of the sixteenth century and the excessively disciplined youngsters of the nineteenth constituted generations of profound respect for authority and superiors in general, and for the king in particular, but not for the constitution. The imperial monarchy represented a continuation of the paternal government of the kings of colonial days. Personal authority rather than the law was what mattered. Paternal authority was rejected both at the beginning and at the end of the Empire. In the first case it was a matter of hatred. In the second, when the monarchy was overthrown, a complex of remorse developed, since, people said, "This was not the republic of our dreams." Even provincial administration was organized in such fashion as to reinforce authority, and not to develop the material resources of the country, Agassiz observed.

[1] Geoffrey Gorer, *The American People: A Study in National Character.*

ilies were large, and paternal authority was as a rule thoroughly
ed. It was a patriarchal society, in which the monarch was a col-
...vc lather, as opposed to a matriarchal society, as exemplified by the
United States of today. The patriarchal complex was also reflected in
the cult of the Iron Marshal, Floriano Peixoto:* the Brazilians felt a
need for a father to govern and discipline them, as Gilberto Freyre
noted in his preface to Luís Martins' study of the complex of remorse
suffered by the generation of parricides that established the Republic.

The various travelers noted the peculiar habit of hand kissing, a
sign of respect for the authority of that taciturn father who since shortly
after 1500 had formed the image of Brazilian society. For it is or was
a patriarchal society, and also an old, traditional society, in the sense of
which Riesman speaks[2]—one in which innovation means little and
adaptation alone, with its ritual and routine, gives direction to social
life. The Brazilian, in consequence, was ceremonious and given to for-
mality; he made much use of long, high-sounding titles. "Your Excellency," "Most Excellent Seignior," "Most Illustrious Seignior" were
current official expressions in 1730, when, by royal decree, the title
"Seignior" was forbidden to everyone. Only in 1841 was it decided that
senators should be addressed as "Your Excellency" and deputies as
"Your Worship." Gradually these formal modes of address became general, ever a reflection of a ritualistic society. The Brazilian is, however,
by nature much less formal than the Portuguese, from whom he acquired
a certain grave solemnity which was common up to the beginning of the
Republic. Today it is disappearing, under the simplifying influence of
the United States.

Attachment to individual personalities is the dominant feature of
Brazilian public and political relations. To place emphasis on direct
relationships and personal liking rather than on relationships of an impersonal, indirect, unqualified nature was a basic feature of Portuguese
character, and, despite all variations, this trait is still strongly evident
in Brazilian character. Political parties have no ideological meaning,
no matter whether they be called liberal, conservative, progressive,
liberal-radical, or republican. For a long time the decisive, dominant
element was the rural aristocracy—the landed proprietors, the plantation masters, and the country "colonels," who commanded a semisovereign people. Political passion was relatively ardent where a tradition of

* Th.. stern and strong President of Brazil from 1891 to 1894.
[2] David Riesman, *The Lonely Crowd: A Study of Changing American Character*, 3d
printing.

freedom had been sealed in the blood of combat, as in Pernambuco and Rio Grande do Sul.

Rhetoric, however, was an obstacle to prosperity and efficiency, the lack of which was decisive. Foreigners, beginning with Mawe, considered the Brazilians loquacious. Bryce observed in 1912 that of greater significance for prosperity than natural resources was the quality of the labor applied to developing the country, and of greater significance yet the quality of the intelligence directing the work. Brazil was less than fortunate in this regard, he said, and the situation could not be otherwise, since the educational process was incomplete. Professional or university education has been instituted only in the present day. Rhetoric perturbs politics, Bryce went on, because many men of unquestionable talent are often betrayed by words and prefer words to deeds. In the United States and England, as Gorer observed, there is an excess of words and of liking for rhetoric, but rhetoric is clearly and consciously recognized as such. In these latter countries rhetoric is rhetoric, and it offers no solutions. In Brazil, rhetoric is an integral part of thought and is presented as a solution.

It was not because of the predominance of law-school graduates in imperial politics that many solutions were delayed. More presidents of the United States have come from the legal profession than from any other, among them men such as Jefferson, Lincoln, and Roosevelt. Of the thirty-five Americans who have exercised the presidency, twenty-two were lawyers, two were judges, and two were trained in law although they did not practice the profession.

A way with words is one of the means of attaining power or political influence. In consequence, the importance of newspapers has grown. The excesses of their attacks on the emperor and their lack of firm opinion were noted by travelers, surprised in 1868 at the extraordinary vitality of Brazilian journalism. The excesses are explained perhaps by the immaturity of the press in Brazil. It had come into being only on May 13, 1808, after a miscarriage in 1747. Corruption and venality are not recent defects. Several travelers pointed out their existence, which goes back to the colonial period. They were treated in *A Arte de Furtar* ("The Art of Stealing"),[3] a classic of Portuguese literature written in the seventeenth century.

[3] First edition published in Lisbon in 1652. See, however, the edition prepared by João Ribeiro, Rio, Garnier, 1928. Corruption began at the top, the authorities accepting graft for the letting of public contracts. See Francisco Adolfo de Varnhagen, *História Geral do Brasil*, 3d ed., Vol. 4, pp. 27, 35.

Miscegenation and the possibility of rising in the social world created an atmosphere of peaceful relations and fellowship. If race prejudice still existed in Minas Gerais in the seventeenth century, discrimination gradually disappeared. As of 1755 marriages with Indians were officially recognized; in 1773 distinctions between "new" and "old" Christians ended.[4] Negroes were favored by their own domestic influence. Under the Empire, along with an increasing awareness of the evils and harms of slavery came a realization of the advantages of free labor, and emancipation became a national goal. Gentleness in dealing with the Negro slave became general, and Brazil ceased to be a hell for Negroes, although it long continued to be a purgatory for whites and a paradise for mulatto women, in the famous words of Francisco Manuel de Melo.

The rise of the mulattoes in the social world was an unquestionable fact, as Gilberto Freyre well pointed out in *The Mansions and the Shanties*.[5] The beauty of the mulatto and other dark-skinned women and the intelligence and the cleverness of the mulatto men favored their rise in the ranks of society. Negroes still constituted the great mass of laborers, although some travelers held that when they were given their freedom they became indolent and lazy. The problem of emancipation was no political bugaboo; it was discussed freely and with feeling, as Agassiz says, by all social classes, and sentiment was generally against slavery. Slavery was an obstacle to progress; its effect on the populace was that of a moral illness. Along with it went the scorn for work which justified laziness, and slaveowners left it to their blacks to earn what was necessary for existence. One of the characteristics of slavery in Brazil was the variety of methods of manumission used for liberating slaves: in 1798 there were 400,000 free Negroes and in the abolition period there were three times as many free Negroes as slaves.The free Negroes had a social standing between that of free European-descended landowners and slaves.

Free immigration began in 1818, but by 1855 only 40,000 colonists had entered the country. At the beginning of the twentieth century Bryce and Pierre Denis pointed out that European immigration served to revitalize rural life and that, because it was not directed to the "North" (i.e., Northeast), that part of the country had the most mediocre rural

---

[4] The "new" Christians were Jews who were obliged to accept conversion in order to escape the tortures of the Inquisition.

[5] Gilberto Freyre, *The Mansions and the Shanties: The Making of Modern Brazil,* translated by Harriet de Onís.

population of all. They attributed to the varying quality of labor the differences between North and South.

Foreigners were unanimous in their praise of Brazilian hospitality. The Brazilians have never been xenophobic. Their nationalism has this peculiar trait: they are not *against* anyone; they are *for* themselves and those who partake of their aspirations, those who come to lend collaboration or merely to share in a common existence.

Lack of freedom, colonial oppression, the shadow of the Inquisition (which as late as the eighteenth century was ever on watch against any sign of heterodoxy), persecution of individuals for political reasons (José Bonifácio being the first victim) were replaced under the leadership of Pedro II, once he attained his majority, by greater freedom of thought, freedom of the press, and freedom of speech.

Koseritz noted the excesses of the press in its attacks on the emperor, whose private life was treated without respect, although Article 99 of the Constitution of 1824 declared his person to be "sacred and inviolable." Advocates of republicanism and positivism propagandized without repression. In consequence, it can be said that there had been a considerable gain: freedom of speech, religious toleration (praised by Protestant ministers such as Kidder and Fletcher), a shedding of racial prejudice, free access to society, peaceful relations among the various ethnic groups, and generous human companionship instead of exclusiveness.

Though the object of attack or disrespect on the part of the press, "Parliament," Ribeyrolles wrote in 1858, "is an institution dear to the people. Its liberties are deeply rooted, and it would take a strong blast to uproot or destroy them." The common people's lot, then as today, was hard, but social mobility and the nonexistence of castes permitted individuals to improve themselves freely. Revulsion was still felt for manual labor, and industry and commerce exerted little attraction. The best part of life was not that devoted to business but that given to leisure. Work was a punishment, and poverty was not a deadly sin. Those in a position to do so aimed at the learned professions. In truth, however, as Wetherell observed around 1850, the Brazilian seemed to have no objective, no aspiration to better his station in life. Political influence was the only goal which interested him, and the plantation masters were masters of the country as well, spending without restraint. Although progressive, Kidder and Fletcher said, the Brazilians had inherited, along with other ancestral characteristics, an antipathy for innovations.

Nothing was done with haste, and the words "Be patient" were among the most frequently heard by those who had to endure the eternal postponement of solutions to their problems. "Time is not money," said the German Canstatt; this shows that the capitalistic spirit had not taken hold in Brazil. No one ever carried a parcel, however small, not even a book. That was slaves' work.

Regional distinctions were readily evident to travelers, whether scholars or mere tourists. Saint-Hilaire referred in 1820 to the appreciable differences in customs among the people of the various provinces. Martius also noted differences and resemblances between Pernambucans and inhabitants of Rio Grande do Sul, for example. The most highly praised were the people of the province of São Paulo. Martius recorded a saying to the effect that in Bahia the men were to be praised, but not the women; in Pernambuco the women were to be praised, but not the men; and that in São Paulo both were to be praised. Certain national defects, mentioned by Canstatt, such as disrespect for the law and natural sensuality, relate to the personal character of Luso-Brazilian culture and to the promiscuous miscegenation to which slavery gave rise. Good qualities listed by Canstatt were hospitality, as previously mentioned, respect for parents, the good nature of the people, and above all their consciousness of their country's history. Martius observed that the citizen of São Paulo told himself, not without pride, that his country had a history. According to the observations made by foreign travelers, from Saint-Hilaire in 1816 to Cooper in 1917, Brazilian patriotism is connected with a consciously developed and preserved history. Brazilian national life suffers, however, from a capital defect: the confusion of words with deeds, aspirations with achievements—in a word, verbalism joined with a lack of political realism.

Few countries offer so many possibilities for change, Bryce wrote in 1912. Cooper's observations, made in 1917, when the domination of European influence—economic and spiritual—was coming to an end, merely stress the traits that have already been pointed out: a lack of industrial initiative, an abhorrence of violence, hospitality, intermittent energy, conservative ideas, an aversion to change, government by oratory, cohesiveness represented by historic consciousness and a common language, domination and rule of an essentially agricultural country by the rural aristocracy, the decisive nature of paternal authority, 70 percent illiteracy (an increase in the number of schools to 13,000 had not compensated for a growth of the population to 20,000,000), a lack of universities, and a spirit of pacifism.

New features in the general picture were higher education for a few women; an increasing practice of sports, especially soccer; a period of twenty years without a revolution (short in comparison with the forty years from 1849 to 1889, when the Empire was unperturbed by revolutions); and, in particular, the assignment of a higher social category to businessmen in São Paulo. There was a beginning of a general suspicion of Americans, who, in the last analysis, were admired for their business efficiency and their practical way of handling things. This struck the Brazilian industrialist or businessman as incompatible with the prevailing ideal of doing everything with decorum. "You love work, and business comes first; pleasure and family life are of secondary importance." "You live to work instead of working to live." These sentences, recorded by Cooper, show the stereotype image which the Brazilians had of the Americans. This image reflected the desire to overcome the idea, of Iberian provenience, of the opposition between the indignity of commercial work and the dignity of the speculative life. It was a step forward.

From 1917 on, a world of transformations took place in the spiritual structure of Brazilian life. New influences were felt: Americanization took the place of Europeanization; economic activity rose in the social scale; work was rationalized; a spirit of boldness and renovation became evident. Strangest of all was the sensation of haste, the dynamism which Monbeig observed particularly in São Paulo. A widespread optimism, intellectual audacity, and enterprising energy characterized the time-conscious men of the frontier regions of the state of São Paulo, decidedly different from those who left everything for the morrow.

The new crops that spread over the pioneer zone, the new techniques of cultivation and production brought new modes of thought. All the young settlers, however, sought to embrace a tradition and to develop a history that would justify their hurly-burly. The energy with which they launched into work and the conviction that fortune awaited them caused Monbeig to believe that the advertising slogan of the national lottery, "Get rich," was, without exaggeration, a collective watchword. To what extent is this pursuit of wealth a continuation of the old dream of rapid enrichment which characterized colonial and imperial times, now joined with the more energetic, bold, independent spirit of the present day?

Like Monbeig, Camacho believes that Brazil is in full process of political, economic, and cultural emancipation. Nothing was so demoralizing to the foreigner, brought up in the tradition of European science, as the climate of the Amazon region, where people died of hunger, Agassiz wrote, a region whose future did not belong to the present generation, Bryce said. The rehabilitation of the Amazon region in foreign eyes was the work of Charles Wagley, who showed that the principal reasons for backwardness were to be sought, not in climate, but in Amazonian culture and society, in the relation of the area to the seats of economic and political power and to the centers of cultural life. The positive values of Brazilian culture, the characteristic features of the Brazilians as a social and national group, all of which Wagley pointed out, will be recalled in the conclusions.

The new thesis of the sociological and geographical school, first presented by Jacques Lambert, then repeated in a new study by Monbeig, later by Morazé, is that Brazil and the Brazilians are divided into two societies, differing in their levels and modes of living—rural or old society and urban or new society. They have not evolved at the same pace and have grown quite distinct from one another, although they are united by the same national feeling. They do not form two civilizations; they are, however, separated by centuries. Old Brazil is the rural zone; the new Brazil is made up of pioneer and urban regions. In the new Brazil the middle classes play a decisive role in politics, for, although their numbers are not great, they insist on the adoption of modern reforms. They meet opposition from rural society, archaic, colonial, resistant to innovations. Indignant over their electoral and political defeats, they frequently call for revolutionary solutions. Lambert repeats the picture of empire days, old but true, of a people which as a whole is relatively indifferent to ideologies, slow to revolt, constituting a classic example of an easily governed nation.

The whole truth is not conveyed by speaking of two Brazils, one archaic, the other new, or one well developed and the other underdeveloped. In reality, as professors Leslie Lipson and Gilberto Freyre recently wrote, there are a number of Brazils, as many as there are specific regions or economic sectors.

Frequent political agitation merely bespeaks an adolescent nation faced with the immense task of economic emancipation and a lack of trained cadres, the latter a consequence of the youthfulness of the population and the poverty of the country's cultural and university resources. Even teaching is being provided hastily, by universities and secondary schools established on inadequate bases. Monbeig and Morazé emphasize the disproportionately small number of adults and the lack of cadres, both of which increase the difficulty of the tasks to be performed and render public administration deficient.

Maurice Le Lannou also observed the rapid, frenzied activity of São Paulo. In his opinion, the fixed-quota immigration system initiated in 1934 could lead a country which had been singularly free of xenophobia to demographic nationalism. The purpose of the system was to safeguard the character of Brazil and to fix the national ethos in accordance with the prevailing racial formula. Into that formula, which was deemed to have given a reasonably homogeneous product, there entered the Lusitanian group, heir to the glories of conquest; a mass of crossbreeds of varying hue, representing on the whole a fine achievement of humanity in the tropics; and minorities of recent European origin, fairly well assimilated, giving their allegiance to Brazil, and accepted as native sons.

This is a European's summation, and the picture it gives is overly colonial and quite unacceptable. The Brazilian no longer considers himself as belonging to a Lusitanian group or his country as subject to colonization. The divorce between feeling and behavior, which Le Lannou noted in the contrast which the Brazilian affords between conservative apathy and a firm belief in riches readily at hand, is to be related to the age-old lack of realism of a people who prefer daydreaming to action.

The foreign view of the Brazilians should be completed by the Brazilians' own view of their national character, and the two should be compared in order to arrive at a better picture.

6. General Traditions and Present-Day Characteristics

Brazil was the only country of the New World to achieve independence under a monarchical regime, similar to that of the mother country.[*] There was no recourse to a foreign dynasty. Political emancipation assumed the air of a natural development, restraining tendencies to civil anarchy, and contributing to preserving intact the territorial heritage of Portuguese America. The immediate consequence of unity was that problems and tasks assumed gigantic proportions—a challenge which

[*] The young heir to the Bragança throne, Prince Pedro, remained in Rio de Janeiro as regent when his father, João VI, returned to Lisbon in 1821. Pedro, influenced by such Brazilians as José Bonifácio, declared Brazil's independence on September 7, 1822.

the governing minorities have had to face since independence. Further complications were represented by the facts that the population had been prematurely scattered over the land and that in its colonial exclusiveness and national isolation it did nothing but regress, coming to display inadequacies of both an economic and a spiritual nature. In its first political action it revealed a high degree of plasticity—a capacity for political accommodation, for temporizing, for adaptation. The solution was facilitated by the reconstitution of a patriarchal society, divided into two castes: masters and slaves.

Brazilian society of colonial and empire days was based on the rural aristocracy. This is a characteristic of societies in old age. Compared with other American countries, particularly Argentina and the United States, Brazil is not a young country in the sense that the past and its traditions make themselves strongly felt in the current political pattern. Pierre Denis observed about 1908 that the Brazilians liked to speak of their country as young, but that the European who had traveled through other Euro-American countries, such as Argentina and the United States, would feel less of a foreigner in Brazil, as he would not there experience the feeling of surprise or shock which the two former countries produced in him by their poorly organized societies, lacking in roots and class distinctions, and having as their sole goals individual freedom and success—characteristics which have become noticeable in Brazil only of late.

Brazilian patriotism is longer in memories. In this sense, Brazil is an old country, full of traditions, constituted for the most part of Brazilians of more than three generations' standing. This is not the case with Argentina and the United States. Between 1850 and 1950 Brazil received only 4,800,000 immigrants, of which but 3,400,000 remained in the country. Of these last-mentioned, a majority is made up of Portuguese. Theirs was the basic personality which predominated in Brazilian character during the three centuries of the Colony (with the addition of certain Indian and Negro variants) and in certain respects it has remained constant, having been reinforced by the current of immigration. Thus there has been a continuity of population, of personalities, and of cultures, contrary to the situation in Argentina and the United States, where peoples from many lands often operated fundamental changes in the personality, the culture, and the very social structure of the country.

It is in the South that first- and second-generation Brazilians are to be found and that historic traditions are less readily felt. Even there, however, the basic Luso-Brazilian personality and culture are preιdominant, and, in consequence, society in the South, even pioneer society, strives to identify itself with tradition and to establish a history for itself. Perhaps, Monbeig thinks, the inhabitants feel the need for seeking in that history, if not a justification for their hurly-burly, at least a source of energy. On the whole, though, as Bryce and Cooper observed, the country is conscious of its past and the Brazilian has a strong national tradition, which renders him zealous for the country's integrity.

A culture and a nationality exist in Brazil which are unique, and which are a source of pride to the inhabitants. They present, however, two different aspects. According to Jacques Lambert, the Brazilians are divided into two societies, differentiated by levels and modes of existence. One is primarily rural and preserves its traditional organization. This is particularly evident in the Northeast. The other is primarily urban; it evidences itself in urban areas throughout the country and in rural areas, also, in the state of São Paulo and in other parts of the South. The first-mentioned is an archaic society; the second represents a new Brazil. Despite the social differences, the two are closely knit, being united by the same national feeling and by other common values. They do not form separate cultures, but represent, rather, different stages of the same culture, separated by centuries. Positive and negative factors, the strength and the weakness of the basic Brazilian culture, are present in both societies. It was the early dissemination of the population of Brazil in the seventeenth century that resulted in the overall predominance of the basic Brazilian culture with its peculiar traditional characteristics, existing even today despite variations produced by urban technical change. (In contrast, the spread of the population in the United States began after 1830, with the coming of the railroads.)

The new Brazil presents a less stratified social structure and an amazing degree of social mobility. The colonial traditions of an archaic society have been brought into sudden contact with new cultural traits, introduced with the rapid importation of new production techniques, new cultures and ways of life, stemming especially from the United States.

The Americanization of Western culture has brought about the rationalization of work, a rise in the social standing of mercantile and industrial activity, and a stimulus to capitalism and to efforts to overcome the past. It has brought in addition all the evils of advertising; it has created the mentality of conspicuous consumption, which leads to inflation; it has led to the debasement of commercial radio and television; it has produced in the middle class sensations of anxiety and alienation. The old-school basic Luso-Brazilian personality has been weakened by the appearance of a new, less formal personality, less attached to personal values, more objective. Since society is divided into old and new sectors, politics has inevitably become a struggle between two different concepts of the nature of political institutions.

The burden represented by three centuries of colonialism, that is, of subjection to metropolitan interests, by four centuries of slavery, by the immensity of the problems facing the country, and by the lack of cadres of leaders, has created a feeling of insufficiency—not of inferiority— which has a psychological effect on decisions and the choice between tasks and solutions of prime importance. Capistrano de Abreu explained the evolution of national characteristics as the gradual overcoming of the feeling of being disdained, as the development of a feeling of superiority in regard to the Portuguese, which led to the proclamation of independence on September 7, 1822. A feeling of inferiority continued with respect to Europe, however, he said. This feeling is not to be interpreted as a complex, since recognition of a scale of values and a capacity for admiration, far from being signs of inferiority, reveal a spirit of generosity indicative of moral health.[1] Only when the attempt is made to dissimulate inferiority, by a pretense of superiority in a dialectic *circulus in probando,* only when the scale of values is inverted, with passion and resentment, does an inferiority complex manifest itself.

This did not happen in the case of Brazil's relations with the great powers of Europe, particularly Great Britain, which exerted a dominant influence on the life of the country. When the optimism and the confidence of the first hours of independence were over, when the Brazilian was still fascinated with the drugs, minerals, grandeur, and power which Antonil had exhibited before his eyes,[2] he choked off his feeling of insufficiency with an endless catalog of his riches—which were not so readily come by as he had previously thought—and as a result of his own natural tendencies he became unrealistic. This is what lies at the root of Brazilian nationalist boasting—riches, not tasks to be per-

[1] Brazilian victories in sports events—Brazilians have twice won the world soccer and basketball championships; they have also won a world lightweight boxing championship and the women's tennis championship at Wimbledon—and in international beauty contests destroy the thesis of the inferiority of crossbreeds, long accepted by the alienated elite under the influence of theories of European and American origin.

[2] André João Antonil [pseud. for João Antônio Andreoni], *Cultura e Opulência do Brasil por suas Drogas e Minas.*

formed; excellencies, rather than economic and spiritual sufficiencies.[3]

It was not recognized that the great sin was poverty, which could be overcome by work and saving. Work was scorned; it was reserved exclusively for slaves. No attention was paid to saving, with the result that the capital required for possession and enjoyment of the riches so greatly vaunted in speeches was never accumulated. A bastard constitution—the fruit of an uncelebrated marriage between unrealistic principle and national reality—was created by copying extracts from Benjamin Constant.[*] Only gradually did it undergo adjustment, and then more in the interest of the elite than in that of the masses. The most persistent element in Brazilian political life seems to have been the habit of adopting solutions that fit principles rather than situations. José Bonifácio's observation that in Brazil the possible exceeds the real seems to bear relation to that lack of realism and attachment to words pointed out by Bryce and Cooper. Or was it José Bonifácio's intention to create a doctrine of political "possibilism," the theory of which would be that possibilities in Brazil are so numerous that momentary reality and current appearances disguise and hide them? In this case, José Bonifácio's phrase would relate to the deceitful vision of hidden riches, to the optimistic view that no effort was required for the Brazilians to possess them, and that sooner or later they would be revealed.

Everything was lacking—both cadres of leaders and cadres of followers. The lack became accentuated under the Republic, with the growth of tasks to be faced, of the welfare needs of eighty million inhabitants, and of the requirements for carrying progress to the more backward areas of the vast territory. Blame for the situation is to be attributed to lack of realism and to verbalism rather than to the predominance of law-school graduates in public life, and to the sacrifice of reality to beauty of form and of sonority, to the world of the word and of sound. It is also to be attributed to the attachment to personalities which characterizes Brazilian national life and the governing minorities. It relates to the basic Brazilian personality, which stresses direct personal relations, based on liking rather than on unconditioned, impersonal, practical relations. Personal liking is above the law.

Attachment to personalities, which historically centered on political

---

[3] Such boasting is of remote origin; its essence, however, was distilled by Afonso Celso de Assis Figueiredo Júnior in his book *Porque me Ufano do meu País.*

[*] The work of Benjamin Constant, particularly his *Cours de Politique constitutionnelle,* greatly influenced the preparation of the Constitution of 1824.

figures (chiefly law-school graduates), cultural leaders, ecclesiastics, and, at the beginning of the Republic, the military, is now dispersed over the most diverse of groups. Beginning in 1930, primarily at the instigation of Assis Chateaubriand, newspapers began to glorify business and industrial leaders, who, through their professional associations, have formed pressure groups and are asserting their demands. Thanks to radio and television new personalities of popular origin give expression to the energies of a semibarbaric populism, counterbalancing the personalities that appear in the society pages of the newspapers.

Thus since 1930 certain personalities have sunk in the general regard and others have risen by acclamation of the populace or of society. If extreme subdivision seems to show signs of a democratization of the processes of history, it also represents the irrational force of barbarized populism, the strength of the conservative classes—more concerned with their own interests than with those of the nation—and, finally, the world of the idle, frivolous personality glorified in society columns.

The sacrifice of the law-school graduate and the intellectual, who today have sunk in the scale of social values and are represented only institutionally, does not denote a gain, any more than the rise of the social personality that is characterized by competition for wealth and by conspicuous consumption—grandiose, useless, a contradiction to the need for savings in the period of development.

Thus, in its greater complexity, the Brazilian personality presents contradictory aspects, some democratic, some oligarchic, corresponding to the fragmentation of power. Both aspects point to a possible future break in the barrier of oligarchic privilege.

The moments of sufficiency in Brazilian history are those in which the minorities took the road of autonomy, or invested their course of action with a certain degree of impersonalness, endowing it with a content of ideas, problems, and solutions. Sufficiency or insufficiency—satisfying or failing to satisfy a series of requirements for a given standard of living—is an economic and moral concept. It is not a matter of Marxist approach, of explaining the lack of the psychological characteristics necessary to capitalism by the poverty of the Brazilian economy, or of viewing the abundance exhibited by the United States as a sign of superiority, as David Potter thought.[4] The thesis of Max Weber[5] aids in understanding how Iberian spiritual insufficiencies impeded or

[4] David M. Potter, *People of Plenty: Economic Abundance and the American Character.*
[5] Max Weber, *The Protestant Ethic and the Spirit of Capitalism.*

rendered difficult formation of the spirit of capitalism. Thus Brazilian spiritual insufficiencies—psychological characteristics—accompanied Brazilian economic insufficiency. Not merely through economic development will that insufficiency be overcome, for if spiritual insufficiencies continue it will be difficult to achieve abundance. Certain psychosocial sufficiencies are indispensable for economic development.

The interplay is functional; there is a mutual interdependence of behavior. The Brazilians have avoided the mistake of rejecting the past: condemnation of the past signifies revolution. They have always managed to maintain a connection with their history; they have acquired a historic consciousness of the unity of their territorial and spiritual heritage. The basic Luso-Brazilian personality has a horror of violence and always seeks a way of smoothing things over, a path of moderation that avoids definite breaks. Cleverness, prudence in shunning extremes, an ability to forget, a rich sense of humor, a cool head, and a warm heart get the Brazilians through difficult moments. These psychosocial characteristics relate to the personal nature of Brazilian culture, to the peaceful human relations of which history bears record, to the patience which forms part of the basic personality and to which slavery gave incentive. Hence the compromises which, upon the proclamation of independence, upon the abdication of Pedro I, upon the proclamation of Pedro II's majority, upon the abolition of slavery, upon the establishment of the Republic, and at the time of more recent civic movements, have softened blows, calmed spirits, favored conciliation, and led rapidly to cooperation.

Conciliation rather than revolution has dominated Brazilian history. In part this is because the people, with their spirit of concord, prefer to gain less rather than have recourse to violence, in part because the dominant oligarchic groups prefer yielding a little to risking much, and finally because the armed forces—democratic, liberal, and progressive in their tendencies—wield a balance of power that is exercised to moderate minorities rather than subjugate majorities.[6] In addition, Brazilian manifestations of lack of conformity—the very revolutions that have occurred—generally are confused expressions of popular demands and of attachment to personalities. They were softened under the Empire by the policy of conciliation, which was represented not only by Honório Hermeto Carneiro Leão, the Marquis of Paraná, but also by Luís Alves de Lima e Silva, the Marshal-Duke of Caxias. The

---

[6] Unfortunately, in 1964 the armed forces broke with this tradition.

only trouble then was—as it is now—that the compromises have been practical from the viewpoint of the personalities involved, not from that of reality. This has always meant the victory of the self-centered interests of the dominant minority rather than national progress. The victories of the common people have been slow in coming, and obtained at the cost of long suffering.

7. Traditional Positive Characteristics

Summing up, one might say by way of tentative conclusions that the traditional positive characteristics of the Brazilians are as follows:

1. A lively feeling of nationalism, which requires foreign elements to undergo a process of Brazilianization; an acute consciousness of the nation's historical heritage.

2. National cohesiveness, represented by a common language.

3. A political tradition of liberalism (although government intervention has always been evident in the economic area) and of civil government.

4. Religious homogeneity, in the form of a highly flexible Roman Catholicism.

5. The relatively peaceful nature of race relations.

6. The importance of family relations, the family still being the nucleus of social life.

7. The fact that the Brazilian people are among the most open-minded and accessible in the world. This trait increases their capacity for adaptation and renders easier the learning of techniques and the application thereof in the exploitation of the nation's resources.

8. The fact that the traditional forms of agricultural cooperation[1] have permitted development of a general spirit of association, as yet exceedingly limited.

9. The fact that, in the mass, the Brazilians are relatively insensitive to ideologies and slow to revolt, constituting the ideal type of an easily governed people.

10. The fact that Brazilian society is characterized by a deeply rooted sense of democracy, based on a profoundly Christian human feel-

---

[1] Under the system of mutual aid known as *mutirão* or *puxirão* the small farmers of a given neighborhood band together to help one of their number with his planting, his harvest, the construction of his house, or some other major undertaking, the beneficiary of such aid being obligated to offer them some sort of festivity in return on the same day.

ing which causes it to view with disfavor inequalities deriving from economic factors.

11. A spirit of conciliation, which favors compromise and the avoidance of extremes; rejection of radical or violent measures or solutions.

8. Present-Day Positive Characteristics

Again summing up, the following can be indicated tentatively as present-day positive characteristics:

1. An overall tendency to optimism and boldness in thought and action, all of which stimulate a spirit of initiative, which formerly was all but inexistent.

2. A tendency toward love of work and toward the setting of a higher value on economic activity, which was formerly held in scorn.

3. Encouragement of capitalism, of the rationalization of labor, and of efforts to overcome remnants of the colonial past.

4. A desire for economic emancipation and social progress. The desire to reform social institutions is very strong, as is the increased awareness of Brazil's geographical possibilities and its historical heritage. Consequently, the former aversion to change and progress is disappearing. A few years ago, speed was considered "the enemy of perfection"; today it is held to be "the enemy of backwardness."

5. Gradual disappearance of the fixed hierarchy of socioeconomic classes, dominant in rural areas.

6. Signs of a belief in fortune acquired by effort and in the social function of money, as opposed to the love of gambling and easy and rapid enrichment so common in the days of the Colony and the Empire. A curious example of the most recent change in the mentality of the young scions of the oligarchy is the seduction exercised upon them by commercial and industrial activity. Formerly their aim was to acquire a notary's office[1] or a post in government.

7. Pacifism, which is related to the rigid discipline to which children are subjected, to paternal authority, and to a horror of tragic solutions.

---

[1] A notary's appointment is a much-sought-after political plum in Brazil, as the office is highly lucrative, represents little work, and enjoys social prestige. Minas Gerais is the state with the greatest number of notaries' offices in Brazil. In 1958, of the 12,258 notaries' offices existing in the country, 2,603 were in Minas. Next came Bahia with 1,637. Men from Minas hold a majority of the notaries' offices in the city of Rio de Janeiro. The so-called notarial class is linked with the Minas oligarchy, which has held the predominant place in the political leadership of the nation.

Brazil has always defended the principles of arbitration and pacific settlement, because its position has a firm legal basis, the country disposes freely of its territory, and the population has no problems of ethnic or linguistic minorities or of racial discrimination. The aversion to violent solutions at home and to war abroad and the belief in Brazilian adroitness at diplomatic negotiation increase the tendency toward a spirit of conciliation. Brazilians are aware that they must live in the mainstream of international life and not in the backwaters of history.

8. Nationalism in the form of loyalty to the country's own aspirations and interests. Disloyalty to the Portuguese crown was possible, but disloyalty to Brazil is not. National individualism and idiosyncrasies impart a distinctive character to Brazilian national and international policy.

9. The moral indignation of the puritanic and moralizing middle class. In its refusal to tolerate mistakes and stains on reputation, it represents a moral force; however, all political solutions that are purely moral in aim are of a negative nature and have preceded movements toward the extreme right.

9. Traditional and Present-Day Negative Characteristics

Still summing up, the following can be indicated tentatively as traditional and present-day negative characteristics:

1. Remnants of the tendency to put off until tomorrow what can be done today; remainders of Portuguese conservatism.

2. Psychosocial instability, resulting from the struggle between the traditions of an archaic colonial society and the cultural elements of the new Brazil.

3. A great lack of trained cadres in Brazilian administration and politics.

4. A limited number of adults in contrast with a multitude of young people. This renders the tasks of the present generation crushing, particularly in view of the immenseness of the problems to be faced.

5. Administrative corruption and lack of truly representative government. The former has historic roots in the colonial period, and was denounced by Father Antônio Vieira and in *A Arte de Furtar* ("The Art of Stealing"). The oligarchies which came afterwards continued the practice of the art, which is gradually being suppressed. The electoral system has been improved, with the banishment of fraud, but it is not

yet productive of results that are truly representative of the nation. Voting continues to represent both the nation and the antination, as Gilberto Amado summed up the situation in 1931.

6. The centering of Brazilian public life on personalities. This can and should be corrected by an emphasis on problems rather than on individuals. Personal feelings complicate the handling of public affairs; hence the favors shown to sons, nephews, and sons-in-law, in addition to other types of nepotism connected with a political system revolving around personalities and with the patron-client relationship which politicians in general, from the most fervent partisans of the oligarchy to the most passionate champions of labor, adopt in their dealings in matters of state.

7. Lack of realism on the part of the ruling minorities. This can and must be corrected by a capacity for meeting challenges with real solutions, not with theories. The lack of realism results from the alienation of those minorities—constantly seduced by foreign marvels—from the everyday reality of national life.

8. The *caiado* complex. Ethnic and cultural crossbreeding has given rise to complexes among the offspring of mixed unions. One of these is that of the *caiado*, which first manifested itself in the colonial period and seems to have been born of a belief in the original sin of miscegenation. It is negative in effect and results in causing mixed-blood sectors of the population to serve antinational interests. This was sensed by the rebels of 1817, who sang that "Brazil is not to be governed by *caiados*."* In Spanish America the royalists counted on the mestizos in the struggles against Bolívar. The *caiados*, light-skinned crossbreeds, who are most frequent in the states of Bahia, Minas Gerais, and Rio de Janeiro, are well-adapted conformists, astute flatterers, band-wagon riders, practitioners of the "art of being a somebody," as set forth in Machado de Assis' short story of that name.[1]

9. The immigrant-settler complex. Another complex which has left its mark on the Brazilian personality is that of the "colonist," which has sprung up in nuclei of immigrant settlers who have not become totally integrated into the Brazilian synthesis. Some of the settlers are possessed by a spirit of discrimination and intolerance; they are racists, antisemites, ultraconservatives, intransigent defenders of the *status quo*,

---

* Reference is made here to the liberal ideology behind the republican revolution in Pernambuco.
[1] The short story by Joaquim Maria Machado de Assis to which reference is made is "Teoria do Medalhão," to be found in the collection *Papéis Avulsos*.

or proponents of a slow, gentle gradualism in reform. They have little understanding of the insufficiencies of other areas of Brazil; they suffer from a sort of superiority complex; they scorn the Indian and the Negro. In an attempt to compensate for the psychological burden of having been born in a nucleus of immigrants, in a "settlement," they have developed by way of defense mechanism a metropolitan, old-country, or viceregal view of Brazil. Today, according to a thesis recognized by many scholars, the "colonial dependencies" of "metropolitan Brazil" (i.e., the East and the South) are the formerly prosperous captaincies and provinces of colonial and imperial days.* For the immigrant-settler mentality, the transformation of areas of recent foreign settlement into areas of influence, in which the nation's destiny is decided, and the decline of the formerly dominant captaincies and provinces to a subordinate position, of colonial dependencies as it were, are causes for inner rejoicing. Neither complex—that of the settler or that of the *caiado*—is a dominant case; it is rather a deformation. I believe, however, that the two figure among the psychological tendencies to be noted among Brazilians, both of the elite and of the mass of the people.

10. Alienation, or cultural expatriation. This is a flight from the inferiority complex, from which the mass of the people does not suffer. The strange predilection for things foreign has led to antinationalism, as Sales Tôrres Homem showed in his *Libelo do Povo* ("Accusation by the People").[2] Sectors of the minority have been alienated, antinational, and antiprogressive. The middle classes vacillate among alienation, acting after the fashion of *caiados*, and truth to themselves.

11. The unceasing, unwearying struggle of all against the state, more particularly against the public treasury.

12. Belief in luck and gambling. Almost all business is not business, but a gamble. This attitude and the excessive number of legal holidays, civic and religious, show that childishness is still dominant and that the Brazilians have not acquired the rational approach and the efficiency required for economic progress.

---

* There is no better example to prove this than Pernambuco. As the most prosperous captaincy during the colonial period, it exported sugar to European markets. Pernambuco managed to maintain its influence if not its wealth throughout the Empire, but coffee came to replace sugar as the country's principal export. By the end of the first decade of the twentieth century coffee-producing São Paulo was contributing 50 percent of Brazil's exports; sugar-producing Pernambuco was barely able to contribute 1 percent. As economic power shifted to São Paulo so did political power. Pernambuco became the "disaster area" of the nation, a poor, backward colony of rich, progressive São Paulo.

[2] Timandro (pseud. of Francisco de Sales Tôrres Homem), *Libelo do Povo.* Reproduced by Raimundo Magalhães Júnior in *Três Panfletários do Segundo Reinado.*

13. Insufficient welfare and educational services. As a nation the Brazilians are still 50 percent illiterate. On the other hand they have twenty officially recognized universities, not to speak of more than two hundred independent institutions of higher learning. Thus there is deficiency in one respect and plethora in another. Average life expectancy continues low (44) and the average length of active economic life is twenty-eight years.

10. Conclusion

The influences which mold character are difficult to fasten upon in the course of their accumulation or dissipation by the processes of history. They can, however, be observed in a prodigious variety of significant personalities. If the social function of character is to ensure patterns of conformity and certain stable elements in productivity, politics, leisure, and culture, and if character, in the contemporary scientific sense of historic social character, is to be considered as standardized reactions in social relationships, it follows that, in a country 52 percent of whose population is nineteen years old or under, youth is to play a role of capital importance.

The children and young people of Brazil must be adequately prepared for the enormous tasks they are called to undertake. Thus investment in education is of as great importance as investment in economic development. Only by attending to needs in both these sectors can the Brazilians remove the inadequacies listed under negative aspects. Abundance must not be merely economic but moral as well. Thus the fight against emphasis on personalities should not mean impersonalness, just as the benefits deriving from conformity should not lead to submissiveness. Without nonconformity there is no progress. Nor should economic nationalism lead to xenophobia.

Industrial and technological transformations should be accompanied by cultural change, so that alterations in traditional ways of life may be accompanied by the execution of programs for technical and educational improvement.

This people, of good disposition in the view of foreigners, is beginning to display, in the positive aspects of its nationalism, an increasing faith in its future and in the main currents of present-day historical development. It does not seem to have any interest in the side paths of history. "This Brazil," wrote Fernão Cardim in 1584, "is already a different kind of Portugal." The progressive acceleration of Brazilian historical development shows that, under the stimulus of new characteristics exhibited by leaders and people alike, Portuguese sobriety and conservatism having been overcome, present-day Brazil is already a different kind of Brazil.

PART II

National Aspirations

Who shall judge between you and us? Who shall be the judge between conservatives and progressives? My answer is: the nation. The nation is not a party.

ZACARIAS DE GÓIS E VASCONCELOS
Speech in the Chamber of Deputies,
January 26, 1864

11. Introduction

Nations, as political societies, are dominated by vital interests which give rise to emotional reactions and rational convictions and are responsible for a historic unity in the behavior of peoples and their leaders. All have permanent aspirations, which are the product of history, the characteristics of the people involved, and the stage of economic development they have attained.

It is by observing the course of historical development that we can detect the emergence of new spiritual vigor, of expanding economic forces, or of political energies that may give expression to national aspirations and ensure the prospect of their future expansion, at home and abroad—all on a larger or smaller scale, in accordance with the capacities of the people, the leadership, and the economic forces in question.

Self-determination can be manifested on a broad or a limited scale in the form of individual liberties, a federal or central-type government, a democratic or an autocratic regime. National integration may or may not be limited to preservation of the national territory or effective occupation thereof, to questions of regional balance or imbalance and of harmony or the lack of harmony between industry and agriculture. Prosperity and well-being may be limited to satisfaction of dominant groups or may be extended to cover all members of the national community. Finally, international prestige may be no more than a matter of recognition of the country's legitimate rights by the international community or, as a natural development of the country's potential, it may become a question of territorial expansion or political hegemony.

Permanent national aspirations are not a mere summing up of present-day aspirations, achieved or frustrated. The latter find inspiration in the structure or superstructure, but are always a reflection of the situation prevailing at the moment. They are the expression of secondary values, accepted without conformity; they are current, contested images of groups, sectors, regions, the elite, or the mass of the people. Permanent aspirations are a historic heritage; they have lasting, living value; they reflect traditional values, unanimously accepted, from

which other aspirations derive; they are truly national, representing
everyone, and not merely the elite or other segments of the populace.
Common to all strata of society, they result from a discriminating selec-
tion made over the course of history.

   The transitory nature of aspirations of the day, their occasional transformation into permanent aspirations, and the increase or decrease in
the number of the latter—since history is the record of change, and a
nation is the embodiment of a uniquely original history—are expressive
of the fecundity of the minority, the cultural advance of the majority,
regenerations, national progress, and development. If there were no
aspirations of the moment, the nation would be a tomb within which the
creative spirit lay dead. The future of the political and the economic
energies of the nation depends on the balance between the permanent
and the temporary, between differing interests and common interests.
If their permanent interests are not defended, nations disintegrate and
perish; but without temporary interests they may grow old and sterile.
That which is permanent is basic and vital, but that which is characteristic of the present day routs the outmoded, gives life to the organic,
and provides for future development. Both, taken together, show the
unity of the course of history—the past (thesis), the present (antithesis), and the future (synthesis) of the nation.

   Although it is not difficult to distinguish between the effects of permanent aspirations on the course of history, it is not easy to classify aspirations. In the first place, the transforming power of history may separate
out from among temporary aspirations those which will prove to be of a
permanent nature. In the second place, owing to the inadequacies of the
representative system or to the control exercised by minorities, constitutions and party platforms, which are the instruments in which aspirations should be most clearly reflected, do not make a neat distinction
between interests of the elite, or party interests, and national interests.
Frequently they evidence an attempt to force the people to support the
temporary objectives of pressure groups, representative of the minority.
National aspirations, common to all, which no Brazilian would hesitate
to consider basic, are represented, for example, by independence, sovereignty, maintenance of territorial integrity, and maintenance and
defense of national unity. Fidelity to the form represented by the federal
republic seems to me a merely temporary aspiration. The permanent
aspiration is embodied in representative democracy, with a harmonious
separation of powers. Centralization promoted and helped the cause
of national unity. Brazil existed as a free nation under the government
of the Empire very nearly as long as it has under that of the Republic.

If we examine Brazilian history we shall observe not merely the variety of forms in which certain permanent aspirations have presented themselves but also—and this seems to me important—how permanent aspirations of a political, economic, social, and international nature often gained added strength from the temporary aspirations of a given moment.

12. Independence and Sovereignty

As in the case of all American communities subjected to colonization, the Brazilians had to struggle to achieve their independence. The early danger of foreign invasions which might have split the national territory was overcome in battles against French pirates, English corsairs, and conquering invaders from The Netherlands. The Brazilians suffered affronts and humiliations, but they maintained the territorial integrity of their land and bequeathed it as a heritage to the nation when it gained its independence. A national consciousness gradually came into being, as a consequence not only of threats from abroad but also of dissensions with Portuguese-born colonists and comparisons between their accomplishments and activities and those of the native-born Brazilians. As agriculture and cattle raising penetrated into the hinterland, fear of foreigners gradually gave way. The growth of Brazilian society increased the responsibility for the common defense and caused an increase in the sense of national security.

Capistrano de Abreu noted that the victories won in the war against The Netherlands, the feats of the *bandeiras*, the abundance of cattle that roamed the vast spaces of the backlands, the huge sums remitted to the government of the mother country, the numerous fortunes that came into being, and the growth of the population had a considerable effect on the psychology of the colonists. They no longer either could or would consider themselves humble, timid rustics, inferior to persons born overseas, as they had done at the beginning of the seventeenth century. By reason of the services they rendered, the wealth they possessed, and the splendors of their native soil, they were to be numbered among the most meritorious subjects of the Portuguese crown.[1] As the author of the "Roteiro do Maranhão a Goiás" (Itinerary of the Route from

[1] João Capistrano de Abreu, *Capítulos de História Colonial*, 4th ed. preparada por José Honório Rodrigues, p. 248; and "A Literatura Brasileira Contemporânea," *Ensaios e Estudos*, p. 75.

Maranhão to Goiás)[2] reports, as late as 1801 an attempt was made to
accommodate the interests of the Brazilians to those of the mother
country and to avoid any loosening of the bond which should always
hold colonies firmly in subjection. The opening of the ports, the entry
and spread of new ideas, the building up of libertarian pressures, the
impracticability of repressive measures, the stimulus to resistance, and
the loss of power by the dominant Lusitanian minority were responsible,
in Capistrano de Abreu's words, for the burgeoning of that feeling of
superiority which resulted in the proclamation of independence on September 7, 1822.[3] At that time the disunion of the provinces hindered
national unity and threatened the achievement of national freedom. It
was in Rio de Janeiro that independence gained form and direction.
Only the provinces of São Paulo and Rio Grande do Sul adhered
unanimously and immediately to the power of Rio de Janeiro; Pernambuco tended toward separate independence; Minas Gerais hesitated between subjection to Rio de Janeiro and autonomy; and Bahia, Maranhão, and Pará preferred obedience to Lisbon.[4]

The War of Independence lasted eleven months and strengthened the
political bond which came into being at that time. São Paulo and Minas
Gerais aided Rio de Janeiro to expel the troops of Avilez, and Pernambuco sent a contingent to help free Bahia from the forces of Madeira.
Ceará and Piauí came to the help of Maranhão, aiding it to overcome
resistance in its capital and to join the Empire. The strong pressure
exerted from without by the parliament in Lisbon had a unifying effect,
and the monarchy, in the person of Prince Pedro, constituted, as Tobias
Monteiro wrote, "a nucleus of attraction for the provinces which rendered independence possible by the incorporation of all into the Empire."[5]

Independence, as an act of secession, showed from the beginning that
the ruling minority, without any leaven of originality, was imitating
European institutions, some of which were not adaptable to the Brazilian social environment. The imitation began on October 12, 1822,
with the caricatural act of proclaiming Pedro I Emperor of Brazil. Now
the title of emperor referred to an ecumenical sovereignty, that of the

[2] "Roteiro do Maranhão a Goiás," *Revista do Instituto Histórico e Geográfico Brasileiro,* 62, 1 parte (1900), 127, 135.
[3] João Capistrano de Abreu, "A Literatura Brasileira Contemporânea," *Ensaios e
Estudos,* p. 76.
[4] Francisco José Oliveira Viana, *Populações Meridionais do Brasil,* 3d ed., p. 328.
[5] Tobias [do Rêgo] Monteiro, *História do Império: A Elaboração da Independência,*
p. 854.

Holy Roman Empire, which had been usurped by Napoleon Bonaparte on May 18, 1804.[6]

The idea of superiority, real or fancied, implicit in the title of emperor persisted and affected negotiations for independence with Portugal.[7] The secret thought of Pedro I was of a future reassemblage of the Lusitanian empire, when he was called to succeed his father in Portugal as Pedro IV.

Recognition was a long and difficult process. On June 14, 1822, José Bonifácio addressed the United States representative with these fine-sounding words, full of pride and independence, which later events were to render weak in effect:

My dear Sir, the Brazils are a Nation and will take its place as such without waiting for or soliciting the recognition of the other powers. Public Agents or Ministers will be sent to them. Those who shall receive them upon that footing and treat with us as Nation to Nation will continue to be admitted in our ports and their trade favored—Those who shall refuse to do so shall be excluded from them.[8]

The United States was the first country to recognize Brazilian independence, the date being May 16, 1824. The destiny of Brazil, however, was bound up with that of Europe, particularly England. The European powers conditioned their recognition on that of the parliament in Lisbon, and this was obtained only thanks to British intervention.[*]

Indefinite postponement of recognition could have had disastrous results for Brazil, which threatened to fall into anarchy and to separate, after the manner of Spanish America, into a number of small republics. The price of recognition, in addition to the sum of two million pounds sterling,[9] included renewal of most-favored-nation privileges (a mere 15% tariff on British goods) for England,[†] whose exactions were later

[6] Arnold Toynbee, *A Study of History*, Vol. 7, p. 22, n. 1; Vol. 9, p. 11.

[7] Charles Webster, *Britain and the Independence of Latin America, 1812–1830*, Vol. 1, p. 57.

[8] William Ray Manning, *Diplomatic Correspondence of the United States concerning the Independence of the Latin American Nations*, Vol. 2, part 3, p. 739.

[*] Portugal recognized the independence of Brazil in 1825. British as well as other European recognition followed thereafter.

[9] "Convenção Adicional, 29 de agôsto de 1825," in Antônio Pereira Pinto, *Apontamentos para o Direito Internacional*, Vol. 1, pp. 339–341; and Hildebrando Accioly, *O Reconhecimento da Independência do Brasil*, pp. 215–216.

[†] The maximum duty that could be placed on English goods was 15 percent. The minimum duty that could be placed on other foreign goods was 16 percent. The treaty signed with England in 1827 is called a renewal, because by a treaty in 1810 Portugal gave Britain preferred treatment in Brazilian ports. That treaty was voided when Brazil broke away from Portugal, but similar terms were reinstituted by the 1827 treaty.

followed by those of other nations, and the odious concession represented by the English conservatorship, which granted Great Britain extraterritorial jurisdiction in Brazil. The bill for services presented by the English, transformed into a treaty, alienated the patriots from Pedro I and was one of the factors which contributed decisively to his abdication. It transformed Brazil into a British protectorate till 1844, when the Brazilians refused to renew the treaty.

The nationalization of the throne and the army, achieved by the deportation of the most violent Portuguese elements and by the struggles in the South, were immediate, temporary objectives, aimed at attaining and securing permanent aspirations. During the Regency (1831–1840) —an experiment with something similar to a federal republic, which proved incapable of assuring order in the vast, as yet poorly structured empire, and of holding the nation together—on several occasions there was imminent danger of dismemberment and of an end to the country's territorial integrity. The throne then became the great symbol of unity, and the conservative politicians who argued in favor of the proclamation of the emperor's majority,* had sufficient national feeling to recognize that there was an affinity between integrity and unity, aspirations dangerously threatened by the innumerable revolts that risked splitting the country into pieces.

Despite the notable services it rendered the fatherland, by consolidating independence and handing Brazil over to Brazilians, the Regency represented an excess of personal power, a fractioning of sovereignty, the division of a house into irreconcilable groups. The political obligation was to avoid extreme or violent positions and to preserve integrity through mutual concessions. The compromise reached, a sign of maturity and experience, well suited to the conformist behavior of the people, was the proclamation of Pedro II's majority. As an aspiration of the day, it served the permanent end of ensuring political stability and, thereby, full and undisputed sovereignty, recognized inside and outside the country.

* In order to reaffirm national unity the politicians resolved to coronate Pedro II at fourteen rather than wait for him to reach the constitutional age of eighteen. He was declared of age to rule in his own right in 1840, and crowned the following year.

13. Territorial Integrity

As José Maria dos Santos said, for the Brazilian people the integrity of the nation was "the dominant idea, until they saw the country definitely consolidated within a system of frontiers which could never thereafter suffer alteration or correction in any restrictive sense."[1]

So strong was this idea at all times that, at the period of the Farrapos Rebellion,* Miguel Calmon, speaking in the Chamber of Deputies in 1837, declared: "Of all political mistakes, the most harmful to the nation is that which leads to violation of its integrity and mutilation of its territory." No group paid more heavily in blood to maintain the country's integrity than did the Pernambucans in the colonial period and the people of Rio Grande do Sul, both under the Colony and under the Empire.

The occupation of an Atlantic seaboard stretching for 4,600 miles—the birthplace of Brazilian civilization—the winning of a vast territory in the interior of the continent, and the creation of a distinctly Brazilian personality form a long, slow process: These developments are evidence that Brazilian history is a vast system of incorporation. Territorial integration was achieved gradually, starting in the colonial period. The first three nuclei of settlement were Bahia, Pernambuco, and Rio de Janeiro. The base of operations for the winning of the hinterland was São Paulo, whose geographical location faced it toward the backlands.† The first burst of activity led to the occupation of the far-reaching seaboard, from the Amazon (1616) to the River Plate (Colônia do Sacramento, 1680).‡ There was but tenuous connection between settlements, but at the settlements the markers of sovereignty were set up. The success of the colonial struggles against French attempts at occupation, the victory over the Dutch establishment, and the expulsion of the Hispano-Argentines from Rio Grande do Sul and Santa Catarina ensured dominion over the entire seaboard, along which nuclei of settlement were scattered at immense distances one from another. The work of the men of São Paulo in pushing back the frontier and incorporating the hinterland into the colony is without parallel in the history of the Americas in the seventeenth century. The astounding physical growth of Brazil is

[1] José Maria dos Santos, *A Política Geral do Brasil*, p. 32.

* The Farrapos or Ragamuffin Revolution in Rio Grande do Sul, 1835–1845, was one of the most serious challenges to national unity. The Duque de Caxias eventually suppressed the revolt, and thereby guaranteed that Rio Grande do Sul would remain within the nation.

† Of the major population centers in colonial Brazil, São Paulo was the only one not located on the coast; consequently, it served well as a center from which exploratory parties radiated into the interior.

‡ In Portuguese this river network bears the name Rio da Prata; in Spanish the name is Río de la Plata.

the result of their efforts, of their unbounded ambition, and of their extraordinary capacity for initiative.*

As early as the eighteenth century the general pattern of occupation was surprisingly like that of the present day. There is no doubt that the population was scattered throughout the territory, for the Treaty of Madrid of 1750, which established frontiers between Spanish and Portuguese America that are practically those of today (save for Acre, whose incorporation into Brazil is owed to the diligence of men from Ceará†), took occupation of the land as its criterion, stating: "Each Party is to retain what it presently possesses." Adoption of this principle is clear evidence that Portuguese colonization effectively extended over the immense area which was to constitute Brazil. Otherwise the principle of *uti possidetis* would not have been invented, invoked, and applied.

The shift of the center of economic gravity to Rio de Janeiro and the transfer thither of the viceregal capital were responsible for greatly increased activity in the East and the South. Population began to increase in those areas and to push toward the center of the country. Readily evident are the sense of direction of Brazilian territorial expansion and the intermittent fashion in which it proceeded. The scantiness of the population and the hardships of travel rendered communication between the seaboard and the hinterland difficult; even so, however, at the beginning of the eighteenth century "all parts of the country were connected, albeit imperfectly, by means of land or river routes."[2]

The ultimate result was the formation of a country of continental proportions, the fourth in the world in contiguous land area,‡ enjoying a highly favorable and important position for commercial purposes and from the viewpoint of world strategy.

* Reference here is to the *bandeira* movement from the coastal zone into the hinterlands. The members of the movement were called *bandeirantes*.

† The devastating droughts of the Northeast drove many from the state of Ceará into the Amazonian interior to extract the lucrative rubber. Those "rubber *bandeirantes*" are credited with the incorporation of Acre, once a part of Bolivia, into Brazil in 1903.

[2] João Capistrano de Abreu, *Caminhos Antigos e Povoamento do Brasil*, p. 117.

‡ Brazil ranks after Russia, China, and Canada. By this reckoning the United States is fifth, since neither Alaska nor Hawaii is contiguous with the continental United States.

14. Effective Occupation of the Land

Effective occupation of the land early manifested itself as a permanent national aspiration. As Brazil was explored at a very early date and occupied very rapidly, inhabitants were few and far between in a large part of the hinterland. The results were great unevenness in the distribution of the population in regions of early settlement, a low level of culture among the inhabitants of the backlands, and an overall low economic level. Unlike the United States, where the Anglo-Saxon colonists as late as 1776 occupied a territory smaller than France, and where expansion to the west, carried out after 1830, was a mass movement that in a few decades occupied the whole country, in seventeenth-century Brazil penetration was undertaken by small groups, which, owing to their limited numbers, could not really carry out the work of settlement. Heinrich Handelmann, writing in 1860, contrasted the two advances of population, saying:

In Brazil, the army of colonizers broke up into a chain of scouts, each of whom in rapid advances achieved great success. Then, however, they were obliged to remain stationary, as isolated advanced posts, without any regular communication with the rear guard. Their sole hope lay in a remote future, with a growth in the number of inhabitants.[1]

Such growth, however, did not come to the aid of the men abandoned in the backlands, separated one from another by distances of several hundred miles.

Under the Empire, since premature dispersion of inhabitants had left the land very thinly populated, thought was given from earliest days to extension of the area of settlement by the establishment of foreign colonies, especially of German or Swiss origin. In 1870 Tavares Bastos proposed the creation of new provinces and territories, with a view to populating the great wilderness areas of Brazil—the upper Amazon region, Mato Grosso, the northern and southern extremities of Pará, the northern corner of Goiás, the southern corner of Maranhão, and the plains which from Rio Grande do Sul to northern São Paulo stretch as far west as the Uruguay River in Santa Catarina and to the Maracaju Range in Mato Grosso.[2]

Rio Branco brought the juridical process of integration, initiated under the Empire, to a definitive end in 1912.* Effective occupation of

[1] Quoted by Leo Waibel, *Capítulos de Geografia Tropical e do Brasil*, p. 285.

[2] Aureliano Cândido Tavares Bastos, *A Província: Estudo sôbre a Descentralização no Brasil*, 2d ed., p. 358.

* José Maria da Silva Paranhos, the Baron of Rio Branco, settled all of Brazil's frontiers except the boundary with Paraguay, established in 1872. He redrew in 1909 the boundary as settled with Uruguay in 1851. Basing all his claims on the principle of *uti possidetis*, he accomplished most of these settlements during the decade he served as minister of foreign affairs, 1902–1912.

the land, however, continued—as it does today—a national dream.
Even in 1940, when the process of nationalizing foreign nuclei of settlement was in full swing, the economically exploited area of the country,
according to the census, covered but 772,000 square miles, or 23 percent of the total national territory. Of this area, only 72,568 square
miles, or 2.2 percent, represent cultivated land, and 320,380 square
miles, or about 10 percent, are used as pasture land. The remainder, or
77 percent of the national territory, either is not or cannot be economically exploited, or is in the hands of "intruders" who escaped the
census takers.[3] Although these figures are for 1940, from that year to
1950 land in use has increased by 1.4 percent, and only slightly more
than 3 percent is being agriculturally exploited. Property ownership is
concentrated in the hands of a few: former Minister João Cleofas asserted at a meeting of the United Nations Economic Commission for Latin
America that in 1953 7.8 percent of the landowners held 73 percent of
the land. In any case, it can be said that more than half the area of
Brazil is unexploited from the agricultural viewpoint,[4] and practically
void of population, since 48 percent of the territory (Amazonas, Pará,
Mato Grosso) contains only 4 percent of the population, and 64 percent
of Brazil (the northern and west central regions) contains only 7 percent of the people.

As the enormous place Brazil occupies on the map is conducive to the
formation of illusions, the more empty spaces, such as the Amazon
region, have excited the international imagination and have given rise
to the idea of their effective occupation by the hungry peoples of the
world. The thesis does not begin with Bryce, but he shows himself one
of its most faithful exponents in asking whether the Amazonian selva,
the vastest and most fertile uninhabited land area of the globe, might
not be reclaimed for man's service. So vast and fertile an area cannot
forever be left idle, wrote Bryce in 1912.[5] Forty years later, Professor Walter Prescott Webb[6] classified the Amazon region, on which
eighteenth- and nineteenth-century pioneers had turned their backs, as
a new frontier, and said that if the United States would use the money it
spends in Europe and Asia on the development of this frontier, prosperity would be re-created, to the general profit of the Western world.

[3] Waibel, *Geografia Tropical*, p. 263.
[4] A typical example is Minas Gerais, of whose 225,133 square miles only 12 percent are
under cultivation.
[5] James Bryce, *South America: Observations and Impressions*, p. 560.
[6] Walter Prescott Webb, *The Great Frontier*, pp. 285, 416–417.

Satisfied in its territorial ambitions, having its full dominion internationally recognized, Brazil is not disturbed by visions of, or desires for, expansion—visions and desires which today have fallen into disrepute. It observes, however, that it has not yet attained one of the most deeply rooted of its national aspirations.

The danger represented by the Amazon region as an empty, unincorporated space, derives, according to Artur César Ferreira Reis, not from possible imperialistic ventures, but from international action to solve the world's problems of hunger, housing shortage, and overpopulation.[7] UNESCO, for example, made an attempt in this direction. Reaction to the project, headed by former President Artur Bernardes, removed the initial danger.

Two conflicting views exist as to the manner of achieving the effective occupation which neither the Empire nor the Republic managed to bring about. The first, which guided the government prior to Getúlio Vargas and which has strong defenders in the ranks of politicians and theoreticians, advocates stimulus to immigration, subsidies for pioneer areas, and consolidation of the East—the center of Brazilian life—as the basis for a slow but steady expansion to the west and northwest. Brazil is an empire within whose confines are to be found areas which are metropolitan in their development and areas in a state of colonial dependency. Expansionist efforts should fan out from the heartland— the triangular area whose angles are represented by the cities of Rio de Janeiro, Belo Horizonte, and São Paulo, a zone of dense population containing the two largest cities, the richest farmlands, the greatest industrial park, and the most highly developed communications network. The aim would be to recuperate old areas of settlement, such as the Northeast, and develop centers of national unity, such as the valley of the São Francisco River, and great land reserves, such as the Amazon valley, without pushing settlement too far west before the East is firmly populated. Population gaps in regions of early settlement would be filled in; support would be given to the work of pioneers in Rio Grande do Sul, Santa Catarina, Paraná, the Doce River valley, and the forest regions of Goiás and São Paulo. Ports would be built, dredging carried out, and a merchant marine provided for a country of extended coastline; roads and highways would be constructed, designed particularly to connect the various economic centers, lest the errors of earlier settlement be repeated. The motto of the partisans of this view is not "Go

7 Artur César Ferreira Reis, *A Amazônia e a Cobiça Internacional.*

80   *The Brazilians*

west," but "Get a firm footing in the East," and carry out works of improvement along the seaboard.

The other view, which found bold and indefatigable champions in Getúlio Vargas and Juscelino Kubitschek, favors immediate advance and occupation of the West, the hopes of many Brazilians being founded on the settlement and exploitation of the states farthest from the seacoast, Goiás and Mato Grosso. In August, 1940, Getúlio Vargas summed up this course of action in the assertion that "the true path of Brazilian nationality lies to the west," in a resumption of the efforts of the *bandeiras* and explorers of the backlands.[8] This geopolitical and politico-economic policy has far-from-modest objectives, and in fulfillment thereof the most grandiose of plans have been drafted. The West is the promised land: it has great reserves of fertile soil that can well substitute for the wasted and exhausted lands of the East.

Location of the capital in the interior was advocated by Hipólito José da Costa Pereira Furtado de Mendonça, the founder of the *Correio Brasiliense* ("Brazilian Mail"),* by José Bonifácio in 1821 and 1822, and by the historian Francisco Adolfo de Varnhagen in 1850. The government of the Empire took no note of this idea. The convention which drew up the constitution for the Republic in 1891 accepted the proposal and incorporated it into Article 3. Floriano Peixoto, attacked by revolutionaries in 1893, sent a commission to the central plateau to mark out the site of the future capital and expressed the desire of transferring the seat of government immediately, on a provisional basis, to some city of the interior.[9] The work of the Cruls Commission, however, was consigned to oblivion, as the administrations of Rodrigues Alves and Afonso Pena† undertook great works for the modernization of Rio de Janeiro "as an indispensable prerequisite for setting all the elements of progress in operation."[10] In 1904 Rodrigues Alves declared to the Chamber of Deputies:

I have come to the firm belief—fortunately one that is generally held—that the economic forces of the country cannot be effectively harnessed until the capital of the Republic becomes a powerful center of attraction for labor and capital, freed of those unhealthful conditions which, exaggerated by some

[8] Getúlio [Dorneles] Vargas, *A Nova Política do Brasil*, Vol. 1, p. 31.
* The *Correio Brasiliense* was an influential Brazilian journal published in London from 1808 to 1822.
[9] "Mensagem Presidencial," *Anais da Câmara dos Deputados* (1893), p. 18.
† Rodrigues Alves was president from 1902 to 1906, and Afonso Pena from 1906 until his death in mid-1909.
[10] "Mensagem Presidencial," *Anais da Câmara dos Deputados* (1907), p. 318.

and exploited by others, have been retarding our development, without our being aware thereof.[11]

In view of the great improvements made between 1902 and 1912 in Rio de Janeiro, no one gave thought to carrying out the provision of the constitution in regard to the location of the capital. The reform of 1926, the decree which established the provisional government, and the charter of 1937 ignored that requirement, though the constitutions of both 1934 and 1946 included it among their transitory articles. It fell to President Juscelino Kubitschek to carry forward, from the first year of his term, 1956, the idea of constructing Brasília and transferring the capital thither.* It is still early to judge the historical efficacy of the change and to what extent the officially victorious "Go west" thesis will show itself capable of expanding the demographic frontier and bringing about effective occupation of the land. The desire is, however, that Brasília should take up, continue, and expand the role played by Rio de Janeiro in promoting national unity and integration.

[11] "Mensagem Presidencial," *Anais da Câmara dos Deputados* (1904), p. 6.
* The Brazilian capital was moved to Brasília in 1960, during the final days of the Kubitschek administration.

15. National Unity

Of more vital importance than effective occupation of the land are maintenance and defense of national unity. This has been the leading theme of Brazilian history, in contrast to the original disunion—later remedied —of the British colonies and the abiding division of Spanish America.[1] At the end of the colonial period Brazil was a unit from the geographical viewpoint only: it was filled with divergency and individualism; the focal point was overseas. The establishment of the Portuguese court in Rio de Janeiro favored a *rapprochement* of the captaincies and marked in a certain fashion the beginnings of the country's unity. The great challenge presented by independence was the creation of a Brazilian ethos and national unity in the face of the enormous economic and social differences between the various regions. It is to the triumph of the central power in Rio de Janeiro over local and provincial authority that the unity of the nation must be attributed. The function which Rio de

[1] Francisco Cavalcanti Pontes de Miranda, "Preliminares para a Revisão Constitucional," *À Margem da História da República*, p. 182.

Janeiro began to exercise in 1808 and which ensured national unity did not, as Oliveira Viana has said, derive from a historic fiat. It was "a slow achievement, a process of evolution full of episodes which the brilliance of imperial majesty cast into the shade but which historical analysis brings to light."[2] It was for this reason that Capistrano de Abreu wrote that "If it was not here [in Rio de Janeiro] that the idea of a nation first arose, it was here that that dream—which came near being no more than a dream—was brought to realization."[3] In addition, Rio de Janeiro was called upon to contribute economically, without assistance, to national unity.[4]

Neither the rule of the governors general in Bahia nor that of the viceroys in Rio de Janeiro succeeded in imparting the character of an organic whole to the various territorial units under the common authority. Different and separate from one another, they led an autonomous existence. Neither the governors general nor the viceroys brought them under one central power, to form a political and administrative unit. Government exercised from faraway Lisbon and the subordination of administrative authority to the Council for Overseas maintained divisions deemed necessary to the subjugation of the Brazilian continent. Brazilian unity had its beginnings on the eve of independence, when Rio de Janeiro began to exercise its functions as a political center for imparting direction to the national will.

The specter of separatism arose on several occasions, but was dispelled even as provincialism was routed. Only with the proclamation of Pedro II's majority was the aspiration to unity fully achieved. From 1840 to 1889, when the monarchy fell, only twice, in 1842 and 1848, was public order seriously disturbed. When peace was reestablished in Rio Grande do Sul in 1845, after ten years of conflict, Pedro II's personal rule shielded the nation like a bulwark against all attempts at shattering national unity. The idea of unity, which lives in every Brazilian and which depends thereon for survival, is a product of a common history and of a belief in a similarly common future.

[2] Francisco José Oliveira Viana, *Populações Meridionais do Brasil*, 3d ed., p. 326.

[3] João Capistrano de Abreu, *Caminhos Antigos e Povoamento do Brasil*, p. 118.

[4] See Dom Pedro's letter of July 17, 1821, to Dom João VI, in Clemente José dos Santos, Baron São Clemente, *Documentos para a História das Côrtes Gerais da Nação Portuguêsa*, Vol. 1, p. 244.

16. National Equilibrium and Regionalism

If unity was a creative achievement of independence, promoted from Rio de Janeiro by the imperial government, Brazil was not *ipso facto* an organic whole, but a congeries of geographic regions or economic sections, each leading a life of its own. Observing them in 1843, Martius was the first to suggest the writing of regional histories. From that time on, attention has been called to the differences between regional groupings and defense has been made of regional interests, suppressed by the imperial policy of centralization. A few historians, such as Handelmann, João Ribeiro, and Capistrano de Abreu, gave attention to the study of certain geographic contradictions, historic traditions, ethnic peculiarities, and specific economic interests that separate geographic regions or economic sections one from another. A large share of political debate under the Empire, well brought out in the work of Tavares Bastos, was devoted to a defense of the province, as a region, against centralization. An understanding of Brazilian development requires that note be taken of the basic similarities and differences that make for the unity of regions, or that group sections together. Reality is not expressed by speaking of two Brazils, one archaic, the other modern, or of one on a high and the other on a low level of development,[1] for in truth there are a number of Brazils, as many as there are specific regions or economic sections, as Professor Leslie Lipson has suggested.[2]

In this sense Brazil is an empire, a federation of sections, a union of regions, although the concept subsists that there are zones of development and underdevelopment, archaic areas and modern areas, metropolitan districts and colonial districts, divided according to their stages of historical development. Evolution has never proceeded uniformly, nor has national power been usurped by a single province or state. Historical, geographical, and economic factors have conspired against regional equality, just as they conspire against human equality. And just as world power is transitory, so the force exerted by the states on national power is transitory.

Brazilian history shows different varieties of regional predominance, through the union of economic and political power. No less a person than Capistrano de Abreu wrote:

[1] Jacques Lambert, *Le Brésil: Structure sociale et Institutions politiques;* published in Portuguese as *Os Dois Brasis.*
[2] Leslie Lipson, "Government in Contemporary Brazil," *Canadian Journal of Economics and Political Science*, 22, No. 2 (May 1956), 189.

If we wished to characterize each century of our history by an appropriate epithet, the sixteenth century would be termed the era of Pernambuco; the seventeenth, that of Bahia and São Paulo; the eighteenth, that of Minas Gerais; and our soon-to-end nineteenth century, the era of the state of Rio de Janeiro.

Fortunately, regional hegemony was not quite so simple as all that. In general it can be said that the colonial period was marked by the predominance of the Northeast, save for the short era in which Minas came to the fore. In the eighteenth century São Paulo suffered a veritable eclipse, from which it did not recover till the middle of the nineteenth. At the beginning of that century the most flourishing captaincies were still those of Rio de Janeiro, Bahia, Pernambuco, and Maranhão,[3] and throughout the Empire these four provinces continued to furnish the great national leaders and the largest share of government revenue.[4] Slowly, owing to the planting of coffee—which had given importance to the province of Rio de Janeiro under the Empire—owing to immigration, and owing to the building of railroads, São Paulo began to come to the fore. In 1874 André Rebouças declared the province of São Paulo, "the Pennsylvania of Brazil," to be marked by destiny. It was "the boldest and most active province in the Empire," for it offered the example, unheard-of in the country, of building with its own capital five railroads at the same time. Its progressive development could find no equal anywhere else in the Empire.[5]

From 1853 on, protests began to be made by the Northeast against the failure of the central government to meet that region's just claims, and it was already said in the Chamber of Deputies that the North and the Northeast were being stifled.

Under the Republic, Rio Grande do Sul made its appearance at the side of São Paulo, Minas Gerais, and the Federal District,[6] its position being strengthened by the revolution of 1930.* The most singular fact

[3] "Roteiro do Maranhão a Goiás pela Capitania do Piauí," *Revista do Instituto Histórico e Geográfico Brasileiro,* 62, 2. parte (1900), p. 104.

[4] *Relatório do Ministério da Fazenda* (1859), pp. 47, 49, 50. See the speech by Carneiro Leão in *Anais da Câmara dos Deputados* (1878), Vol. 2 (2 agôsto 1831). In 1855 Pernambuco was still considered a rich province, *Correio do Brasil* (Rio de Janeiro), 23 abril 1855.

[5] André Rebouças, *Garantia de Juros: Estudo para sua Aplicação às Emprêsas de Utilidade Pública no Brasil,* pp. 2, 3, 23.

[6] It held first place in industrial expansion. See the message of President Nilo Peçanha to the Congress, in *Anais da Câmara dos Deputados* (1910), p. 458.

* President Getúlio Vargas was a native son of Rio Grande do Sul and he brought to office with him some capable politicians from the southernmost state.

to be noted is that Minas Gerais, the only province which ever since the days of the Empire has maintained its political power unshaken—strengthened under the Republic, and escaping the total eclipse that overtook São Paulo after 1930—has not always made an economic contribution to the union commensurate with its political dominance. If it is true that national power has not always been the appanage of the South and that of all the provinces it can be said that they have not always enjoyed the same prestige, it cannot be disputed that Minas Gerais has always shared in the political direction of the country. Without the support of Minas Gerais, no political movement has ever met with success and its exclusion from a movement has meant sure defeat.

The fact is that national power has not always been held by a single province, nor have all of them always enjoyed the same prestige in the course of Brazilian history. The Empire has often been accused of aggravating the problem, by its work of centralization. Tavares Bastos was among those who fought hardest to show that cohesiveness depended on sectional liberty. Under the Republic, however, owing to the policy pursued by the several states or groups therof, regional or sectional progress was either choked off or put off.

No one believes that the North or the Northeast, which have suffered from so many disadvantages, desire radical changes of a separatist or sectional nature. They represent every bit as much as other sections the traditional principles of the Brazilian people, and they have viewed the transfer of the capital to the center of the country and the monumental constructions of Brasília as neglect of their aspirations and of their most urgent needs. Perhaps they have lived too much in the past, but it is almost a crime on the part of the federation to disregard the fundamental problems of those traditional peoples who have contributed so much to national unity and to create a new city in the midst of a wilderness. Brazil is synonymous with the Brazilian people, and if a part of that people which may be described as the nation's firstborn, which struggled to create an original civilization, is abandoned in favor of achieving effective occupation of the land in unpeopled areas, the federation is not serving its purpose.

The country has abandoned the reality represented by the people of the North and the Northeast for the possibility of creating a new capital, the national spirit of which remains to be developed. The Northerners recognize the South's superiority in material wealth, but against the nullity of the wilderness they set their ancient virtues and see a lack of realism in ruining a large area of the nation. It is obvious that the South cannot remain prosperous while the North and the Northeast sink into the category of dependencies or colonies. It has become a commonplace —although the argument is fallacious—to say at the United Nations or in studies on colonialism[7] that Brazil has one of the world's largest colonial empires, though it is not the object of accusation as a colonial power.

As a body, the nation is one and indivisible; it can survive only if each section or region carries out its functions without impoverishing the others or reducing their work. The obligation of attending to imbalance—not with any idea of eliminating it, for that would show lack of understanding of history, but of lessening its impact—is temporary. The obligation of avoiding secession and maintaining unity, however, is permanent. Brazil was never divided against itself and I trust it never will be.

The constitutions of 1934 and 1946, particularly the latter, sought to provide for a just balance between the several regions of the country. In order to promote improvement in the valley of the São Francisco River, the Amazon region, and the Northeast, it was established that for a period of twenty years sums should be applied in these areas amounting to no less than 1 percent, 3 percent, and 3 percent, respectively, of the national revenue.

The basin of the São Francisco, with an area of 243,952 square miles and a population exceeding five million, is a region of great political and social contrasts. This was the scene of the great Canudos campaign, which provided the subject for Euclides da Cunha's book *Rebellion in the Backlands*. The river, whose length totals 1,960 miles, connects important ports and cities of the valley. The construction of highways and electric plants, the reclamation of low-lying river lands, the building of water-supply systems in a number of cities, a campaign against malaria, the regularizing of navigation over a stretch of 800 miles, and the erection of a number of hydroelectric installations, notably those of Três Marias, are the principal achievements of the São Francisco Valley Commission.[8]

The Plan for the Economic Improvement of the Amazon Region is concerned with a problem far vaster in scale, since, for legal purposes, the region includes not merely the state of Amazonas with its 611,146

[7] Robert Strausz Hupé and Harry W. Hazard, *The Idea of Colonialism.*

[8] The law creating the Commission is No. 541, dated November 15, 1948. See "A Recuperação de um Vale," *Observador Econômico*, No. 170 (março, 1950), and No. 240/241 (fevereiro–março, 1956). See also *Represamento do São Francisco, Dois Irmãos e Pirapora.*

square miles but, wholly or in part, eight other units of the federation —the territories of Amapá, Roraima, and Rondônia; the states of Pará and Acre; and sections of Mato Grosso, Goiás, and Maranhão—for a total area of 1,930,000 squares miles, or more than half of the country. Even before the delegates to the constitutional convention of 1940, Getúlio Vargas championed the task of mastering the great equatorial valley and slowly won adherents to the idea of freeing the Amazon region from one of the lowest levels of underdevelopment. The definite incorporation of that region into the economic body of the nation, as a factor for prosperity and creative energy, requires the mastery of forests and rivers and the establishment of an economically stable society. The Plan is one of the boldest ever undertaken in Brazil and is on the same scale of grandeur as the hydroelectrification of the São Francisco (Três Marias) and of the Rio Grande (Furnas), the recuperation of the Northeast, and the creation of the iron-and-steel or automobile industries.[9]

The attempt is also being made to correct regional imbalance by the recuperation of the Northeast, a region comprising eight states covering 14 percent of the area of Brazil (471,527 square miles), with more than twenty million inhabitants. This, one of the longest-settled areas of the country, is also one of the most underdeveloped in the Western Hemisphere. As a problem area—characterized by short life expectancy, by a high rate of infant mortality, by poor health conditions, by deficiencies in food and housing, and by low per capita income—the Northeast inspired from the first years of the Republic a movement for its restoration, aimed at avoiding or reducing the increasing disparity between the Northeast and the East and South. Despite the resources offered by the 1946 constitution, the fact is that the Northeast's share in the total national income fell from 15.5 percent in 1948 to 11 percent in 1959. On the basis of the conviction that a policy of combating drought was not enough and that what was called for was an all-out attack on underdevelopment, which would bring the economy of the region into adjustment with that of the nation as a whole, the Superintendency for the Development of the Northeast (SUDENE) was established on December 15, 1959. It coordinates all federal agencies in the region, unifying national action.[10]

[9] See the publications of the Superintendency of the Plan for the Economic Improvement of the Amazon Region (SPVEA), particularly Sócrates Bonfim, *Valorização da Amazônia e sua Comissão de Planejamento*, No. 6; Adriano Menezes, *O Problema da Colonização da Amazônia*, No. 7; Agnello Bittencourt, *Navegação da Amazônia & Portos da Amazônia*, No. 8; and Waldir Bouhid, *Amazônia & Desenvolvimento*.

[10] Stephan H. Robock, *Projecto de Planejamento Global para o Nordeste do Brasil;*

Complementing the foregoing is the Plan for the Economic Improvement of the Southwest Frontier Region,[11] created in 1956 to raise the standard of living for the people in frontier areas of Rio Grande do Sul, Santa Catarina, Paraná, and Mato Grosso, and to incorporate them into the national economy. These initiatives show that interregional balance has not yet been achieved—nor will it be attained in the near future. They indicate, however, that the attempt is being made to achieve coherence, to do away with the most flagrant examples of imbalance, and, by unequal treatment, to favor regions suffering from inequality.

Nevertheless, in recent years—since the 1946 constitution—the fact of the matter is that economic progress has been concentrated in certain states, such as São Paulo and Paraná, whose income has risen from 36 percent to 38 percent of the total for the country, to the detriment of other regions, such as that of the Amazon, whose income declined from 2.4 percent to 2.2 percent of the total, or the Northeast, where the decline was from 16.2 percent to 14.3 percent. Juscelino Kubitschek's development policy has been accused of aggravating regional disparities, and even of provoking a crisis of impoverishment in Rio Grande do Sul, which has lost capital to the extent of forty billion cruzeiros just in the last ten years.[12] The increasingly grave situation of the Northeast, the disaster in the South, and an exodus of inhabitants from Minas Gerais which exceeds that from the Northeast (1,200,000 as against 980,000 from 1940 to 1950) call for a watchful integration policy, since the whole of Brazil is becoming tributary to the industrial center of São Paulo.

Jimmye S. Hillman, *O Desenvolvimento Econômico e o Nordeste Brasileiro; Análise Estrutural da Economia Nordestina;* Celso Furtado, *A Operação Nordeste.*

[11] Created by Law No. 2976, of November 28, 1957; for practical purposes it is not as yet in operation.

[12] Franklin de Oliveira, *Rio Grande do Sul: Um Nôvo Nordeste.*

No attempt has been made to translate monetary values into terms of present-day currency, for lack of adequate studies on which such calculations might be based. Some idea of the fluctuations that have occurred may be suggested, however, by the fact that the cruzeiro, which in 1945 stood at about 19 to the dollar, in early 1966 stood at 2,200.

17. Communications and National Unity

Another great national aspiration which has stirred Brazilian hearts from the earliest times is the development of communications, via river navigation or railroads. Under the Empire people believed more strongly than today in river navigation and in the role to be played by certain rivers in promoting unity and regional development. Brazil has always had enthusiasts of its rivers—fluvial highways, sources of energy, providers of irrigation for arid zones. The São Francisco River, which has won the name "river of national unity," the Araguaia, and the Tocantins were the objects of greatest study. Miracles were hoped of the São Francisco—the possibility of settlement of the Northeast followed later by that of the Amazon basin.[1] The Araguaia was held preferable to the Tocantins by General Couto de Magalhães for purposes of navigation, since, by bringing Goiás into contact with Mato Grosso, Pará, and Maranhão, the Araguaia would link the mouth of the Amazon with that of the River Plate and give not merely Goiás but the whole Brazilian interior "a coast as important as the Atlantic seaboard." Even today river navigation in Brazil extends for a distance of but 27,280 miles, 15,500 of which are in the Amazon basin.[2]

The policy of free river navigation, so ardently championed by Tavares Bastos,[3] was finally established in 1866 when the Amazon, the Tocantins, the Madeira, the Negro, and the São Francisco were opened to merchant ships of all nations.[4] The hopes of the moment were not realized in fact, and existing evils were not corrected by the political action proposed. Development continued to be slow. The Amazon region, achievement of whose destiny was promised in Getúlio Vargas' famous speech of October 9, 1940, today finds another source of unimaginably great promise in the recently opened highway between Brasília and Belém.

Under the Empire and the first era of the Republic the railway seemed the ideal solution to the communication problem. As early as 1835 the first law was passed authorizing the government to grant exclusive rights for a forty-year period to one or more companies for the construction of railways from the capital of the Empire to the provinces of Minas Gerais, Rio Grande do Sul, and Bahia.[5] These and other initiatives having come

---

[1] The bibliography concerning the São Francisco and its valley is extensive. See in particular Teodoro Sampaio, *O Rio São Francisco e a Chapada Diamantina*, and Luís Flôres de Morais Rêgo, *O Vale do São Francisco*.

[2] Ceçary Amazonas, "Navegação Fluvial do Brasil," *Revista Brasileira de Geografia*, 21, No. 4 (outubro–dezembro 1959), 499–515.

[3] Aureliano Cândido Tavares Bastos, *O Vale do Amazonas*.

[4] Decree No. 3749, of December 7, 1866.

[5] Decree No. 101, of October 31, 1835. This had its origin in a draft drawn up by Bernardo Pereira de Vasconcelos.

to nought, it was only on April 30, 1854, that the first railway was in-
augurated—a little line running barely nine miles. By 1861 Brazil had
414 miles of track, but in 1862 Ferreira da Veiga protested from the
rostrum of the Chamber of Deputies that, although Minas Gerais was
the source of supply for Rio de Janeiro, paid a third of the duties col-
lected by the customs service, and accounted for a sixth of the population and of the seats in the Parliament, it was not provided with a single
railway.[6] The Empire did not succeed in facilitating rail communication,
and it fell to the Republic, after the financial consolidation of Campos
Sales,* to give greater—although insufficient—stimulus thereto, with a
view to meeting the needs of the country.

The development of a rail system is a prime factor in the progress of
any nation, Afonso Pena declared to the Congress in 1907, and by the
following year rail lines extended for 11,160 miles. In 1910 Nilo
Peçanha informed the Congress that the Central Railway of Brazil had
reached the banks of the São Francisco River, the goal of Brazilian
statesmen in ratifying the grandiose treaty.[7] Between 1910 and 1930
rail mileage in operation doubled, but after the latter date highway
construction came to the fore in official planning and was emphasized
in the programs of Getúlio Vargas and, especially, Juscelino Kubitschek.
Air transport, initiated in 1927, has in reality best fulfilled the long-
standing aspiration for unity, owing to the ease of communication which
it offers. Today the entire national territory is supplied with air service.

[6] *Anais do Parlamento Brasileiro*, Câmara dos Deputados (1862), Vol. 2, p. 135.
* President Campos Sales, through his efficient minister of finance, Joaquim Murtinho,
put Brazil's usually chaotic finances into better order during his term of office, 1898–1902.
[7] *Anais da Câmara dos Deputados* (1910), pp. 407, 431.

18. Psychosocial Integration

If the great task of consolidating the union and strengthening the bonds
of national solidarity was not completely realized, through failure to
achieve the aspiration for easy communication, it was carried forward
by psychosocial integration, by miscegenation, and by the Brazilianization of immigrants. The various ethnic groups were obliged little by
little to adjust to one another in a progressive advance toward harmonious community relations, rejecting racial intolerance and discrimination
on grounds of color. Differences at first were deep-seated. The native-
born were distinguished from arrivals from Portugal, Europeans from

Indians, colonists from slaves, whites from blacks, The three races, originating in three different continents, seemed totally incompatible, and nothing favored the spread of feelings of benevolence. In addition to ethnographic factors of a separative nature, others of a psychological character likewise exerted an influence. Europeans born in Brazil (*mazombos*) were discriminated from those born in Portugal (*reinóis*); so too Negroes born in Brazil were discriminated from those born in Africa, the former being known as *moleques*. Catechized Indians were distinguished from pagan savages: the term *caboclo* (now confusingly applied to pure-blood Indians, halfbreeds, copper-colored mulattoes, and backwoodsmen) originally designated the former.[1] It fell to the common people to overcome these differences. The minority of Lusitanian origin still imposed legal distinctions, avoided crossbreeding, and scorned the savage Indians and Negroes of all types.

If the Jesuits sought to pacify the Indians and convert them—in other words, to dominate them and turn them into *caboclos*—the colonists were pitiless in their combat against the bravest and most indomitable. The War against the Indians that took place between 1683 and 1713 and the subsequent pacification of the Cariris is but one episode in a process of extermination of the recalcitrant, begun in earliest days against the Tamoios and other Tupi groups and culminating in the Royal Edict of May 13, 1808, ordering war against the Botocudos of Mato Grosso. Though a rather common practice in Spanish America, this was an unusual course for Brazil and was prohibited after 1831.[2] Before the war of 1808 new methods were employed: in 1755 the Indians were freed from slavery, privileges were conceded to persons marrying Indians, and the use of Portuguese was made obligatory in São Paulo, and Maranhão (i.e., the present states of Maranhão, Pará, and Amazonas). A new word, which appeared in 1775, synthesized all this effort toward harmony: civilization.[3] While this change was taking place in official methods, miscegenation was carrying out its work, and a feeling of solidarity was fostered by the pressure of threats from abroad. The result was the end of bilingualism, which posed so great a threat to linguistic unity in São Paulo and Amazonas (with their multitude of tongues, as Father Antônio Vieira wrote), and the subjugation

---

[1] See Capistrano de Abreu's introduction to the *Diálogos das Grandezas do Brasil*, p. 18.

[2] Law of October 27, 1831.

[3] José Honório Rodrigues, "Civilização, Palavra e Conceito," *Diário de Notícias* (Rio de Janeiro), 24 maio 1953.

of the Indians by acts of atrocity, extermination, and expropriation of their lands—methods employed for centuries, which gave way only before miscegenation. Nothing positive was done for the Indians in the nineteenth century. The lands of mission Indians, once the missions were suppressed, passed into the hands of the municipal councils; those of other Indians were taken by force of arms.

The establishment of the Indian Protection Service in 1910, thanks to the impassioned efforts of Cândido Mariano Rondon, represented the beginning of positive action. However, we are presently witnessing the last days of a number of tribes. Some, such as the Xicrins, Canelas, and Pacaás-novos, were massacred by backlanders or brought to extermination by those who deprived them of their lands through chicanery. Others, such as the Suruís, have been decimated by disease. In all truth, both the colonial and the national governments denied the Indians their civil rights, and present-day civilization condemns them to extermination. Action for their protection has been so insignificant that today, according to the best estimates, there are but 68,000 to 100,000 Indians left. A Brazilian Indian policy has yet to be developed.[4]

[4] Darcy Ribeiro, *Língua e Culturas Indígenas do Brasil*; and Ministério da Agricultura, *A Política Indigenista Brasileira*.

19. Miscegenation and Racial Tolerance

Miscegenation was at first a new and exotic phenomenon, a rarity which engaged minute attention, aroused the senses, and was measured and weighed with a precision that is unknown in Brazil today, accustomed as the Brazilians may be to classification by skin color and blood percentages.[1] The first passions to be aroused were those of the seamen[2] in Cabral's fleet. From the moment of discovery, Brazil was populated by an ingrafting of men. Despite prejudice, because of biological necessity, the influence of the slave-master relationship, and the celebrated Portuguese preference for dark-skinned women, the Brazilian people took unbridled miscegenation as a way of life. Crossbreeding, accompanied by social and cultural transformations, offered a means of rising in the world, besides making for weakened prejudice and bringing about tolerance, in contrast to slavery, which was an obstacle to social integration.

[1] See Capistrano de Abreu's introduction to the *Diálogos das Grandezas do Brasil*, p. 17.
[2] Two of whom deserted, remaining in Brazil.

Racial discrimination existed at one time in Brazil. It manifested itself in segregation among troops and in exclusion of nonwhites from the priesthood and from the bureaucracy. The shade of color of the child born of the union of master and slave decided its social fate—whether it would be admitted to the upper class, given freedom but consigned to the lower classes, or kept in slavery.[3]

Prejudice gradually centered on the Negro, who was excluded from land ownership as late as 1809. Slavery, which provided the master class with its living, is very possibly responsible for a number of complexes, among them the objection to manual labor. Even though the members of the master class exercise mechanical offices they do not abandon their presumptions to being white or noble, Brother Domingos do Loreto Couto wrote in 1757.[4] It is in consequence of all this that abolition represented a momentary goal on the path to achievement of a permanent aspiration to harmonious relations among the various races. By 1855 Brazilian public opinion was not divided between liberals and conservatives but between partisans of immediate abolition and those favoring the continuation of slavery. In 1872 Tavares Bastos declared that one of Brazil's three great needs was acceleration of the emancipation movement.[5]

Abolition was one of the aspirations which touched most deeply the national conscience. It did not, however, free the Brazilians from color prejudice, which continued, although in a gentler form. There are those —Oliveira Viana,[6] for example—who believe in the progressive Aryanization of the Brazilian people. There are also those like Gilberto Freyre who, though highly critical of the former, asserts that: "Negroes are now rapidly disappearing in Brazil, merging into the white stock; in some areas the tendency seems to be towards the stabilization of mixed-bloods in a new ethnic type, similar to the Polynesian."[7] This has led an American historian to say that the Brazilians consider the progressive whitening of the population a national ideal, a supposition which is broadly confirmed by observations made in the present century, and that Brazilians thus seek to avoid the existence of a racial minority which

---

[3] Harry William Hutchinson, *Village and Plantation Life in Northeastern Brazil*, pp. 99, 117.

[4] Domingos do Loreto Couto, "Desagravos do Brasil e Glórias de Pernambuco," *Anais da Biblioteca Nacional* (1904), Vol. 24, p. 227.

[5] Aureliano Cândido Tavares Bastos, "A Situação e o Partido Liberal," *Os Males do Presente e as Esperanças do Futuro*, 2d ed., p. 151.

[6] Francisco José Oliveira Viana, *Evolução do Povo Brasileiro*, 2d ed., pp. 191–194.

[7] Gilberto Freyre, *Brazil: An Interpretation*, p. 96.

might perturb internal peace.[8] The limited degree of racial intolerance
or color discrimination that exists has economic and social bases; those
who overcome disadvantage by education find the gates of society open
to them. Colored men, particularly mulattoes, have attained and continue to attain fame and high position. Examples are Brazil's greatest
writer, Machado de Assis, Gonçalves Dias, André Rebouças, Teodoro
Sampaio, Lima Barreto, and Nilo Peçanha. In all truth it must be admitted, however, that, despite miscegenation and racial tolerance, the
lowest places in society continue to be taken by those who are darkest
of skin.

[8] William Lyttle Schurz, *This New World: The Civilization of Latin America*, p. 172.
The same idea is expressed in Hutchinson, *Village and Plantation Life*, p. 101.

20. Acculturation and Nationalization of Immigrants

It was only after 1818 that a more intense phase of ethnic and cultural
crossbreeding began, with the arrival of new ethnic groups. This is not
the place to recall the history of immigration, recruited or spontaneous,
limited or unlimited, burdened with restrictions or free thereof.[1]

Immigration was originally exclusively European in origin—Germans and Swiss, followed by Italians, Spaniards, and Portuguese. It
became diversified with the arrival of Japanese, Syrians, and Lebanese.
In all, it totaled 5,000,000 arrivals between 1850 and 1950. All stocks
have shared in the cultural-relations process, and, with few exceptions,
they have intermarried. In general it can be said that no other country
has received so many Japanese, and that only the United States has
admitted a larger number of Germans. Only Argentina and Mexico have
received more Spaniards, and few other countries have received so
many Italians and Slavs. Even so, however, in 1950 immigrants represented less than 3 percent of the total population, whereas in 1920 they
came to 5.11 percent.

European immigration did not have the consequences that are generally imagined. In the first place, it was not the prime factor in the
growth of the Brazilian population from 4,000,000 in 1822 to 50,000,-
000 in 1950. The principal factor, despite a death rate which has been
and continues to be high (18 per 1,000 inhabitants), has been the high

[1] See José Fernandes Carneiro, *Imigração e Colonização no Brasil*; and Artur Hehl
Neiva, "A Imigração e Colonização no Govêrno Vargas," *Cultura Política*, No. 21 (novembro 1942).

birth rate—43.05 per 1,000 inhabitants. Immigration accounts for but 8,000,000 persons, 4,000,000 of which represent the excess of immigration over emigration, the other 4,000,000 being offspring of immigrants. Second, the whitening of the population which was noted between 1872 and 1940, a period in which whites rose from one third to two thirds of the population, is to be attributed not merely to immigration but also to the superior economic position of the whites and their higher rate of survival, and also to crossbreeding, since color gradations, facial features, and type of hair determine the imprecise statistical classifications of "white" and "brown."[2]

In the 1950 census the percentage of whites fell 3 percent and that of browns rose 5 percent. Immigration was less important by reason of its numbers than by reason of the reinforcement it represented for the western-European element in the process of ethnic and cultural crossbreeding. Foreigners and naturalized Brazilians numbered 1,212,184 individuals in 1950, or 2.34 percent of the total population, the separate percentage for naturalized Brazilians being 0.25. This means that these elements have little more significance for the national picture than do the Indian groups, which at best represent 0.2 percent of the total population today.

Before their considerable reduction in numbers, almost to the point of extinction, the Indians made their contribution to Brazilian life through ethnic and cultural crossbreeding. European immigrants strengthened the white element and Occidental features among Brazilians. The Japanese have accentuated Oriental features and have had an influence on the Brazilian diet. As none of these groups were preponderant factors in the growth of the population, however, they have not modified the basic Brazilian personality.

Assimilation has gone forward without encountering undue difficulties, and the Brazilian economy owes the various ethnic groups important contributions. In agriculture, particularly as regards the growing of grapes, coffee, wheat, and other grains, the Italians and the Germans have distinguished themselves; in industry Italians, Germans, Syrians, and Lebanese have made their mark.[3] The majority have gone to southern Brazil, where today, along with people who have come from the

[2] Giorgio Mortara, "A População do Brasil e seu Desenvolvimento nos Últimos 125 Anos," *Boletim Geográfico*, 19, No. 161 (março–abril 1961), 271–272.

[3] See Manuel Diegues Júnior, *Etnias e Culturas no Brasil*; Orlando Valverde, *A Velha Imigração Italiana e sua Influência na Agricultura e na Economia do Brasil*; Lourdes Magalhães de Matos Strauch, "Atividades Econômicas da Região Sul," *Boletim Geográfico*, No. 145 (1958), 507–515; and Clark S. Knowlton, *Sírios e Libaneses*.

Northeast and Minas Gerais, they make up the working force in the pioneer zones.

Two groups in particular assumed a position of isolation, owing either to their great ethnic difference from the Luso-Brazilian environment, to differences of cultural background, or to feelings of superiority. These were the Germans and the Japanese, who thus avoided integration.

Under the Empire there were those, both conservative and radical, who opposed the granting of favors to immigrants, to the detriment of rural Brazilians. Antônio Pedro de Figueiredo wrote in 1847 that the bringing of colonies of immigrants to Brazil was inopportune, and that the obstacle to agricultural development was the latifundium, which impeded access to the land. There were also those who did not believe in the superiority of the settler to the Negro as a tiller of the soil. Such, for example, was the case with Martinho de Campos, when, on taking over the cabinet in 1882, he declared himself opposed to the recruitment of immigrants. Despite this opinion, Germanic groups gradually grew in the South, and by the end of the Empire the minutes of the municipal councils in Santa Catarina were kept in German, because no one knew Portuguese. When Baron Cotegipe learned this from Viscount Taunay, he declared in the Senate that it was "time that they learned, for this is Brazil, not Germany."

Under the Republic the government paid no attention to the problem, despite the warnings given by Sílvio Romero, particularly in his book *O Alemanismo no Sul do Brasil: Seus Perigos e Meios de os Conjurar* ("Germanism in Southern Brazil: The Dangers It Represents and Means of Combating Them"). Later, in 1917, when the question of the boundary between the states of Paraná and Santa Catarina came up in the Senate, Rui Barbosa proclaimed the dangers of German dominion and German expansion, showing that a large part of the land in the area in dispute had been granted as a concession to a German company, which, in selling lots, accepted only settlers of Germanic origin. The outcry raised by Rui Barbosa against the Germanization of Santa Catarina had no repercussion, and the endogamic groups continued to exist, offering no immediate peril to national security until German and Japanese expansionist activities rendered them a menace.

Integration of the Germans was always a problem, as they considered ideas of fusion and of conformity with Brazilian customs whims of the natives, from which the latter would have to desist. Handelmann wrote in 1860 that the Brazilians would have to

... offer guarantees that they were resolved to respect and protect the German nationality of the immigrant; consequently they will have to make it as easy as possible for immigrants to set up independent communities of their own and, instead of appointing administrators therefor, allow them to choose directors for themselves.[4]

The persistence of these ideas, particularly among groups in Santa Catarina and Rio Grande do Sul, transformed them into cysts in the body of the nation. Some of the groups, as for example the 25th of July Federation,[5] maintained antinationalist policies. The isolation of the nuclei has retarded their ingathering, but the processes of urbanization and industrialization have facilitated the assimilation and integration of about 200,000 Teutons, who have immigrated to Brazil over a period of eighty years. The 1950 census registered more than 65,000, almost all (96.2%) in the states of the South.[6]

As for the Japanese, they have not always enjoyed official favor. In the nineteenth century the proposal for importing Chinese and other Asiatics was greatly criticized,[7] and in 1934 Miguel Couto fought in the constitutional convention against Japanese immigration. The result was the establishment of the quota system, which rendered immigration difficult.[8]

Despite these obstacles, from 1908 to the present, with the exception of the war years, Japanese immigration has continued, reaching a total of about 450,000, or 0.6 percent of the population of Brazil. The largest number settled in São Paulo (78.8%) and in Paraná (19.1%). The World War and certain terrorist and nationalistic organizations, such as the Shindō Remmei (League of the Way of Subjects) rendered the process of racial and cultural assimilation difficult. Adaptation to Brazilian types of dress and dwellings, abandonment of the Buddhist cult for attendance at the Catholic mass, intermarriage, and participation in

[4] Heinrich Handelmann, *História do Brasil*, translated by Lúcia Furquim Lahmeyer, *Revista do Instituto Histórico e Geográfico Brasileiro*, Vol. 162, t. 108, pp. 971–1000.
[5] Aristóteles de Lima Câmara and Artur Hehl Neiva, "Colonização Nipônica e Germânica no Sul do Brasil," *Revista de Imigração e Colonização*, 2, No. 1 (janeiro 1941), 39–119. See also *Documents on German Foreign Policy, 1918–1945*, p. 859.
[6] Emílio Willems, *Assimilação e Populações Marginais no Brasil*. See in particular Emílio Willems, *Aculturação dos Alemães no Brasil*.
[7] See [José Pedro Xavier Pinheiro], *Importação de Trabalhadores Chins*. See also Salvador Menezes Drummond Furtado de Mendonça, *Trabalhadores Asiáticos*, and *Imigração Chinesa*.
[8] José Honório Rodrigues, *Brasil e África: Outro Horizonte*, pp. 86–90; 2d ed., Vol. 1, pp. 89–92.

politics, with the election of Japanese deputies, show that the process of acculturation is definitely under way. Industrialization, migration to the cities, religious influence, and compulsory military service have hastened its progress. General acceptance of Japanese immigration and the terms of the latest agreement—that of 1960—show that mutual respect has overcome past prejudice and discrimination. Contributions to Brazilian culture, economic and industrial development, and agriculture have been clearly evidenced.[9]

In 1938 the Council on Immigration and Settlement was created; in 1954 it was transformed into the National Institute for Immigration and Settlement. Among the Council's functions was that of accelerating the process of adaptation, acculturation, and integration—of Brazilianization, in short. Basic points in the nationalization policy were the breakdown of geographic and social isolation, avoidance of forming new homogeneous nuclei of immigrant settlers, incentives to the inclusion of Brazilian families in existing nuclei, and multiplication of other environmental factors (e.g., schools) which have a nationalizing effect. At the same time the attempt was made to take due account of the interest which immigration has for economic development.[10] The predominance of national interest in immigration matters, as established in the 1934 constitution, was reinforced in that of 1946. Since that time the cysts have disappeared.

Immigration today has been reduced by the cutting off of currents from eastern Europe and more particularly from Italy. The only steady flow of immigration is from Japan, and at the present moment (1964) severe restrictions are imposed thereon: no Japanese is given an immigration visa without first transferring at least $5,000 in United States currency to Brazil. From the Amazon to Paraná the Japanese have been actively engaged in agriculture. Tea and black-pepper production is 100 percent in their hands and 90 percent of Brazilian peppermint is grown by them. They have provided workmen for São Paulo industry, and their presence in the country is a stimulus to Japanese investment in Brazil.

Prospects now present themselves of the coming of white colonists from Asia and Africa—Netherlanders from Indonesia, Belgians from

---

[9] Concerning the Japanese, see Antônio Rubio Muller and Hiroshi Saito, *Memórias do I Painel Nipo-Brasileiro*; James L. Tigner, "Shindō Remmei, Japanese Nationalism in Brazil," *Hispanic American Historical Review*, 41, No. 4 (November, 1961), 515–532; Hiroshi Saito, *O Japonês no Brasil*.

[10] Rui Ribeiro Couto, "O Problema da Nacionalização," *Revista de Imigração e Colonização*, 2, No. 1 (janeiro 1941), 18–34.

the Congo, Frenchmen from Algeria, and Englishmen from Kenya. The advantages they offer are disputed in view of possible racial complexes. Even so, for a variety of reasons Brazil holds fifth or sixth place among the preferences of those seeking to emigrate from their native countries.

Immigrants have not altered the basic Brazilian character, for in the South, in which first- and second-generation Brazilians are readily found, they are integrated into Brazilian culture and the Brazilian historical tradition. Under the administration which governed Brazil from 1956 to 1960, officials of non-Portuguese descent included the president of the Republic, the vice-president of the Senate, the presiding officer of the Chamber of Deputies, the chief justice of the Supreme Court, and numerous senators, deputies, cabinet ministers, judges, and other persons of high rank.[11]

Thus the most serious problems of psychosocial integration in Brazil are gradually finding solution. The Afonso Arinos Law (No. 1390 of 1951), which makes the practice of racial discrimination a rapidly punishable crime, and the creation on June 20, 1910, of the Indian Protection Service, charged with protecting, educating, and assimilating Indians into the economy and the cultural life of Brazil, complete the picture of what the country has done to achieve ethnic democracy based on respect for the individual regardless of his origin and to further the work of national integration. Even so, much remains to be done. In January, 1961, Deputy Abel Rafael called for the granting of land titles to Indians, particularly in the states of Amazonas and Pará, where they are most common, and where they are being driven from their homes by adventurers.[12]

The question of the rights of naturalized citizens presents a more serious problem. Ordinary laws in more than fifty instances prevent such citizens from exercising specific activities. In general, for naturalization purposes, a year's residence is required of a Portuguese, three years' residence of a person engaged in agriculture or industry, and five years' residence of foreigners not included in the foregoing categories. Once he has become naturalized, however, the new citizen is confronted with innumerable restrictions upon his participation in Brazilian life, set forth in the constitution and in ordinary laws.

[11] President Juscelino Kubitschek de Oliveira, of Czech origin on his mother's side; Paschoal Ranieri Mazzilli, president of the Chamber of Deputies, of Italian descent; Filinto Muller, vice-president of the Senate, and Nelson Hungria Hoffbauer, chief justice of the Supreme Electoral Tribunal, both of German descent.

[12] *Diário do Congresso Nacional*, 17 janeiro 1961, p. 201.

Some of the more exaggerated restrictions are those prohibiting the naturalized citizen from being principal of a rural school or a teacher in the elementary grades, and from giving instruction in Portuguese, geography, or history. Deputy Castilho Cabral recently presented Draft Amendment No. 11 to the constitution, which would revoke existing constitutional provisions and confer upon the naturalized Brazilian, five years after acquiring citizenship, all rights possessed by the native-born save that of election to the presidency or vice-presidency of the Republic or the governorship or lieutenant-governorship of the states. The question of granting naturalized citizens almost all political rights has naturally stirred up much controversy, and the nationalist members of the Chamber of Deputies insist on every precaution. As Deputy Nelson Carneiro pointed out in the debate in the Chamber, a dividing line should exist between the rights of native-born and naturalized citizens, but this should neither mean denial of facilities for naturalization nor be an obstacle to repeal of excessively harsh restrictions on the naturalized. The dividing line is represented by national interest.[13]

In reality, the Brazilian people are far more homogeneous in terms of culture, language, and stage of historical development than the peoples of other countries of comparable size or population. India, China, the Soviet Union, Indonesia, and Pakistan are inhabited by peoples of greatly differing cultures, who speak a variety of languages. The peoples of Asia are divided into sharply differentiated linguistic and religious groups; loyalty to language, religion, caste, and local divisions is strongly accentuated in countries such as India, Ceylon, and Pakistan.

The Brazilian people have learned a common language (it must not be forgotten that Tupi predominated in São Paulo and Amazonas up to the middle of the eighteenth century); they have fostered national unity; they have defended the integrity of their territory; they are bringing up their children and preparing them for life with but scanty resources; they possess strong national feeling. All consider themselves equally Brazilian, whatever their ethnic and cultural background.

The serious problem is that of the differences in stage of historical development which today sharply separate rural and urban areas, and divide the North, Northeast, and Center from the East and South. Rural insurrections such as those which took place at Canudos and in the disputed border region between Paraná and Santa Catarina, the excesses committed by outlaws and religious fanatics, and the demands

[13] Speech delivered on January 17, 1961; see *Diário do Congresso Nacional*, 17 janeiro 1961, pp. 208–210.

currently being made by backlanders and rural workers show the need
for the reforms that so often have been promised by the national governments from 1831 till today—promises the fulfillment of which has
always been avoided or postponed.

21. Classes and Social Justice

The processes of acculturating the various ethnic groups and integrat-
ing them into Brazilian society should culminate in harmony and, if
possible, cooperation among the different social classes. In the early
stages of its history Brazilian society was composed of but two castes,
masters and slaves. Intermediate social classes began to appear in the
colonial period. Their ranks were composed of free men who owned no
lands and of a great variety of crossbreeds. A rigid caste system lasted
but a short time, since crossbreeding tended to break down caste distinctions and bring about a general leveling. Strictly speaking, no class
struggles occurred in Brazil. This was not, as Oliveira Viana wrote, because conflicts were rare, of short duration, discontinuous, and local, but
because the only struggles that took place were between masters and
slaves. Free men who were not landowners were so few in number that
they did not dare form a group or resist the impositions of the landed
proprietors. The cases which are commonly cited have a social character, in that popular demands and economic factors had a part therein,
but they fail to show any division along class lines, unless masters and
slaves be taken as classes rather than castes. The same can be said of
rural movements and banditry, in which social aspirations are mingled
with religious mysticism.

By the end of the slave period,* crossbreeds exceeded the white
master class in numbers, and Negroes constituted the lowest level of the
social hierarchy. The free immigrants who arrived during the nineteenth
and twentieth centuries swelled the ranks of the middle and lower
classes, but the dominant group continued to be represented by the
rural aristocracy—the landowners, the sugar and coffee planters. The
descendants of the old rural aristocracy, who until recently alone held
sway in Brazil, have today been joined by the *nouveaux riches* of industry and the upper ranks of commerce in a small but powerful class
that still reigns over the society. Social instability and mobility prevent

* Slavery was abolished in 1888.

the formation of rigid class lines. The abolition of slavery gave rise to rural and urban working classes. To be sure, free city workers and peasants existed prior to that event, but they had no particular social significance, since, whenever possible, they themselves made use of slave labor. It is the move to the cities and industrialization which, in this century, have fostered the formation of an urban working class. As a class, however, field workers, living under more primitive conditions, still represent a little more than half of the mass of the people in Brazil, or 55.24 percent of the total.[1]

Urban and rural workers alike were always immobilized by ignorance, paternalism, and the dominance of the rural aristocracy, all of which ensured victory for the oligarchy. Political inertia characterized the working classes of the cities, at least until 1930, and field workers found in banditry the means of manifesting a spirit of rebellion. The 1930 revolution, although it did not at first seriously threaten the *status quo*, marked an advance, in that workers began to take part in political life. Getúlio Vargas appreciated the potential value of the political support of the working classes, which until that time had been prevented from forming associations and furthering their demands by labor-union action. For this reason the regulations established to protect the rights of labor or to improve working conditions do not represent gains won by the workers for themselves but a concession on the part of the state.

Today, with more than two million urban workers, Brazil is ceasing to be a rural country, despite its agrarian structure and the fact that a slight majority of the population lives in rural areas. Living conditions in those areas are primitive, but the voice of the rural population is beginning to be heard. In addition to the increasingly rapid movement to the cities, one should note that the industrial sector, which in 1939 contributed 17.9 percent of the national income, in 1959 contributed 25.3 percent; industrial establishments, which numbered 40,983 in 1939, reached 128,769 in 1958.[2]

Despite all these signs of change, power remains in the hands of

---

[1] The first returns of the 1960 census show a great increase in the movement to the cities. The number of rural dwellers declined from 68.76 percent of the total population in 1940 to 63.84 percent in 1950 and to approximately 55.24 percent in 1960. See *Desenvolvimento e Conjuntura*, 6, No. 3 (março 1962), 9.

[2] "Retrospecto Parcial da Economia Brasileira," *Desenvolvimento & Conjuntura*, 5, No. 7 (julho 1961).

representatives of the rural oligarchy, supported by a strong contingent of traditionalists from the ranks of commerce and industry.[3]

The latter do not form a solid group, for their interests divide them. The men of commerce are more conservative; they are identified with their own interests rather than with those of the nation; their action is carried out for the most part behind the scenes. The industrialists, in whose ranks foreign elements—naturalized immigrants or first- or second-generation Brazilians—are more numerous, show themselves to be more progressive and take a more open part in public debate. They boost economic nationalism, since that fits in with their interests. Industry, thanks to its leaders, has everywhere proved a revolutionary force. Aggressive, versatile, untrammeled by doctrinaire principles, it is of far greater significance than a multitude of libraries filled with revolutionary works or a university overrun by liberal professors. In Brazil it is not yet altogether a force for progress: it vacillates; it both supports and fears basic reforms; its stand on national and international issues is now ahead of the times and then behind them; it struggles for open possession of positions in the executive branch of the government. The leaders of the commercial class—who refer to it as "productive"—have taken a frankly conservative position. Some commercial sectors have had a hand in speculation in foodstuffs in periods of crisis, and they often set their personal interests above those of the nation. Leaders of the commercial class have also been accused of conspiracy and of connection with reactionary sectors of the nation. Commercial and industrial groups exert strong pressure on the government by opinions expressed behind the scenes and by economic influence. The executive and the legislative branches do not readily take fright—save for those who listen to the opinions of conservative leaders—but they do not tolerate demonstrations by the working classes, whether urban or rural, as they always view such activities as a prelude to revolution. The opinion registered by the wielders of economic power or by the popular classes is, as it were, a barometer by means of which one may measure the strength of the government, constantly fluctuating in accordance with the pressures exerted upon it.

Left in the lurch is the middle class, which has also grown with the move to the cities, but which has not constituted in Brazil the basic, decisive element which has brought about stability in Europe, particu-

[3] See the excellent study by Raimundo Faoro, *Os Donos do Poder: Formação do Patronato Político Brasileiro.*

larly in the United Kingdom, and in the United States.* The Brazilian
middle class is marked by indignation rather than by influence. The
indignation of the moralizer is not only an ingredient but also an instrument in the struggle for power. It is in this last respect that the
struggle against corruption is of service. It also provides a pretext for
stifling the voice of tolerance in the conflict between ideologies and
modes of thought. It is a common happening along this byway of history
that indignation ends as indignity. It is the indignant who are the greatest threat to public liberties in the United States, just as the tolerant are
those who do most to facilitate corruption. The middle class had as a
program at the moment of its greatest indignation what it called the
moral rehabilitation of the country. At that point it acted as an independent group, although it served the interests of the various conservative sectors. It was not an element for stability, in accordance with the
role assigned it by Aristotle. It sought, according to its leaders, to
storm the citadel of power, without sullying itself by alliances with the
masses, but aided by elements of distinction, however antinationalistic
and void of enthusiasm for economic development they might be. The
position taken by the middle class in Brazil in 1954–1955 was precisely
the opposite of that assumed by the middle class in Europe, where it has
been and remains a key factor in democracy and industrialism, or even
of that taken by the middle classes in the emerging countries of Africa
and Asia, which have helped the cause of independence and nationalism.

Jacques Lambert, who has studied the role of the middle class in
Brazil, noted that its strategic location in the cities gave it an authority
which bore no relation to the numbers in its ranks, particularly in
comparison with the rural masses. As the latter and the urban proletariat exist at a low cultural level and have low standards of living,
the middle class could take a vanguard position. Its leaders, however,
have deprived it of the political role which it has had in Europe and in
the United States; they have made indignation an end in itself; they
have exploited the tendency to inflict punishment that characterizes the
lower middle class, which lives in a perpetual state of restriction and
frustration. Extreme moral indignation is a form of resentment which
the Nazis put to use, whereas the Anglo-American middle classes have
cast off indignation and insisted on morality as a normal discipline, representing an important factor for stability. The Brazilian middle classes
failed to achieve this result owing to poor leadership in 1954–1955.

* The Brazilian middle class has been estimated to comprise approximately 15 percent
of the population.

Today, crushed by inflation, they have no prospects of arriving at the political role and influence which they might have exercised at a more favorable hour.

The clash between the current interests of the several classes is imparting new life and vigor to the country. Out of the opposition between them the national interest gradually emerges. The momentary visions of a given group do not constitute national aspirations, although the vision entertained by the majority reflects the essence of the objectives of that fundamental element in the nation, the common people. In view of the state of abandonment in which the populace found itself, a few of its aspirations to social justice were incorporated into the 1934 constitution, which sought to nationalize the economy, to render it more democratic, and to favor the worker. Labor tribunals and the corresponding judiciary were the creation of the 1946 constitution.

22. Representative Government and the Harmonious Division of Powers

Ever since the proclamation of independence, when the question of choosing a form of government first arose, the most varied of tendencies have continued to manifest themselves, ranging from radical republicanism to absolute monarchy. It soon became clear, however, that the essential aspiration of the majority was for representative government, with a harmonious division of powers. Dom Pedro I declared to the Constitutional Assembly on May 3, 1823, that he hoped it would bring forth a wise constitution, the sole aim of which would be the happiness of the people in general. To this end it should have

. . . solid bases—bases which the wisdom of centuries has shown to be true —providing the people with the freedom which is their due and the executive with whatever power may be required. A constitution in which the three branches of government are clearly divided, so that they cannot arrogate to themselves authority that is not theirs, but at the same time one in which they are organized in such harmonious fashion that it will prove impossible, even in the course of time, for hostility to develop among them, so that, in close union, they will contribute increasingly to the general happiness of the state.[1]

[1] *Anais do Parlamento Brasileiro, Assembléia Constituinte, 1823* (1876), p. 41.

Antônio Carlos Ribeiro de Andrada was to say a little later, on May 16:

... the nation has already laid certain bases: it has chosen a dynasty, proclaiming an emperor, who is the protector and perpetual defender of Brazil; it has therefore declared its preference as to a form of government, namely constitutional monarchy, essential points of which are the division of powers, harmony thereamong, and the intervention of the executive in legislative matters.[2]

The idea of a harmonious division of powers and a strong executive predominates in both statements.

Brazil was ruled by a hereditary constitutional monarchy of the representative type from 1824 to 1889. In the latter year a federal republic was established, likewise representative in character, and—with intervals of dictatorship from 1891 to 1894, from 1930 to 1934, and from 1937 to 1945—this was the form of government which prevailed until recently (1964). Although the 1824 constitution declared that the emperor's ministers were answerable to Parliament, it did not provide for a parliamentary system. Holders of portfolios were the personal choices of the emperor, who named and dismissed ministers at his pleasure. The constitution established no difference of rank between the houses of Parliament, although seats in the Chamber of Deputies were held on a term basis and those in the Senate for life. Only in 1847 was a decree[3] issued creating the office of chairman of the Council of Ministers, the appointee to which, in consultation with the sovereign, selected the remaining members of the cabinet. The novelty lay in this manner of exercising a choice which had formerly been the exclusive prerogative of the emperor, not in the institution of votes of confidence or lack thereof. No cabinet fell without an expression of this sort on the part of the Parliament; none failed to present its program. Each chairman of the Council headed a ministry, usually that of finance, "in order that this ministry, through which all expenses are channeled and controlled, may enjoy greater prestige in relation to the other ministries," as Dom Pedro II was wont to say. When the chairmanship was not combined with the Ministry of Finance, it was joined with the Ministry of the Empire. This, however, occurred less frequently, contrary to the British tradition, which was followed in the case of the republican parliamentary system.

Cabinets had to have parliamentary backing in order to survive.

[2] *Ibid.*, p. 90.
[3] Decree No. 523, of July 20, 1847.

Feijó, despite his great qualities, his dignity, and his high moral character, was obliged to resign for lack of parliamentary support. Bernardo Pereira de Vasconcelos acquired the strength to combat the disorder and anarchy that threatened the country in 1837 by organizing a cabinet whose members were drawn from the Parliament. It was not the longest lasting, since the cabinet headed by Viscount Rio Branco (the twenty-fifth in the history of the Empire), likewise organized on a completely parliamentary basis, had an existence of more than four years, from March 7, 1871, to June 24, 1875. (There were also cabinets that lasted no more than six days, such as the seventeenth, organized by Zacarias de Góis e Vasconcelos.) The Marquis of Olinda, in replying to Martinho de Campos in the Chamber of Deputies, insisted, however, that the emperor had the right to choose his ministers freely.[4]

The parliamentary regime made for instability of executive power. From 1826 to 1889, discounting the period of the Constitutional Assembly of 1822 and the dissolution of the Legislature in 1823, the average Brazilian cabinet had a life of 1.1 years. Even if one consider but the forty-nine–year period from the proclamation of Dom Pedro II's majority to his overthrow (1840–1889), there were thirty-six cabinets, each lasting an average of 1.3 years.

The constitutional remedy of dissolving the Chamber of Deputies, a prerogative of the sovereign of which the regents were deprived, was not often applied by Dom Pedro II. In his "Advice" to Princess Isabel in 1871, he viewed it as an appeal to the nation to which resort should be had only in the gravest of instances. And he acted accordingly. Of the thirty-six cabinets of the period in which he exercised the executive authority, twenty-seven were overthrown by the Chamber of Deputies, and only nine times was the latter dissolved by the emperor.

It was the parliamentary custom to discuss general policy in the debate on the budget of the Ministry of the Empire. Special policies were debated in the discussion of the individual ministerial budgets. The parliamentary regime—which always requires complete independence of the sovereign or the president in relation to parties—made for greater unity in cabinets, laid greater responsibility on parties and leaders, led to greater stability and cohesiveness in the government, and permitted the system to function with a greater degree of regularity.

[4] Speech delivered on June 28, 1862, recorded in *Anais do Parlamento Brasileiro* (1862), Vol. 2, pp. 254–256; transcribed by José Honório Rodrigues in "O Parlamentarismo e o Conselho de Ministros," *Jornal do Brasil* (Rio de Janeiro), 15 julho 1962.

The dominant minority, whether or not it enjoyed popular support, always considered monarchical government a permanent aspiration. José Antônio Saraiva, in a speech to the Chamber of Deputies, declared, to prolonged applause:

... from the first deputy of the majority to the last deputy of the opposition, we all recognize that the only regime possible in Brazil is constitutional monarchy. From the first deputy of the majority to the last deputy of the opposition, I repeat, we all recognize that the Crown is the chief protector of our institutions, the greatest and surest guarantee of our rights.[5]

The ministerial crisis of 1868, however—which was not provoked by Parliament, since the cabinet did not resign as a result of a vote of lack of confidence, having as it did almost the whole of the Chamber of Deputies on its side—showed that executive leadership, exercised by the ministers of state and the emperor, was the dominant force in the country. It was from this point that "disbelief in the virtue of the parliamentary monarchy and an increasing aspiration to a new regime and a new order of things" date.[6]

With the return of the parliamentary regime, the fall of the cabinet in 1962 likewise resulted from extraparliamentary causes, having been occasioned by incompatibilities among its members, who were candidates in the forthcoming elections.[*] In this case the crisis was the consequence of the shotgun wedding of a parliamentary regime to a presidentialist constitution.

If monarchy did not represent a permanent aspiration, if parliamentarism did not enjoy lasting vigor, if the federal republic appeared as an aspiration in 1869–1870 but became a reality only in 1889, it seems logical to conclude that the political principle which was asserted in 1823, which was confirmed in 1824, which prevailed until 1889, which was reaffirmed in 1891, and which is valid even today is representative government and a harmonious relation between powers, although the predominance of the executive has always been accepted.

With or without a monarchy, with or without a republic, with or without federation, with or without presidentialism or parliamentarism, the permanent aspiration has always been for a democratic regime of the representative type, with a harmonious division of powers. Ideo-

---

[5] Speech delivered on May 27, 1862, recorded in *Anais do Parlamento Brasileiro* (1862), Vol. 1, pp. 64–65.

[6] Francisco José Oliveira Viana, *O Ocaso do Império*, p. 24.

[*] Tancredo Neves, the first prime minister under the new parliamentary system, which began in September of 1961, lasted nine months in office.

logical problems were never of essential importance to either the majority or the minority. There was in fact a considerable overlapping of the parties in this regard. José Maria da Silva Paranhos, Viscount Rio Branco, in a speech in the Chamber of Deputies, expressed the amorphous character of the parties there represented, saying:

We are conservatives because we wish to preserve and defend the institutions to which we have sworn allegiance; we all recognize that the monarchy is the most precious inheritance that we have received from our ancestors, that the integrity of the empire is essential to the great and glorious future which we desire for our country. We are also liberals, because we desire monarchy, but monarchy in perfect harmony with public liberties. This is required by the century in which we live; this is the manifest aspiration of the country.[7]

It is for this very reason that the policy of conciliation and alliances has proved so satisfactory to the personal interests in dispute, especially those of the dominant minority, despite the violence of mutual criticism. One of the principles of conciliation, Tôrres Homem said in a speech in the Chamber of Deputies, is that mutual offenses are to be forgotten. In the view of this man, who had come from the liberal camp and was accused of being a "heterogeneous element among his new ultra-conservative allies," it was the conservatives "who had done more for reforms and liberal principles than their official champions."[8] Fundamentally, the policies of the two parties were the same: a broad area of agreement existed between them on the basic issues raised with a view to appealing to the same group of voters. With rare exceptions the politicians were all exceedingly changeable, which led Francisco Otaviano to say, quoting Seneca, "You may be sure that it is a difficult thing for a man to remain at all times the same."*

The experience of the various regimes has proved the realism of Dom Pedro I and Antônio Carlos Ribeiro de Andrada, not only with respect to the intervention of the executive in legislative matters, but also as to the subordination—open or disguised—of the legislative and judicial branches to the executive. Thus parliamentarism in Brazil never meant the predominance of the legislative branch, since the sovereign, as such, gave the executive a natural preeminence. Whether or not the balance of

[7] Speech delivered on June 2, 1862, recorded in *Anais do Parlamento Brasileiro* (1862), Vol. 2, p. 258.

[8] Speech delivered on June 25, 1862, recorded in *Anais do Parlamento Brasileiro* (1862), Vol. 2, p. 216.

* The similarity and interchange between the two major parties under the rule of the second emperor prompted the Visconde de Albuquerque to remark, "There is nothing so much like a Conservative as a Liberal in power."

power between the several branches be disturbed by the special importance attributed to one or to the particular strength gained by another, the fact is that it would not have been possible to preserve the state, had not all in partnership shared the burden of national responsibilities, just as nations would lapse into endless warfare and anarchy were not a balance of power maintained in world politics.

23. Oligarchy and Democracy

The great democratic aspiration the principle of which is expressed by the representative system is being achieved very slowly, for two reasons. In the first place, representation used to be fraudulent, and still is restricted. In the second place, although under the Empire the public enjoyed many liberties, as Tavares Bastos, one of the monarchy's greatest critics, recognized, the Penal Code of 1841 and the reform of 1871 set limitations thereon. These limitations, however, did not go so far as those imposed during the regression that took place under Floriano Peixoto or during the Vargas dictatorship, which practically abolished civil liberties. Since Empire days the Brazilian government has been oligarchic, founded upon the interests of slaveholders, of great landowners, of sugar and coffee growers—traditional forces who, as Nabuco wrote, have ascribed unto themselves not only glory but government as well.

Brazilian conservatism has its roots in the family groups which since colonial times have been masters of the land and which since the proclamation of independence have taken the lead in politics. Independence was the achievement of the intellectuals and the youth of the country, aided as always by a few Portuguese allies, blind but men of goodwill. They were able to write a constitution and debate it within limits, but real power remained in the hands of the great landowners, and Dom Pedro I clipped the wings of the authors of independence, conferring upon the country a constitution that maintained intact the already obsolete, static socioeconomic structure of the Portuguese colony, a structure which has been an obstacle to national progress or has deadened incipient impulses thereto. The whole history of Brazilian radicalism can be summed up as a frustrated effort against the powerful economic oligarchies, in whose hands lie the reins of power. The whole of conservative action, seconded by the so-called moderating power, has consisted in avoiding a decisive conflict, the battle which would bring down in ruins the remainders of Portuguese colonialism in Brazil.

The oligarchies have always been active. However, it has already been noted that the political leaders of Minas Gerais have always shared in the direction of national policy, whether or not the state itself shared to a major extent in the national income. Participation by the Northeast in such direction has always depended upon its role in the economic life of the country. The same cannot be said of the minority from Bahia, which was neither so indispensable as that of Minas Gerais nor so easily dispensed with as that of other regions. Its strength was not in direct relationship to its economic resources, but the latter were not a dispensable factor as in the case of Minas.

Brazilian conservatism has its roots in family groups in the states of Rio de Janeiro, Bahia, and Minas Gerais, especially the last-mentioned —groups which since colonial times have skillfully manipulated the nation's politics. The Minas oligarchy is composed of 174 family lines, of which 135 are of Lusitanian peasant origin, only 39 being descendants of members of *bandeiras*.[1] Like the other oligarchies, it is traditionalist and conservative and is composed of large landowners. It makes up the greatest part of the white population of the state with the largest number of Negroes in the country—a fact which strengthens its attitude in defense of the *status quo*. This, together with its facility for adaptation, which has been noted since the time of Saint-Hilaire by the most observant travelers, may explain the refinement of political art exhibited by the dominant class in Minas. Wrote José Bonifácio to Dom Pedro I: "Let Your Royal Highness not believe all that the people of Minas Gerais tell you, for they have the reputation in Brazil of being the cleverest deceivers in creation. They make black out to be white and white black."[2]

Without support from Minas Gerais no political movement in Brazil has ever met with success, and exclusion of Minas from the government means failure as long as the agrarian structure which is the basis of power persists. This position of favor was also assured by the predominance of representatives of Minas, followed by those of Bahia, in the Chamber of Deputies, from the time of the first elections until 1875.

This situation was further emphasized under the Republic. From

[1] Cid Rebêlo Horta, *Famílias Governamentais de Minas Gerais*.

[2] Tobias [do Rêgo] Monteiro, *História do Império: A Elaboração da Independência*, p. 473. I am indebted to Professor Francisco Iglésias for bringing to mind the role played by oligarchy in the state of Rio de Janeiro.

1889 to 1930 the state of Minas was dominated by a single party, the PRM (Republican Party of Minas). Despite local struggles between families, it remained unified in making demands at the national level. The Minas oligarchy and similar groups in Bahia and the state of Rio de Janeiro—whites who are also surrounded by a multitude of Negroes and crossbreeds—aided by *caiados,* have constituted the substance of the ruling Brazilian minority. Oligarchs from Minas, the state of Rio de Janeiro, and Bahia, principally the first-mentioned, are wont to speak of politics only in an intimate whisper;* they are the sliest representatives of Brazilian adroitness, of the spirit of moderation and conciliation. The skill of this dominant minority stems from the fact that it is ever on watch to defend its privileges, ever concerned with maintaining docility in the masses, who have been castrated and bled white.

On the national level the same socioeconomic antagonism has called for similar ability, hence the remarkable talent for directing the nation's affairs which they have exercised without encountering any special opposition. Conciliation, as a political doctrine, was well represented by Honório Hermeto Carneiro Leão, afterwards Marquis of Paraná. He was the symbol of the spirit of adjusting differences between members of the dominant class and measuring out concessions to those under their domination. Moderation suited the aspirations of the oligarchy and sought to bring about compliance on the part of the oppressed. Control of the states of Rio de Janeiro, Minas, and Bahia by an ethnic minority developed in the members thereof a flair for the direction of national affairs, in which the same capacity for self-defense was required on a grander scale. Hence the predominance of men of Minas, Bahia, and the state of Rio in national leadership. That predominance, challenged but invincible, had no corresponding economic consequence, nor did it bring any particular advantage to the states in question and the people thereof.

The preeminence of these groups was beneficial in that it meant that Brazilian history has been marked by relatively little bloodshed; it was detrimental, however, in that it meant the persistence of the social structure of preindependence days, dominated by a landowning oligarchy. Features of this economic system which cannot escape notice are the social and psychological solidarity of family groups and what Arnold Toynbee has called the patron-client relationship. In the case of the last-mentioned, an ethnic and emotional tie is incompatibly coupled

---

* They have perfected the use of the political rumor as an instrument for political maneuvering and bargaining.

with the crudest of economic exploitation and social injustice. These institutions are the product of a society—Luso-Brazilian colonial society —whose history shows no sign of advance. They still exert an influence on the Brazilian social structure, which is full of reminders of the past. Some are readily observable—open-air markets, for example. Some survive in disguise. Others are represented by psychological vacuums— the archaic characteristics exhibited by rural workers when they move to the city and swell the ranks of the urban proletariat. The patron-client relationship is an expression of the oligarchic *gens*, of the dominant minority which has not yet been put in its place, which refuses to yield to the demands of an economic development that can be achieved only with its extinction.

The low level of production which characterizes the agrarian structure of Minas Gerais, the movement of people to the cities,[3] the decrease in cultivated areas (about 1,235,000 acres), and the enormous growth of uncultivated areas (25,194,000 acres in 1940; 38,038,000 acres in 1950) in the nine Northeastern states (Maranhão, Piauí, Ceará, Rio Grande do Norte, Paraíba, Pernambuco, Alagoas, Sergipe, Bahia)[4] show that the end is near. In addition, recent studies show the breakup of oligarchic groups in Minas Gerais and the decline of the political parties of the center, accompanying the decrease in the rural population, which dropped from 68.8 percent in 1940 to 63.8 percent in 1950.[5]

Thus even prior to agrarian reform—on which subject the oligarchies entrenched in the Congress have sought to delude the populace by introducing no less than 212 different bills—the inequitable traditional agrarian structure of the country, which has caused Brazilian creative impulse to lose impetus, is already showing symptoms of decay. It is the active ingredient in the broth which the demagogic forces of the time are bringing to a boil. The monopoly of power traditionally exercised by the oligarchy cannot be terminated if the oligarchy's economic basis is not first destroyed. It is for this reason that the breaking up of the great landed estates is an issue of central importance. So too is tax reform. The current tax structure of Brazil evidences the domination of the oligarchies, which own the country but do not pay its expenses: 80 percent of the burden falls on those who are least in a position to

[3] Domício de Figueiredo Murta, "Nota Prévia sôbre a Estrutura Agrária de Minas Gerais," *Revista Brasileira de Ciências Sociais*, 1, No. 1 (novembro 1961), 62–78.

[4] "Agricultura no Nordeste," *Flagrantes Brasileiros*, No. 16 (1960), 28.

[5] Orlando M. Carvalho, "Os Partidos Políticos em Minas Gerais," *Segundo Seminário de Estudos Mineiros*, pp. 23–41. In 1960 the rural population fell to 55.24 percent of the total.

bear it. As early as 1847 Antônio Pedro de Figueiredo, writing in
O Progresso, a political review published in Recife, criticized a tax
system which took from the poor to give to the rich, to the landowning
potentates. His sentiments were echoed in the Chamber of Deputies in
July, 1964, by César Prieto in his criticism of the bill modifying the
income tax, when he said that henceforth that tax "will merely be a
translation of the sweat of the Brazilian worker instead of an indication
of the taxpayer's degree of economic prosperity." Instead of combating
tax evasion, he said further, the bill contributed to the "enrichment of
the powerful and the shocking impoverishment of the wage-earning
classes."

It was always thus, however. Antônio Felício dos Santo declared in
the Chamber of Deputies in 1880 that "in Brazil almost all taxes are
indirect. We have lived under a system whereby the taxpayer has his
money taken from him by treachery."[6] To all this must be added
illiteracy and the dominant influence of personalities on politics—
serious obstacles to political progress.

New forces which tend toward the elimination of the oligarchy are
the urban middle classes, the new industrial and commercial class,
workers' organizations, intellectuals, demagogic populism, the political
education of the masses, and the development of national parties, as a
result of which the tendency to sectional or regional voting is defeated
by national consciousness. The secret ballot, guaranteed by the electoral
system instituted in 1934, is an ever-more important factor in the
choice of national leaders and in voting for the president. Whereas only
276,783 ballots were cast for Prudente de Morais (1894), 3,077,411
persons voted for President Juscelino Kubitschek (1955) and 5,600,000
for President Jânio Quadros (1960). As a rule, only 2 percent of the
population voted under the Republic up to the time of Eurico Dutra
(1946), when the percentage rose to 13. At the time of the election of
Jânio Quadros it reached 19.14. The road to democracy lies through an
increase in the ranks of voters. To this the constitutional requirement
of literacy has proved an obstacle. If the representative system is to
survive as a legitimate, authentic expression of the will of the people
and meet the challenge of the present, an effective majority must be

[6] *Anais da Câmara dos Deputados* 5 junho 1880. Direct taxes currently represent
20 percent of the total tax burden in Brazil, whereas they represent 75 percent in the
United States and 50 percent in Canada and in Japan. Indirect taxes are the mainstay
of the Brazilian tax system, and fall mainly on the common people. Direct taxes are
subject to many types of exemptions and frauds.

established on the basis of a truly national vote, free of the coercions of economic power. If it is to merit trust it must represent all sectors of national opinion, not merely dominant minorities.

Joining forces, the lords of economic power seek through pressure groups—powerful institutions or organized interests—to exert influence on elections and government policies. Marshaling the means of exerting pressure on public opinion, arming themselves with abundant resources, they exact promises of those to be elected and seek to turn the present process of economic development and the advance of social justice from their course. Social justice still takes the form of a paternal or patronal favor. By dulling civic consciousness the economic power structure seeks to continue its rapid enrichment by speculation and by promoting governmental corruption. It goes arm in arm with the state, in partnership therewith. In the name of freedom of enterprise—freedom for private capital, that is—it seeks to defend deliberate prejudice to certain classes for its own benefit, defrauding popular aspirations. The more backward economic groups do not desire the democratization of business capital, the sole effective arm against the excessive concentration of economic power.

Brazil is not the only country in which the benefits of civilization have been monopolized by small oligarchies or economic groups. Nor will Brazil provide the only instance in which the power of the oligarchy or group is broken and benefits are extended to a majority of the members of society, raising the productive capacity of the entire community. History will not come to an end if the majority is benefited. As Arnold Toynbee recently said, the movement toward social justice is not opposed to economic productivity; the two are complementary. Those who insist on preserving intact an archaic, obsolete, static, traditional social system are the public enemies of the representative system and civil liberties, for they force the unfortunate masses into the arms of extremists.

24. Centralization and Federation

Like monarchy and republicanism, centralism and federalism are changeable aspirations, representing an attempt to meet the objectives of the moment. An examination of Brazilian history shows that the colonial legacy is diffuse, contradictory, careless, lacking in coherence and sequence. The unity deriving therefrom is much more the product of varied behavior—behavior which is thereby better able to serve regional difference—than of a uniform and symmetrical aspiration toward integration. The latter was the objective in the case of the Spanish Empire, disunited by the very idiosyncrasies of the Spaniards; its later division derived from the attempt to impose uniformity. When in 1549 a central government was created for Brazil, the desire was to provide a higher authority, which would operate at a level above the donataries,* would be respected by all, would resolve disputes, and would prevent conflicts. The centralizing principle began at this time, but it did not succeed in imposing itself nor was it ever entirely accepted and adopted. The divisions and the units which were established and reestablished show the practical realism with which passing conditions were faced. In 1621, when Spanish dominion was fully established in Brazil, the division made between the state of Brazil and the state of Maranhão, each entirely independent of the other and linked directly to the metropolis, offered a grave risk of disintegration and separation. In consequence, the city of Salvador was never really the capital of Brazil.† The viceroy, invested with full powers in war and exercising authority over a few governors and captains to the south, strengthened the centripetal spirit, without impeding the centrifugal tendency, which worked against the general interest.

Against the accentuated autonomy of the captaincies must be set, as centripetal forces, the uniformity of Portuguese character, which overcame the sharpest of divisions, the spirit of accommodation, inconsistencies in behavior that worked toward unity through diversity, and, above all, in time, the unifying force of enthusiasm for the land. No colonial movement therefore possessed a national character, save to some extent the war for the expulsion of the Netherlanders and, later, the proclamation of independence, which, as we know, was not received with unanimous approval. It was Dom João, the regent, later king, who, during the thirteen years of his residence in Brazil, centralized the government, united the captaincies, dissipated prejudices, and, through the experience provided in common living, paved the way for the

---

* In 1534 Brazil was divided into fifteen captaincies, which were given to twelve different donataries. As that system did not function as the crown had hoped, in 1549 a central government under a governor general was created.

† Salvador served as the capital of the state of Brazil from 1549 to 1763. Since the state of Maranhão was separate from the state of Brazil, however, Salvador never served as capital of the entire area known to the contemporary world as Brazil, which, of course, includes both old colonial political divisions, the state of Maranhão and the state of Brazil.

consolidation of the country. From that time on Rio de Janeiro was the real capital of Brazil.* It was under leadership from Rio de Janeiro that order was imposed, that secession was avoided, and that the triumph of the conservatives, who found support in the rural areas and identified themselves with the aspiration to order, tranquility, and unity, led to a realization of the uselessness of anarchy. The excesses of liberals and conservatives were restrained by the moderating power of the emperor,† which power, in turn, was identified with two of the most authentic aspirations of the Brazilian spirit—conciliation and compromise.

The moderating power, which was the emperor's exclusive prerogative, was the key to the entire political organization of the country. It can be said that up to 1964 such a power was discreetly exercised by the armed forces, which moderated, on behalf of national interests, the excesses of the political parties.‡ Side by side therewith, although lacking in military might, goes the power originating in the people, often exercised not through their representatives but through the opinions they express and through their behavior. This may or may not take the form of civic pressure, sometimes persuasive, sometimes understanding in nature.

Disbelief in the monarchy began to manifest itself about 1868, on the occasion of the crisis that arose between the liberals and the emperor. When the Paraguayan War came to an end, the aspiration arose for a new form of government, republican and federal in nature. The idea of federation seemed to serve the interests of the regions composing the nation without any longer representing a threat of dismemberment, as had seemed to be the case formerly, particularly in the instance of the Farrapos Rebellion (1835–1845). After the manifesto of December 3, 1870,§ the republicans took to maintaining that it was impossible to reconcile monarchy with federation.

* The capital had been transferred from Salvador to Rio de Janeiro in 1763. A few years later, in 1774, Pombal incorporated the state of Maranhão into the state of Brazil, forming thus the territorial outline of modern Brazil.

† This power is the famous *poder moderador*, the fourth branch of government, which gave the emperor the power to balance the political elements of the nation and the other three branches of government for the sake of harmony and stability. The constitution of 1824 detailed the extent and characteristics of the moderating power.

‡ No constitution after 1824 mentions the moderating power. It is clear, however, that after 1889 the army regarded itself as the sole depository of the emperor's moderating power. This extraconstitutional power was called upon in April, 1964, by the army to rationalize both its action and its position.

§ The Republican Manifesto of 1870 initiated a campaign to substitute a federal republic for the monarchy.

In 1889 along with the Republic came federation, revolutionary unrest, despotism, domination of the small states by the large, and militarism. A marked conflict was evident between national interests and those of the states, or between the latter and the interests of the municipalities. There was an absence of any organizing principle to preside over national development. The states, particularly São Paulo and Minas Gerais, took to setting their interests over those of the nation. In 1902 President Campos Sales declared to the Congress:

> It is my unshakable conviction that, under this system, true political power, which under the unifying restraint of the Empire resided in the central government, has been transferred to the states. State policy—that is the policy which strengthens the bonds of harmony between the states and the union —is, then, in its essence national policy.[1]

As Pontes de Miranda observed, however, the country remained divided into two parts, some of which were subordinated unto others—into masters and slaves, into metropolitan states and colonial states.[2] The federal system did not function under the 1891 constitution, although beginning with the administration of Prudente de Morais (1894–1898) composure was maintained in political relations, abandonment of legality and tumultuous changes of government being avoided. No national parties existed: voting by state blocs in the Congress and the way in which elections were conducted meant a continuation of the falsification of the representative system that had prevailed under the monarchy.

The revolution of 1930 took place in opposition to all this. If it brought benefits as regards economic emancipation and electoral justice, it also brought dictatorship and an imitation of monarchical centralization. Since 1946 the nation has operated under a new federal system. As the embodiment of a present-day aspiration, the federal government can, with more than half of the resources of the union at its command, draw up and execute national programs of modernization and development; it can correct regional insufficiencies; and thus it can contribute to strengthening the permanent aspirations to democracy and unity.

From the practical viewpoint, however, the federal government is poor. In 1959 it could count on but $900,000,000 for administering a

[1] Message to the Congress, recorded in *Anais da Câmara dos Deputados* (1902), Vol. 4, p. 4.

[2] Francisco Pontes de Miranda, "Preliminares para a Revisão Constitucional," *À Margem da História da República*, p. 174.

nation of 65,000,000 inhabitants—less than half the resources at the command of the city of New York for administering a metropolis of less than eight million people. In 1962 the federal budget estimated receipts, for a population of 70,000,000, at 439,000,000,000 cruzeiros, of which only 17,000,000,000 were to be applied to regional assistance.[3] The new federal system, then, represents little more than an expectation, for it promises much but as yet does little in comparison with the needs of the country.

Whether the prevailing system be federal or not, compromise has been the easiest political solution. Conciliation is always sought and always found; it takes inspiration in the conditions of the moment; it is emotional; it believes that the possible exceeds the real; it brings unique advantages to the oligarchies and the minorities, defrauding the common people, exhausting their patient expectation, destroying their faith in a prompt solution to their problems. It seems to me that, under the present circumstances, it is no longer possible to mislead the populace, much less turn aside the course of history. There can be neither peace nor quiet until the dominant minority is disposed to make indispensable concessions and to heed the need for essential reforms. The balance of power is tending to be dislocated toward the side of the common people, who are more truly representative of the nation than are the oligarchic minorities.

[3] Superintendency for the Development of the Northeast (SUDENE), 3,875,979 cruzeiros; São Francisco River Valley Commission, 993,500 cruzeiros; Superintendency of the Plan for the Economic Improvement of the Southwest Frontier Region, 760,000 cruzeiros.

25. Economic Development and Well-Being

The idea of development is not new. It is naturally linked with that of prosperity, written into the 1824 constitution, which attributed to the legislature the task of promoting the general good of the nation. As an aspiration, it was so vague that Parliament and the executive could abstain from espousing it. Besides, how was it to be stimulated if Brazil was stigmatized from birth by the original sin of subordination to Great Britain? Tariff preferences extended to the English as early as 1810 and renewed in 1827 transformed the country into a vast British market. Suffice it to note that in 1825 English exports to Brazil were almost half as great as shipments to the United States and that they all but equaled those to the rest of South America and Mexico combined. England, however, bought very little from the Brazilian Empire.[1]

The virtual monopoly which Great Britain exercised over Brazilian commerce up to 1844,* the serious financial crisis that arose with independence when the public debt was estimated at eighteen million cruzados,[2] the assumption by Brazil of the Portuguese debt, and the loans negotiated in London in 1824–1825 and 1828 all bespeak Brazilian dependence on British financing. The abrogation of the trade treaty in 1844 did not affect the preeminence of Great Britain in commerce and investment, but it did free the Brazilian treasury and permit the advance in economic development which is to be observed after 1850.

Under these circumstances, even though the aspiration to prosperity had inspired the builders of nationality, as can be seen from the appeal made in the manifesto of August 6, 1822, to European enterprise or from the 1824 constitution, the truth of the matter is that only after 1850 was the emperor able to give thought to the matter. From that time on the idea frequently appears in the speeches from the throne. "I thank you," the emperor said to Parliament in 1850, "for the assistance you have lent my government. I count on the effectiveness thereof in uniting the great Brazilian family in the common intent of promoting the consolidation of public order and national prosperity."[3]

Despite the efforts of a few and the aspirations of the many, the backwardness of Brazil was manifest. Tavares Bastos rightly accused the government of "indifference and neglect with respect to stimulating national progress."[4] The slow pace of reform, ingrained routine, laziness, and timidity impeded growth. The programs proposed by the various cabinets included only routine measures; they were limited to guaranteeing defense of the constitution and the laws and to balancing the budget; they were concerned with urgent questions of the moment and but little with basic reforms.

It was for this reason that, after calling the Conservative leader Eusébio de Queiroz "the *permanent* Governor General of Brazil," Martinho de Campos said that "the government—if not the present one,

[1] Alan Krebs Manchester, *British Preeminence in Brazil*, p. 207.

* In that year the trade-preference treaty of 1827 expired and the Alves Branco Tariff raised import duties.

[2] "A Correspondência do Barão de Wenzel de Mareschal," *Revista do Instituto Histórico e Geográfico Brasileiro*, Vol. 80, p. 36.

[3] *Anais do Parlamento Brasileiro*, Câmara dos Deputados (1879), Vol. 1, p. 7.

[4] Aureliano Cândido Tavares Bastos, *A Província: Estudo sôbre a Descentralização no Brasil*, 2d ed., p. 296.

then that of the *rightful possessors of power*—must undertake reforms."

The constitution of the Republic,* which was also a product of the elite, failed to charge the legislative branch with promoting the national welfare and reduced the union, in the words of João Barbalho, "to what was strictly necessary to existence." Under the administrations of presidents Rodrigues Alves and Afonso Pena the aspiration to development became obvious. Said the first, referring to public works, "I never lost heart in the endeavor to give them proper development nor could I entertain a moment's doubt as to their effectiveness as necessary factors for promoting the prosperity of the country."[5] The program of reforms and improvements undertaken by the latter required large sums of money. Said Afonso Pena to the Congress: "To claim that public expenses should not increase, particularly in a new country such as Brazil, which lacks a strong stimulus to the development of its inestimable natural riches, is to advise that a halt be made on the road to progress."[6]

The 1934 constitution incorporated the old concepts of stimulating economic development and defending Brazil's interests as an underdeveloped country. The idea of accelerated growth is modern: to all intents and purposes it arose with the Second World War. Vigorous nationalistic movements gave birth in underdeveloped areas to independent nations, which at once identified the poverty in which they lived with the exploitations of the colonial powers. The revolution of rising expectations is a worldwide phenomenon, varying in intensity and in priorities. No society, great or small, complex or simple, capitalist or socialist, stable or unstable, has remained untouched.

These expectations have given rise to new and expanded forms of international cooperation. It would be unwise, however, to suppose that economic development is necessarily tied to peaceful procedures. The revolution of rising expectations is advancing more rapidly than real possibilities of rapid and substantial satisfaction. If the phenomenon is worldwide, inspiring Asiatic and African peoples who until recently lay in bondage, it encourages Brazil, free for more than a century, to believe in a quick end to its afflictions. A few concrete achievements, such as the building of the steel mills of Volta Redonda (1946), the establishment of the Doce River Valley Company (1942) and the São Francisco River Hydroelectric Company (1945), the construction of the power plants of Três Marias and Furnas, the setting up of the gov-

---

* The constitution of 1891.

[5] "Mensagem Presidencial," *Anais da Câmara dos Deputados* (1905), p. 10.

[6] "Mensagem Presidencial," *Anais da Câmara dos Deputados* (1909), p. 376.

ernment petroleum company Petrobrás (1953), and the creation of an automobile industry foster and build hopes for the future.

Volta Redonda was born of government initiative, in the face of the need to establish and develop an iron-and-steel industry in Brazil. In 1930 the country produced a mere 36,000 tons of pig iron in eleven charcoal-fueled blast furnaces. The chief enterprises were the Belgo-Mineira Iron and Steel Company and the Esperança Mill. On March 4, 1940, the Executive Committee of the Iron and Steel Plan was set up, and in January, 1941, the National Iron and Steel Company came into existence. The Export-Import Bank provided a loan of $25,000,000, later raised to $45,000,000, for the acquisition of equipment, and with 1,400,000,000 cruzeiros the national aspiration to possess a steel industry took concrete form. In 1946 pig iron was poured for the first time at Volta Redonda; in 1954 the second blast furnace began operation; in 1955 ingots produced at Volta Redonda totaled 646,000 tons; and in 1963 production reached 1,267,560 tons. In the decade from 1940 to 1950 the iron-and-steel industry grew to fourteen enterprises and by 1962 the number reached forty-five. They employ a variety of processes, but overall ingot production totals 2,500,000 tons. Next in rank after the National Iron and Steel Company, with a production of 250,000 tons, is the Belgo-Mineira Company.[7] Founded in 1917 under the name of the Iron and Steel Company of Minas Gerais, it became the Belgo-Mineira Iron and Steel Company in 1921, the principal shareholder being the Bank of Brussels.

More recent private or mixed-economy enterprises—Usiminas, Mannesmann, Cosipa (Iron and Steel Company of São Paulo), Acesita, and several other plants under construction in various states—are expanding production to meet Brazil's steel needs. Before the planned expansion could show any results, however, an unprecedented crisis overtook the iron-and-steel industry in July, 1964, immediately after the *coup d'état* of April of that year.

The Doce River Valley Company is closely bound up with the history of exploitation of the corresponding area, which forms a natural corridor between the iron deposits of Itabira and the sea.[8] Beginning in the

---

[7] See Armando Soares, "Da Pequena para a Grande Siderurgia," *Correio da Manhã* (Rio de Janeiro), 15 junho 1951; *Conjuntura Econômica*, 15, No. 12 (dezembro 1961); 16, No. 3 (março 1962).

[8] Concerning the valley, see Luciano Jacques de Morais, "Os Recursos Naturais do Vale do Rio Doce," *Boletim da Sociedade Brasileira de Geografia*, 1, No. 3 (novembro–dezembro, 1950); and Ney Strauch, *Zona Metalúrgica de Minas Gerais e Vale do Rio Doce*.

last years of the monarchy, attempts were made, by the granting of concessions, to establish the link with the ocean, but only around 1907–1908 were the ores of Itabira properly evaluated. English groups failed, though in 1911 they had set up the Itabira Iron Ore Company. After the First World War, Percival Farquhar,[9] an American connected with the world of international finance, and, in the years of his activity in Brazil, the intermediary through whom more than $200,000,000 were invested in the country, sought financial backing for the Itabira Company. Farquhar's venture met with an obstacle in the nationalistic opposition of President Artur Bernardes, who thought that Farquhar's projects were not in the best interests of the country and would leave the nation in bondage to foreign industry with regard to products already in use in Brazil. Only in 1928–1929, when the hostile Bernardes administration had given way to that of Washington Luís Pereira de Sousa, who favored foreign capital, did Farquhar, his contract assured, begin execution of the plans that had been drawn up, only to have them paralyzed by the advent of the depression in the United States. Failure by Farquhar to fulfill his contractual obligations permitted Getúlio Vargas, in May, 1931, to declare the 1920 contract null and void. For eight years a great struggle went on, in which, with the aid of powerful Brazilian groups, the attempt was made to have Vargas reconsider his decision, but on August 11, 1939, he issued a decree whereby it was rendered irrevocable.

In 1939, then, the Brazilian Mining and Steel Company was set up by a group of Brazilians, with the participation of Farquhar, having a capital of 2,000,000 cruzeiros. It took over not only the property of the Vitória-Minas Railway, controlled by the English, but also Farquhar's studies and projects, and it obtained a concession for building a road to Itabira. Farquhar and his group continued in possession of 48 percent of the stock of the company, which was directed by Brazilian groups, with the aim of lessening nationalist opposition. That opposition increased, however, as it was proved that in reality the national treasury had financed the construction of the Vitória-Minas Railway, which had been incorporated into the new Brazilian Mining and Steel Company. The capital of the latter was insufficient to permit it to carry out the obligations into which it had entered under the 1939 contract, nor did it obtain financial backing from the United States, since American

[9] Excellent documentation on the activities of Percival Farquhar is to be found in the National Library and the National Archives of Brazil. Charles A. Gauld is the author of a biography defending Farquhar, *The Last Titan: Percival Farquhar, 1864–1953.*

capitalists insisted on a guarantee from the federal government—a guarantee that was refused them.

Goaded by nationalists and faced by the threat of war, the Brazilian government decided to solve the iron-ore problem by setting up the Doce River Valley Company. By the terms of an agreement signed in Washington on March 3, 1942, Great Britain and the United States promised to cooperate in executing the plan for creating not merely the steel complex of Volta Redonda but also the Doce River Valley Company, the purpose of the latter being to exploit the mineral and water resources in which the region was rich.

With a loan of $14,000,000 from the Export-Import Bank and a government contribution of 200,000,000 cruzeiros, the Doce River Valley Company bought up the rights of the old Mining Company and obtained a guarantee from the United States and Great Britain that they would buy 750,000 tons of ore a year for three years. Difficulties were great at the beginning and were aggravated at the end of the war by lack of interest on the part of the Americans; however, a new loan of $5,000,000 was received from the Export-Import Bank in 1945. In 1948 came a third loan of $7,500,000, and in 1955 a fourth, of $3,900,000. The 34,849 tons of ore exported in 1942 rose to more than 1,500,000 in 1952, of which the United States was the principal buyer.[10] In 1959 the total came to 3,300,000 tons, valued at $35,800,000; in 1960 tonnage reached 5,000,000.[11]

The Doce River Valley Company, born of nationalist struggle, now saw its interests threatened by a government act of December, 1964, whereby the greatest of concessions were made to the Hanna Mining Company.* The government decree marked one of the greatest capitulations in Brazilian history, similar to those made by Dom João in 1810

[10] Résumé based on Edward J .Rogers, "Brazil's Rio Doce Valley Project," *Journal of Inter-American Studies*, 1, No. 2 (April 1959), 123–140.

[11] This figure is taken from the *Mensagem* of President Kubitschek for 1960 (p. 127), the best prepared of recent presidential reports. President Quadros' *Mensagem*, presented in March, 1961, makes no mention of the Doce River Valley in its chapter on regional imbalance, but the chapter on industry says that exports reached 5,000,000 tons in 1960. The "Bases" of Chairman of the Council of Ministers Tancredo Neves make no reference to the subject, but the *Mensagem* of President Goulart asserts that the Company's program of expansion is based on forecast sales of 20,000,000 tons beginning in 1965. In 1960 Brazil exported 5,160,266 tons; from January to September of 1961 exports came to 5,676,000 tons.

* The Brazilian nationalists, bitterly opposed to the granting of concessions to foreign companies, are particularly sensitive about the exploitation of natural resources. The military government offended the nationalists by its concessions to the Hanna Mining Company.

and by Dom Pedro I in 1827 in their treaties with Great Britain.

Although the country is rich in water-power resources, Brazil has suffered from a chronic shortage of electric power. Production has been marked by a multiplicity and dispersion of small producing systems and by the preponderance of two foreign-capital consortia, the Brazilian Traction group (an affiliate of Canadian Light and Power) and the Brazilian Electrical Enterprises group (an affiliate of the American and Foreign Power Company). Only half the population of the country is provided with electricity, and in order to meet the demands of industrial consumption it has been necessary to resort to a high percentage of private sources of power, including small diesel generators, some with a capacity of less than 1,000 kilowatts.[12] The Second World War made it impossible to import equipment and expand electric-power facilities precisely at the moment when the country was undergoing a surge of industrial development. An important step toward supplying electrical needs is represented by the authorization given in 1945 by President Getúlio Vargas for the organization of the São Francisco River Hydroelectric Company, which was established in 1948. The plant which was built has an installed capacity of 180,000 kilowatts, but even without any regulation of the flow of the São Francisco it could be made to provide an additional 60,000. Immediately upon completion of the Três Marias dam the figure can be raised to 1,000,000 kilowatts.

Of late the federal and state governments have taken an ever-more-active part in providing electrical service for the country, especially in underdeveloped regions. This is done either by nationalizing existing enterprises, by participating in the establishment of new developments such as Furnas, or by promoting the needed connections between power facilities. One of the greatest of the undertakings initiated is Furnas, where a gigantic dam has created a reservoir reaching for almost 250 miles. It regulates the flow of the Grande River, it has an installed capacity of about 1,000,000 kilowatts of electricity, and it permits an increase of 70 percent in the capacity of the Peixoto plant, which the Brazilian Electrical Enterprises group is building farther downstream.

---

[12] The government which came into being as a result of the April, 1964, revolution, and which has shown constant compliance in the face of United States demands, acquired the American and Foreign Power Corporation (AMFORP) in a transaction that was deemed detrimental to national interests in view of the form it took, of the price that was paid, of the fact that no accounting was taken or any assessment of value made, and of the haste exhibited in honoring an engagement supposedly entered into by the government that had been overthrown. Concerning the purchase, see the *Diário Oficial* (Brasília), 15 dezembro 1964.

Owing to its regulation of the river flow and its exceptional geographic location—equally distant from Rio de Janeiro, São Paulo, and Belo Horizonte—the Furnas dam is a work of note. The Três Marias dam on the upper São Francisco, south of Pirapora, provides the great reservoir for regulating the flow of the river. It was built by CEMIG (Central Electric of Minas) and the São Francisco River Valley Commission; 60 percent of the financing represents domestic capital, the remainder is in German and American funds. The inauguration on July 25, 1962, of the first two units of the Bernardo Mascarenhas Hydroelectric Plant increased electrical production by 132,000 kilowatts. In the future the figure will rise to 520,000 kilowatts. The flow of the São Francisco is regulated, guaranteeing navigation for vessels of up to 900 tons over a stretch of 810 miles between Pirapora and Juàzeiro. When the two plants, both in Minas Gerais, operate at full capacity, Brazilian electrical production will be increased by 1,780,000 kilowatts.

In addition to Furnas and Três Marias, other undertakings nourish hopes for a substantial increase in electric-power production. The greatest of them is Urubupungá, which, when completed in 1965, will generate 3,000,000 kilowatts—the equal of the total generating capacity of Brazil in 1956. This exceeds the production of the Asswan plant in Egypt (2,080,000 kilowatts) and the Grand Coulee plant in the United States (1,944,000 kilowatts). The impulse imparted by the Kubitschek administration, the federal projects that have been initiated, Urubupungá (the concession for which was granted to the state of São Paulo), and the establishment on June 11, 1962, of Elctrobrás, which is to serve as the capstone of a system of mixed-economy enterprises, show the existence of a nationwide development policy in the electric-power sector. Through subsidiaries which extended credit or made loans, the federal government collaborated in increasing productive capacity by 350,000 kilowatts in 1962 and 650,000 in 1963. Thought is now being given to the construction, in agreement with Paraguay, of a hydroelectric plant at Sete Quedas, on the Paraná River. This would provide the country with more than 10,000,000 kilowatts. However, the electric-power policy of the government which came into being with the *coup d'état* of April, 1964, is limited to regulatory, supplementary action, which may hamper the force of progress, limit state activity, and increase the number of enterprises controlled by foreign shareholders.

Total electrical capacity of the country increased from 1,106,517 kilowatts in 1940 to 3,993,100 kilowatts in 1958 and 4,800,082 in 1960. Even so, per capita electrical consumption (423 kilowatts) continues to be extremely low when measured by the standards of the United States, Canada, Japan, Australia, New Zealand, South Africa, and Europe,[13] although it is one of the highest in Latin America, being exceeded only by that in Costa Rica (695 kilowats). The increase in consumption of electric power—about 10 percent in the Rio de Janeiro-São Paulo area from 1960 to 1961—reflects expanded industrial production.

The São Francisco River Valley Commission, in addition to constructing the Três Marias dam, is building highways, reclaiming lowlying ground along the lower São Francisco, promoting regulation of the river flow, constructing hydroelectric plants, and providing medical and sanitation services for the population. It is working admirably for the development of an important area entirely within Brazilian territory, covering 243,180 square miles and having 4,000,000 inhabitants.[14]

Another positive achievement is the government petroleum company, Petrobrás. It began activities in 1953, although oil was first discovered near the city of Salvador on January 21, 1939.[15] By 1959 Brazil ranked nineteenth among thirty-four producing countries; in refining capacity it held twenty-fifth place.[16] Continued progress is shown by the following figures: in 1955 more than 2,000,000 barrels were produced; in 1959, about 24,000,000; in 1960, more than 29,000,000; in 1961, more than 43,000,000. By the last-mentioned year 43.5 percent of the crude oil consumed in the country was of national origin. From the industrial viewpoint, refined petroleum represented 65 percent of total national consumption, as against 39 percent in 1955. Two Petrobrás refineries (those named for President Bernardes and Landulfo Alves) alone accounted for 57 percent of the national total, the remaining 43 percent being produced by eight private refineries. Despite increased consumption, Brazil is on the road to self-sufficiency. This holds true, moreover, for petroleum by-products.[17]

The leading Brazilian concern, Petrobrás, does 400,000,000,000 cruzeiros' worth of business annually; its personnel numbers about

[13] See Yves Leloup, "A Produção de Energia Elétrica no Brasil," *Boletim Geográfico,* 19, No. 163 (julho–agôsto, 1961), 469–482; and "Energia Elétrica na América do Sul," *Conjuntura Econômica,* 15, No. 12 (dezembro 1961), 83–90.

[14] *Recuperação de um Vale,* Rio de Janeiro, Comissão do Vale do São Francisco, Documentário no. 3. Reproduced from *O Observador Econômico e Financeiro,* Nos. 240, 241 (feveréiro–março 1956).

[15] Gerson Fernandes, "História da Descoberta de Petróleo no Recôncavo Baiano," *Boletim Geográfico,* 16, No. 144 (maio–junho 1958), 390–393.

[16] "Aspectos da Lavra do Petróleo no Brasil," *Desenvolvimento e Conjuntura,* 16, No. 144 (dezembro 1959), 37–50.

[17] "Indústria de Petróleo," *Conjuntura Econômica,* 15, No. 10 (outubro 1961), 73–81.

25,000; it produces about 80,000 barrels a day; it constructs pipe-
lines; it has a fleet of 40 tankers; it makes an annual investment of
20,000,000,000 in exploration, drilling, and production development;
and only 2 percent of its income derives from government sources, the
remaining 98 percent being represented by receipts from industry. It is
aiding the nation in capital formation, a point very much to its credit.
The government took over the privately owned refineries by a decree of
March 31, 1964. The resulting wave of feeling contrary to expropriation
contributed to the circumstances which brought about the fall of President João Goulart and encouraged attack on Petrobrás. Petrobrás currently lacks the support of nationalistic conviction, which had aided its
growth.

The petroleum industry has brought about social changes in the
area surrounding All Saints Bay (Baía de Todos os Santos), in Bahia.
It has upset the balance between the sexes, increasing the relative
number of men; it has created new symbols of status, prestige, and
power, forming new urban middle classes; it has created social and
economic problems; and has opened up a new frontier of prosperity.[18]

Finally, one of Brazil's greatest achievements has been the creation
of an automobile industry. Started in 1956, it was firmly established by
1961, when 145,674 vehicles were produced—heavy- and medium-
weight trucks, buses, pickups, jeeps, and passenger cars. By that year it
had become thoroughly integrated into Brazilian industry: it no longer
depended on the large-scale imports that had been required during the
preceding three years, and it was able to dispense with most of the
official favors that had been extended to it on its initiation. In 1962
production reached 198,684 units, but the total fell to 183,968 in 1963
and to a still lower figure in 1964.

The new shipbuilding industry, represented by three yards, is a still
further factor in the development of an independent Brazilian economy.
Going into production in 1961, it has already launched bottoms totaling
more than 30,000 dead-weight tons, employing a large percentage of
locally made parts.

The growth of the iron and other metal industries, the manufacture
of basic equipment (chiefly heavy machinery, with particular emphasis
on equipment for the electric-power industry, 93% of whose needs are
met), and the great expansion of the automobile and petroleum industries mean that Brazilian industrialization is a factor on the credit

[18] Tales de Azevedo, *Problemas Sociais da Exploração do Petróleo na Bahia.*

side of the national ledger. It fulfills one of the greatest aspirations of the Brazilian people and has won for the country leadership in Latin America, Brazil now accounting for almost one fourth (23.3%) of the net value of Latin American manufactures.

The aspiration to economic independence is being realized at an accelerated pace by a strengthening of the industrial structure which aims to ensure, on the basis of the country's natural resources, a satisfactory degree of self-sufficiency, capable of supporting any effective exercise of national sovereignty. There is, however, a serious lack of adjustment between agriculture and industry.

26. Education

One of the greatest benefits of independence, Capistrano de Abreu wrote, was that it prevented the citizens of the country from going overseas, as they had in colonial days, to seek a broader field of action for the realization of their ambitions. Another benefit was freedom of the press; still another, the hope that education might be extended to a greater number. This hope was realized neither under the Empire nor under the Republic, both of which favored the elite. Although Brazilian efforts in the field of education were limited, from the beginning they exceeded those made by the Portuguese. The most negative aspect of Portuguese colonial rule, especially as compared with Spanish, was lack of attention to, and even scorn for, the dissemination of culture, whether or not that culture was dogmatic, subject to censorship, and limited to theology, philosophy, and law, as in Spanish America.

In early times, religious plays and comedies were the only form of literature available for those who did not know how to read. And that included very nearly everyone, with the exception of the landed proprietors, some of whom too were illiterate. The schools founded by the Jesuits and other religious orders were for a long time the only institutions of learning in Brazil. Public instruction as provided by the mother country was restricted to the teaching of Latin, Greek, rhetoric, grammar, mathematics, philosophy, and theology: it prepared the scions of the gentry to go on being gentry. It was only in 1759, 259 years after the discovery of Brazil, that, in the slow fashion which characterized Portuguese dominion, there was a reform of teaching, with a view to preventing its "total ruin." At that time two royal institutes were created in Rio de Janeiro; four in Bahia; four in Pernambuco; and two

each in Mariana, in São Paulo, in Vila Rica (today Ouro Prêto), in
São João del-Rei, in Pará, and in Maranhão. These institutes were intended to prepare pupils for the university in Portugal. In 1772 a new
reform strengthened the selective bases of elementary education, directed toward the sons of the gentry. The whole of education was subject
to the Board of Censors, a tribunal which was also charged with book
censorship. It was maintained by a single tax of one real on each pound
of meat cut in the butcher shops and ten reis on each two-and-a-half-
quart measure of rum. In 1786 the viceroy, Dom Luís de Vasconcelos,
wrote that "the state of elementary schools was lamentable throughout
the captaincies of Brazil." The legacy of the Colony was deplorable.

The coming of Dom João brought some small improvements. The
teaching of medicine, surgery, and military science was begun, and
courses in agriculture, design, economics, and commerce were initiated.
As always, the principle concern was with educating the sons of the
dominant minorities. Only after 300 years of the Colony were a few
advanced courses started. No single center was created at which the
personality of the Brazilian elite could take shape and grow. Anyone
who wanted to attain to a higher degree of culture had to go to Coimbra,* to which the sons of the landed gentry continued to direct themselves. The surgical courses started in Rio de Janeiro in 1813 and in
Bahia in 1815 offered no attraction to most of the young men, who were
to seek in the study of law the basis for a political career.

The builders of Brazilian nationality soon perceived the country's
lacks. José Bonifácio, in his *Lembranças e Apontamentos* ("Recollections and Notes"), written in 1821, did not fail to make mention of
public instruction, from elementary schools to universities. Convinced
that constitutional government could not succeed without "a greater
degree of education and morality among the people," he suggested the
establishment of elementary schools in every city, town, and parish; of
a secondary school for the study of "useful sciences" in every province;
and of a University of Brazil, comprising four faculties—philosophy,
medicine, law, and economics and government.[1]

It was José Feliciano Fernandes Pinheiro, later Viscount São Leopoldo, who proposed to the Constitutional Assembly the creation of a
university in São Paulo. It was a suggestion of great importance, aimed
at meeting the aspirations of the young men of Brazil, who, uncertain of
being able to continue their studies in Coimbra, were anxious to com-

---

* Coimbra is the seat of Portugal's oldest university.
[1] Otávio Tarqüínio de Sousa, *José Bonifácio, 1763–1838*, pp. 114–115.

plete them at home.[2] It was Martim Francisco who presented a memorial[3] on the reform of elementary education and on teaching in general—basic, professional, and scientific. In his view, the aim of public instruction was national prosperity. The Constitutional Assembly did not merely take cognizance of these expressions of opinion. It included in the bill on the form of provincial government "promotion of the education of youth,"[4] and it examined a bill which recognized as a public benefactor the citizen who by the end of the year presented the Assembly with the best treatise on physical, moral, and intellectual education for young people.[5]

The first national action in the educational field consisted in the creation of law schools, one in São Paulo and one in Olinda; in continued support of the schools of medicine and surgery in Rio de Janeiro and Bahia; in the law of October 15, 1827, which called for the establishment of elementary schools in all the cities, towns, and other population centers of the Empire; and in the law of November 11, 1831, which established secondary courses in the capital and in the largest town of each judicial district in every province of Brazil. These were very modest beginnings, particularly in view of the Portuguese heritage, and they show that the dominant minorities—the oligarchy and the elite—did not have education of the masses in mind.

The reports of ministers and of presidents of provinces[6] continually show the lamentable state of education, particularly at the elementary level. The state of discouragement and neglect characterized not merely the provinces but even the imperial capital. Suffice it to say that in 1840 there were but 1,503 students in the public elementary schools of that city; in 1850 they numbered 1,517; in 1860 they totaled 4,022. In the whole of the Empire in 1851 there were 43,732 pupils in elementary schools; in 1860 there were 115,953.[7] In 1851 there were only 3,749 pupils in secondary schools throughout Brazil; in 1860 there were 10,911. In 1869, for a population of over 8,000,000, the Empire pos-

---

[2] *Anais do Parlamento Brasileiro: Assembléia Constituinte, 1823* (1877), Vol. 2, p. 63. It must not be forgotten that it was the cabinet over which the Viscount presided that established, on August 11, 1827, the law schools in São Paulo and Olinda.

[3] Published for the first time by Primitivo Moacyr in *A Instrução e o Império*, Vol. 1, pp. 119–147.

[4] *Anais do Parlamento Brasileiro: Assembléia Constituinte, 1823* (1876), Vol. 1, p. 69.

[5] *Anais do Parlamento Brasileiro: Assembléia Constituinte, 1823* (1877), Vol. 2, p. 80.

[6] Summarized in Primitivo Moacyr, *A Instrução e o Império*. See also his *A Instrução e as Províncias*.

[7] *Relatório do Ministério do Império* (1840, 1851, 1860).

sessed 3,962 institutions of learning, with 126,846 students[8]—an average of 1 establishment for every 2,019 inhabitants, of whom 1 in 63 was in school.

Expenditures for education during the Empire came to 3,030,929,301 reis; as the overall revenue of the provinces amounted to 103,000,000,-000 reis, the appropriation for education represents 3 percent, or, according to a report of the period, 348 reis per inhabitant. Minister Paulino José Soares de Sousa, who had these figures compiled, compared them with data for the United States to show how little was being done in Brazil. The United States had 7,000,000 children in school, 200,000 schools, and 350,000 teachers, for which expenditures amounted to 180,000,000,000 reis. As the American population was then estimated at 37,000,000, the expenditures for education came to 4,864 reis per inhabitant.

Confronted by this disheartening comparison, Paulino José Soares de Sousa wrote words which were not heeded, but which today are worthy of remembrance:

Let us, however, do our utmost to ensure that we are not the last on the road which civilized nations are taking. . . . The sums you appropriate for the development of popular education will soon be compensated by a decrease in expenses for law enforcement. They will return, multiplied, to the public coffers under various categories of revenue; they will bear fruit in a thousand benefits to society, in ways as varied as they will be important. Public schools, considered as instruments of civilization, work as do the primal forces of nature in fashioning the elements that are to enter into the composition of our globe: they create the present while preparing the future. Public instruction is a powerful tool for removing many causes of political backwardness; it is the basic element in the establishment of morality; it softens manners; it confirms with the light of reason the good sentiments the seed of which God has planted in the heart of man. I refrain from other considerations to say that you cannot initiate the new era of peace in a more worthy and noble fashion than by encouraging public instruction throughout Brazil.[9]

Despite this appeal, progress continued to be slow. In 1876 the number of schools reached 6,000; attendance totaled about 200,000. In 1882, although the number of schools had risen to 6,350, the number of pupils remained stationary. In 1889, however, schools numbered 7,500 and pupils 300,000.[10] Plans, suggestions, bills, debates in the

[8] There were 3,156 elementary schools with 115,939 pupils; 467 secondary schools with 10,911 students. See *Relatório do Ministério do Império* (1870), p. 29.

[9] *Relatório do Ministério do Império* (1870), pp. 29–30.

[10] Frederico José Sant'Anna Nery, "Instruction publique," *Le Brésil en 1889*.

Chamber of Deputies, and reforms followed one upon another, but nothing practical was done to remedy the deplorable state of basic and professional education either in the provinces or in the capital, the latter, however, being better cared for than the former.

It can be estimated that under the Empire only a quarter of the population of school age received instruction. The achievement of the Empire surpassed that of the Portuguese colony, but it fell far short of national aspirations. Only an occasional soul of a more serious and alert nature, aware of a sad reality which he did not try to escape, called attention to the lamentable state of elementary education and instruction for the common people. These were neglected for secondary and higher education, which in turn were of inferior quality but preferred in that they satisfied the requirements of the dominant oligarchy. In 1852 Gonçalves Dias showed his awareness of the problem, writing that "the great drawback of our secondary education is that it concerns itself solely with preparing boys for a career in medicine or law. Our institutes are mere preparatory schools for the academies, and of poor quality at that."[11] In 1865 the president of the province of Minas Gerais, Judge Pedro de Alcântara Cerqueira Leite, called the Assembly's attention to the fact that "We, the people of Minas, tread ground which is primarily metallic in content, yet not a single course in mineralogy is given anywhere in the province."[12]

The greatest failing of the Empire, however, lay, as Gonçalves Dias noted, in neglecting the great mass of the population, the slaves and the Indians, who received no instruction whatever, although the former were the mainstay of the national labor force. Brazil, Rui Barbosa wrote in 1882, spent only 1.99 percent of the general budget on education, whereas 20.86 percent went to military expenses.[13]

In 1890 schooling was provided for but 250,000 pupils, and the illiteracy rate was 79 percent. The economic and social structure—based on large holdings, slavery, and the cultivation of a single crop—and the oligarchic political superstructure were not propitious to educational development.

The Empire had not broken with the colonial past, and was thus incompatible with progress. Although Dom Pedro II in his "Political

[11] Antônio Gonçalves Dias, "Relatório sôbre a Instrução Pública," *Publicações do Arquivo Nacional*, 39 (1957), 345.

[12] Moacyr, *A Instrução e as Províncias*, Vol. 1, p. 149.

[13] Rui Barbosa, *Reforma do Ensino Primário*. Republished as Vol. X, 1883, tome 1 of the *Obras Completas de Rui Barbosa*. See pp. 163–164.

Advice to the Princess Regent" in 1871 recognized that public education "is the chief need of the Brazilian people,"[14] and though his adversary Tavares Bastos wrote that "after the emancipation of labor, the worthiest object to which the Brazilians can give thought is the emancipation of captive spirits from ignorance,"[15] the truth was, as Tavares Bastos further said, that "the landowning oligarchies and their representatives in the legislative and executive branches take no interest in popular education in such countries [i.e., ones employing forced labor]."[16]

The Republic came into being, and illiteracy continued to represent a social evil that guaranteed the victories of the oligarchy, owing to constitutional restrictions on the right to vote. The 1891 constitution did not include in its Declaration of Rights the right to free elementary instruction. It did give the Congress the repsonsibility—not an exclusive one, however—for establishing institutions of secondary and higher education in the states. It was easy to assert in the beginning, as in the report for 1891, that the former monarchical regime had notably neglected public instruction, to the point that it could be "averred that, far from progressing, in a sense we have gone backward."[17] Then it became common, in presidential messages or ministerial reports, either to state that there had been no notable change in the area of public instruction or to devote only a few lines to the topic.

There were no significant gains as regards either the expansion of public instruction or the improvement of education. The few advances that were made were not in proportion to the rise in the population and the increased demand for education. The creation of the Ministry of Education and Health in 1930, the proclamations in 1934 and 1946 that education is the right of all, and the announcement that 10 percent of the nation's revenues and 20 percent of those of the states and municipalities were to be applied to maintaining and developing education would make one believe that the time had at last come when one of the most legitimate and deeply felt of national aspirations would be met.

[14] Taken from a photographic copy of a manuscript in the possession of Dom Pedro de Orleans e Bragança. Limited private edition, without title page.

[15] Aureliano Cândido Tavares Bastos, *A Província: Estudo sôbre a Descentralização no Brasil*, 2d ed., pp. 239–240. The author shows that in 1870 there was one student in school for every 90 inhabitants in the Empire. In the Neutral Municipality [i.e., the district in which the capital was located] the figure was 1 for every 42. In seven of the provinces the average was 1 in 100; in Piauí it was 1 in 200. In the United States the average was 1 for every 7 inhabitants (p. 216).

[16] *Ibid.*, p. 238.

[17] *Relatório do Ministério da Instrução Pública, Correios e Telégrafos* (1891), p. 11.

Statistical data, though they show an unprecedented expansion, fail to confirm the hope raised.

Save in a few states, Lourenço Filho says, "No appreciable educational progress was noted in the first years of the Republic. For the country as a whole progress continued to be slow up to 1930. If in 1889 the number of pupils per 1,000 inhabitants was 18, twenty years later it was still only 29; in 1920 it reached 41; in 1929, 50." In 1930 it was 65; in 1940, 80; in 1958, 94.[18]

This might seem considerable progress, but the truth is that in 1958 there was a 30 percent deficit: one third of the population of school age was not attending school. As a result of the population explosion and the shortage of schools, illiteracy has not diminished to the extent that could be desired. In 1948, on noting that from 1890 to 1932 the rate of illiteracy had fallen from 79 percent to 52 percent, Lourenço Filho expressed the hope that the 1940 census would show a rate of less than 40 percent.[19] The hope proved illusive, for in 1940 the literacy rate was only 43.04 percent and in 1950 only 48.35 percent—this on the basis of those over ten years of age, for if those aged five and over be taken as the basis the literacy rates are 38.2 percent in 1940 and 42.66 percent in 1950.

Literacy in the various divisions of the country shows very low percentages between 1940 and 1950. The six states with the highest rate of literacy in 1950 were (1) the Federal District (the present state of Guanabara), 84.56 percent; (2) Rio Grande do Sul, 65.83 percent; (3) São Paulo, 65.37 percent; (4) Santa Catarina, 64.2 percent; (5) Paraná, 52.68 percent; and (6) Mato Grosso, 51.25 percent. The six states with the lowest rate of literacy in 1950 were (1) Alagoas, 23.65 percent; (2) Maranhão, 25.22 percent; (3) Piauí, 25.59 percent; (4) Paraíba, 29.18 percent; (5) Ceará, 31.19 percent; and (6) Bahia, 31.55 percent.[20]

As Brazil is a country 51.85 percent of whose inhabitants in 1955 were aged nineteen years or less, the school network has not grown to meet educational requirements. If one compares the total population of school age with the number of those actually in school, one will note that the percentage of the latter rose from 45.1 percent in 1954 to 54.3

---

[18] Manuel Bergström Lourenço Filho, "Educação, 1889–1941," in Ruben Borba de Morais and William Berrien, *Manual Bibliográfico de Estudos Brasileiros*, pp. 159–166.
[19] *Ibid.*, p. 163.
[20] "A Alfabetização no Brasil Segundo o Censo de 1950," *Contribuições para o Estudo da Demografia no Brasil*, pp. 387–437.

percent in 1958; nevertheless this meant that in the latter year 46 percent of the children between the ages of seven and fifteen had not attended elementary school.[21]

If the structure of the Brazilian population by age groups shows a high percentage of children, of the economically unproductive, the percentages for schooling and literacy are incompatible with the economic potential represented, and have an adverse effect on productivity rates. Even in 1960, out of 14,200,000 children between seven and fourteen years of age, only 7,500,000 were enrolled in schools. An impressive number of adults and adolescents also are completely or functionally illiterate—a total of 20,000,000.

Secondary education presents no better picture. About 150,000 pupils were in secondary schools in Brazil in 1933; in 1950 enrollment reached 620,000; in 1958 it was 990,000; and in 1961 it was 1,308,000. The increase would seem to indicate enormous progress, but it involves only a fraction of the population. For every 100 elementary-school pupils there are but 16 enrolled in secondary schools. Moreover, secondary education was predominantly (73.4% in 1961) of the college-preparatory type, as opposed to agricultural, industrial, commercial, and normal-school education. Dominated by the preparatory-school spirit, academic in character, secondary schooling meets the aspirations of only the ruling and upper-middle classes, whose aim is represented by the learned professions.

Agricultural and industrial courses are insignificant in comparison with the real needs of the labor force. As against 960,489 young people enrolled in academic-type secondary schools, there are but 6,694 in agricultural schools and 30,759 in industrial schools.[22] Vocational training, aimed at improving lower- and middle-level working standards, is not provided to the extent required for economic development. In the bitter struggles that lie ahead, labor and industry, working in collaboration, will take an increasingly active role in politics to ensure the reform of vocational education, so that it may take on new meaning and meet adequately the needs of our day.

Higher education shows great progress from the statistical viewpoint. The 20,000 students of 1933 rose to 43,958 in 1950, to 77,000 in 1958, to 93,202 in 1960, and to 98,982 in 1961. The distribution of students by curricula, however, shows the continued dominance of those that do not meet the needs of a changing society and an expanding economy. A

[21] *Comentários*, pp. 10–11.
[22] *Sinopse Estatística do Ensino Médio.*

traditionalist minority insists on maintaining, counter to the interests of a semisovereign people, a type of education which is altogether inadequate—one which does not teach how to share in the creation of wealth, one which is not in keeping with the times, one which is purely ornamental, one which bears no relation to the vast and complex tasks of bringing about a new social and economic order. Suffice it to say that the most numerous groups of students are those seeking law degrees (23.85%), or degrees in philosophy, science, and letters (22.6%). Students of engineering account for only 11.6 percent of the total; medical students, 10.5 percent; and students of economics, accounting, and actuarial sciences, 9.1 percent.

If the courses offered by the faculties of philosophy, science, and letters meet the requirements for training secondary-school teachers, and if the teaching of engineering sciences is expanding less in the area of civil engineering than in specialized areas which meet personnel needs in the petroleum, steel, shipbuilding, automobile, and machine industries, the results are as unimpressive as in the case of chemistry, agronomy, and medical courses. The former show no advance: whereas the population grew by 25 percent from 1952 to 1961, enrollment increased by but 10.5 percent—the lowest rate registered in any field of learning. Of the 16,893 students who graduated in 1960, engineering graduates in general numbered 1,521—731 in civil engineering, 163 in mechanical engineering, 121 in electrical engineering, 11 in naval engineering. Only 36 obtained first or second degrees in industrial chemistry. That same year, however, law graduates numbered 3,274; graduates in romance languages, 713; graduates in classical languages, 256.[23]

The data for 1962 confirm the tendencies which have been noted. Of the 18,226 graduates of the various institutions of higher learning 52 percent were bachelors of law or of philosophy. The most serious aspect of the matter is the decline in enrollment in medical schools, for Brazil, with its current demographic explosion, has one of the world's lowest ratios of physicians to total population—a mere 4 for every 10,000 inhabitants. The Soviet Union has 18; Italy, 14; Argentina, 13; the United States, 12.

Public expenditures for higher education are constantly on the increase, absorbing more than 50 percent of the total educational budget, whereas expenditures for primary education are declining. The sum

[23] *Sinopse Estatística do Ensino Superior, 1960; Sinopse Estatística do Ensino Superior, 1962.*

spent on higher education is four times that for secondary education and slightly more than thirty times that for elementary education. In 1961, 15.8 percent of the budget went for elementary education; 22.5 percent for secondary education; and 44.3 percent for higher education.

There still is no ready solution for the problem of illiteracy. Compensation is provided only by new, extra-educational instruments, such as the movies, radio, and television. In the absence of schools, they act like pole stars guiding the ignorant to the discovery and judgment of values. Their positive side consists in the fact that they accompany the changes of popular culture in taste and consumption, especially as regards music and amusements. Radio, with 920 transmitters, and television, with almost 30, represent merely the beginning of the mass production of novelty-oriented popular culture. The informal education thus provided stimulates and makes for uniformity; it is not active, promoting rather mass conformity; it alienates by making no allowance for participation; it produces no differentiation, even of a marginal variety. The all-but-total commercialization of radio and television is a crime which threatens to barbarize an entire people, 50 percent of whom are illiterate. Judgment is weakened by abandonment of intellectual for irrational principles and by childishness, that is, the confusion of serious things with play. An overproduction of words and images, launched upon the air without any critical or educational control, increasingly provides too broad a horizon for those who are lacking in knowledge. It also leads to knowledge, however—knowledge of a varied and superficial type—and provides an informal education which, in the lack of any other, serves as an adjustment to society.

The illiterate of today, then, is not the same as the illiterate of thirty years ago. Informally he has learned much more. He is also far more subject to the pressures of producers and promoters at the service of the great economic interests to whose advantage it is that he be subjected, alienated, and misled. The intimate relationship between the development of information media and economic and social development led the United Nations Economic and Social Council to recommend that underdeveloped countries consider the possibility of drawing up, as part of their economic development plans, national information programs which would serve educational ends and the needs and interests of rural people. In view of the potential of television as a teaching instrument, it recommended further that educational programs should have priority.[24] Nothing of what was proposed has been done in Brazil.

[24] *Development of Information Media in Underdeveloped Countries; Report by the Director-General of the United Nations Educational, Scientific and Cultural Organiza-*

The Ministry of Education and the Congress have taken no interest in the problem, permitting commercial cupidity to settle upon the barbarization of the populace.

Training continues to be provided then only for cadres of leaders, in the interest of the dominant minority, despite declaration of the right to education or recognition that equal opportunity should be provided for all. Those who rise in the world do so unaided by the facilities which the state should offer, simply because mobility permits rising.

The fact that illiteracy impedes a truly national vote, by restricting the exercise of democracy, and that rapid industrialization calls for the training of technical and professional cadres are not the only reasons why Brazil should broaden the system of public education. Above all, education is the longest-lasting basic factor in national security and one of the fundamental requirements of national strategy. The Americans, with one of the world's best teaching systems and an illiteracy rate of only 2.7 percent, feel it indispensable for their security, in the light of Soviet progress, to review their entire educational structure. This is not only with a view to obtaining more scientists and engineers, as one might think, but also to producing more social scientists and more men trained in the humanities, in order to provide the nation with basic human resources.[25]

Elementary education in Brazil is extremely inadequate; secondary education is devoted to training for the privileged; the universities, their sights set on the examples of Europe and the United States and their backs turned to national reality, are dedicated to defense of the *status quo* and the preservation of aristocratic concepts and colonial traditions; and withal the country's educational problems are growing worse from day to day. The existing shortage of elementary schools, the shortage of space in secondary schools and universities that will come about as a result of a population growth rate of 3.1 percent, and the desperate shortage of technicians and manpower that alone can satisfy an expanding industry bring clearly into view the specter that threatens Brazil. Poverty and the lack of education go hand in hand and are characteristic of underdeveloped peoples. The challenge to poor nations, said Anísio Teixeira, is to get education organized before achieving wealth, or at least during the process of attaining it.[26]

tion, New York, United Nations Economic and Social Council, 31st Session, January 19, 1961.

[25] G. B. de Huszar (ed.), *National Strategy in an Age of Revolutions*, pp. 226–227.

[26] Anísio Teixeira, reply given to the "Inquérito sôbre Diretrizes e Bases," *Diário de Notícias* (Rio de Janeiro), May 13, 1962. Concerning this problem, see F. Benham, "Edu-

Whatever the road may be, aspirations of this sort—general education preparatory to citizenship, and selective higher education for those with the capacity for it—cannot be neglected. The nation awaits a statesman-educator.

---

cation and Economic Development in the Underdeveloped Countries," *International Affairs*, 35, No. 2 (April 1959), 180–187.

27. Health

Public health has been neglected to an even greater extent than education by governments both Portuguese and Brazilian. Epidemic disease did not exist in Brazil; it was brought by the colonists or immigrants. "Water supply and sewerage were left to private initiative and cadavers were buried in the churches. Public sanitation was provided by rainwater, sunshine, and the ever-active vultures."[1] Only in 1797 did the first sanitary code come into effect, Brazil having gone without one for three centuries. With the arrival of Dom João in Brazil the office of chief health officer of the Court and State of Brazil was created, to see to the preservation of public health. However, the opening of the ports and the arrival of colonists brought epidemics which carried off large numbers of Brazilians.

From that time on dates a consciousness that "matters of public health cannot be left to the discretion of nature, particularly in Brazil, which, with its abundance of vast ports and safe anchorages maintains extensive intercourse with foreigners, who often, in the course of trade, present us with gifts of a most sinister nature." These words were written in 1832, after the statement had been made that "Brazil, by the bounty of its sky and soil, is without any exaggeration one of the healthiest countries in the world," one in which intermittent fevers were endemic only in swampy spots, one which knew only sporadic diseases such as those which afflict humanity in any part of the world. Save for recognition of the existence of leprosy and censure of the lack of physical education for children, the government considered the nation's state of health good,[2] although it is known that periodic famines attacked the populations of the hinterland, particularly in the Northeast. A law of

---

[1] João Capistrano de Abreu, *Capítulos de História Colonial*, 4th ed., preparada por José Honório Rodrigues, p. 335.
[2] *Relatório do Ministério do Império* (1832), pp. 1–2.

September 25, 1827, permitted free import of grains and other food-stuffs into the provinces of that region. The average life expectancy of slaves was only fifteen years.

Yaws, trachoma, and hydatid disease, which seem to have existed since the colonial period, were not recognized. Smallpox raged throughout the Empire in 1850 and yellow fever and cholera morbus were beginning their deadly work. The state of health was, then, melancholy,[3] with epidemics carrying off thousands. Despite this, only in 1850 were public cemeteries and burial services established and the Board of Public Health created. The last-mentioned was reorganized in 1886 and again in 1890, under the Republic. In 1903 it was turned over to Osvaldo Cruz, who, besides wiping out yellow fever and cleaning up both capital and country, awakened a national consciousness of health and hygiene problems. In 1920 the National Department of Public Health was created, and in 1930 the Ministry of Education and Health came into being. The Ministry was more concerned with the former than the latter, however, and a separate Ministry of Health was established in 1953.

A number of accomplishments may be singled out: the defeat of the plague; the eradication of yellow fever and malaria, with the aid of the Rockefeller Foundation and the Pan American Health Organization; and the fight against yaws, trachoma, endemic goiter, Chagas disease, schistosomiasis (which affects from 3,000,000 to 4,000,000 persons), and ancylostomiasis or hookworm (which attacks more than 23,000,000 persons, half of whom may be classed as ill).[4] These, however, represent but one aspect of the intensive sanitary activity which is being carried out on behalf of a population whose situation is aggravated by malnutrition; by a lack of the most elementary hygienic conditions, of hospitals, and of medical services; and by the fact that the pharmaceutical industry is controlled by international cartels. In consequence, the infant mortality rate, though dropping, is still exceedingly high, and the overall death rate for the decade from 1940 to 1950 was 20.6 per 1,000 inhabitants. Average life expectancy was only 43.7 years, which is insignificant when compared with 68 years in the United States and 70 to 71 years in Sweden.[5]

I do not believe that the ideal of public health has constituted a na-

[3] *Relatório do Ministério do Império* (1850), pp. 41–46.
[4] Mário Pinotti, *Vida e Morte do Brasileiro.*
[5] "Mortalidade da População Natural do Brasil" and "Nota sôbre a Vida Média Brasileira nos Diversos Estados do Brasil," *Contribuições para o Estudo da Demografia do Brasil*, pp. 80–90 and 97–102.

tional aspiration. It has been more a private than a public concern. All
—the elite and the masses alike—suffer from its neglect. It is well known
that the ruling minorities suffered great losses from the middle of the
past century to the beginnings of the present. In 1882, addressing Parliament, Martinho Campos said: "Unfortunately for the fatherland, the
life of senators gets shorter and shorter. Fate has persecuted all our
parties; our most eminent men have disappeared rapidly."[6] It is not
surprising therefore to discover that no concern for public health had
been expressed in the constitution. The 1824 text limited itself to the
assurance that "no type of labor, cultivation, industry, or commerce may
be prohibited provided it is not detrimental to public morality, security,
and the health of the citizens" (Article 24). The 1891 constitution made
no prohibitions whatever. Under the impact of the success obtained in
campaigns, beginning with those of Osvaldo Cruz, the 1934 constitution,
and later that of 1946, gave the federal government authority (also
granted to the states under the 1934 constitution) to pass legislation
regarding general standards for the protection of health (see Article 5,
XV, b, Constitution of 1946). Unlike the case of education, however,
they make no specific provision of funds for health programs.

I do not think that constitutions are the sole mirror in which the
aspirations of minorities and majorities are reflected. However, do not
the lack of reference to health matters in so many documents and the
mere attribution of legislative authority in the last two constitutions
show that the ideal of public health is of relatively recent origin? It
cannot be argued that public health services would benefit the populace
alone, and that for that reason the elite has taken no interest therein.
In truth, Father Antônio Vieira was right when he wrote: "I do not
know which has ever been of greater harm to Brazil, disease or dark
ignorance."[7]

Although the problem is real and merits preferential attention, it took
a work of education, however slight it may have been, to transform public health into an aspiration, as I believe it is today. Many ideals of the
moment are in the process of becoming permanent, and this is one of
them. This has been especially true since the Second World War. The
aspirations to economic development that have arisen in Latin America,
Asia, and Africa reveal the various causes for their low standards of

[6] "Discurso Programa do 29. ° Gabinete de 21 de janeiro de 1882," *Organizações e
Programas Ministeriais*, p. 192.

[7] Antônio Vieira, "Sermão da Visitação de Nossa Senhora," June 5, 1640, *Padre Antônio Vieira: Sermões Pregados no Brasil*, edited by Hernani Cidade, Vol. 2, p. 202.

living and levels of productivity: sickness, poverty, and illiteracy seem inevitably to be the characteristics of those areas. Linked by an insolvable bond, education and health have become instruments for attaining that efficiency which is indispensable for the development of power. Arnold Toynbee prophesied in 1934 that the little European world would find itself surrounded by powerful giants when, along with India and China, Brazil acquired the gift of efficiency.[8]

[8] Arnold Toynbee, *A Study of History*, Vol. 3, p. 303.

PART III

The Permanent and the Transitory:
A Summing Up

The past cannot be reconstructed; the past cannot be relived.

> José Tomás Nabuco de Araújo
> Speech in the Senate,
> June, 1864

And what right does antiquity confer upon what is bad and undesirable?

> Francisco Gonçalves Martins,
> Baron São Lourenço
> Speech in the Senate,
> June, 1864

28. The Permanent and the Transitory:
A Summing Up

In the foregoing historical and political analysis of national aspirations, note was taken that permanent and transitory aspirations have interacted, that some of the former have not been achieved to this day, and finally that some of the latter have become permanent. If obstacles have impeded Brazil from fully asserting its independence and sovereignty, it is nonetheless true that, despite all political and economic pressures from without and the limitations deriving from international agreements, the country's position has a firm legal basis, the nation disposes freely of its territory, and the population is ethnically and culturally homogeneous and highly conscious of its national integration.

The feeling that independence had not been fully achieved in 1822 led to the abdication of Dom Pedro I in 1831 and to the nonrenewal of the treaty with Great Britain in 1844. A single line of action has been constantly and watchfully followed, aimed at the consolidation of Brazil's political emancipation. A greater or lesser degree of firmness has been exhibited, depending on the capacity for leadership and the chances for resisting potential aggression existing at a given moment.

It is by their manner of holding back or advancing that movements and men are distinguished from one another. Some, traditionalistic and conservative, with origins in colonial society, have preferred to hold back, maintaining the *status quo*. They have thwarted the course of historical development, deceiving the common people, who have played a secondary rather than a leading role on the political scene. Others, of mixed-blood origin—to use João Ribeiro's expression—have made up the bulk of that genuinely national radicalism whose existence can be noted from the time of the first struggles in the eighteenth century to our own day. For these latter, independence has not yet been achieved.

If Brazil's territorial integrity has never really been affected, despite the fact that the country was potentially the object of aggression (since only during the Paraguayan War did Brazilian naval forces rank among the largest in the world), the truth is that effective occupation of the

2/3 of the territory and
1/14 of the population

1/3 of the territory and
13/14 of the population

FIGURE 1. Contrast between the northern and west-central states and those of the Northeast, East, and South with respect to area and population.

national territory continues a dream. Even in 1950 there still persisted the "contrast between the very low density of population in the northern and west-central regions and the relatively high density (high by national standards of comparison that is; low by international ones) in the Northeast, East, and South" (see Fig. 1).[1] The northern and west-

[1] Giorgio Mortara, "A Distribuição Territorial da População," *Contribuições para o Estudo da Demografia do Brasil*, pp. 53, 56.

central regions together comprise 64.1 percent of the area and but 6.86 percent of the population of the country; whereas the Northeast, East, and South, with but 35.9 percent of the area contain 93.11 percent of the population. In 1957 the west-central and northern regions still had but 3.57 percent and 3.52 percent of the population; the East had 35.38 percent; the South, 33.67 percent; and the Northeast, 23.86 percent.[2]

Thus the growth of the population has not been accompanied by a better distribution thereof over the national territory, nor has it increased the area of effective occupation. It is imperative, then, that the nation funnel toward the North and the Center its explosively expanding population. In this sense, the construction of Brasília has been of positive benefit, since it has served as a lodestone in attracting people into unoccupied territory. Its initial cost and maintenance expenses represent one of the country's most awesome investments in the area of national integration, the objective being to complete the work begun with the delimitation of frontiers. Historically it symbolizes the prevalence of optimism; functionally it meets boldly the challenge of a situation that recalls the division made at Tordesillas, which was not respected by the pioneer explorers and the mestizos. Their action won legal recognition, but their achievement was not rendered effective by succeeding generations. By its objective, Brasília represents the continuation of a fundamentally national line of development and an abandonment of the conservatism of the alienated minorities, whose faces are turned toward Europe.

The growth of the population and the opening of a new frontier for human occupation in western Brazil are causing the Brazilians to shake off their historic inertia and are broadening their confidence in their ability to face the future. Conditioned estimates forecast that the country will have 98,000,000 to 113,000,000 inhabitants by 1980. Even so, it will still have an average of only 12.4 inhabitants per square kilometer.[3] The estimate for the year 2000 is for 149,000,000 to 168,000,000 inhabitants.[4] These estimates may be on the conservative side, since the population growth rate of Brazil has jumped to more than 3 percent a year. The population of São Paulo all but doubled in the decade from 1950 to 1960 and that of Rio de Janeiro grew by about one half. In

---

[2] *Ibid.*, p. 58.

[3] *The Population of South America*, p. 15.

[4] Giorgio Mortara, "Previsões sôbre o Desenvolvimento da População do Brasil na Segunda Metade do Século XX," *Contribuições para o Estudo da Demografia do Brasil*, p. 46.

large measure this is to be attributed to abandonment of the countryside by the rural population, with a consequent growth of the shantytown districts of the metropoles.

The greatest exodus is not from the Northeast but from Minas Gerais, which from 1940 to 1950 lost 1,200,000 inhabitants; 16 percent of the state's sons now live beyond its confines. The movement to Rio de Janeiro and São Paulo does not favor effective occupation of the land, and were it not for the attraction of Brasília and the population explosion such occupation would have to wait. With the population increase, however, comes a corresponding growth in the social and cultural problems that affect the populace, perturb the nation, and hinder its possibilities of overall development. Present-day negative tendencies in the social and cultural fields may provide an obstacle to historical development. Problems of health, medical care, food production, high prices, inadequacies of housing and education must be solved in proportion to the growth of the population and of national production.

Malaria, which had apparently been eradicated, has reappeared in serious epidemic form in Maranhão and Amapá. The whole basin of the Tocantins River, from southern Maranhão to northern Goiás, is affected by the disease, which has become more frequent and obvious since the opening to traffic of the Belém-Brasília highway. Infectious disease causes the death of 200,000 children during their first year of existence. In the Northeast, life expectancy is but twenty-seven years, and only one third of the population wears shoes. There are places in the Northeast and other parts of the Brazilian hinterland where a worker's monthly wages come to less than the price of a pair of shoes. The dominant elite is indifferent to this spectacle of genocide; it has always been opposed to such structural reforms as would do away with these social monstrosities. The situation is aggravated by the fact that of the 3,720 countylike units, known as *municípios*, into which Brazil is divided, 1,419 are completely without physicians' services. In 2,600 *municípios* sewerage systems are nonexistent outside of the urban centers that form the seats of government. In 2,100 there are no water-supply systems.

According to a recent estimate of the National Nutrition Commission, during the period from 1960 to 1962 average per capita food consumption for a population of 73,000,000 came to about two pounds a day. The apparent shortage of housing is estimated at 6,000,000 units. In the state of Guanabara alone, abandoned children number 300,000.

It is not surprising then that there should have been a rising wave of unrest, disadjustment, and demands for salary increases which produced more than 309 strikes during 1960 in São Paulo alone. This was attributed by some members of the elite to Communist agitation and the follies of recent popular administrations, and not to the formidable resistance which certain groups offer to reform.

The interrelationship of economic and social development calls for attention to the consequences of industrialization and the movement to the cities, to the difficulties of transition from a rural to an urban environment, to the abrupt substitution for archaic social patterns of others which subject everyone to the winds of demagogy, populism, disintegration, and delinquency. Resistance to economic development may come from the imbalance between growth in production and population increase, interaction between which takes place along lines that are as yet obscure and form the subject of controversy. No constitutional change has been more greatly recommended than agrarian reform; nevertheless, the Congress has shelved 212 bills directed at such action.[5]

Education has a capital role to play both in the defense of permanent aspirations and in the achievement of goals. Nevertheless, education for the elite continues to predominate in Brazil. Its end is cultural enrichment through the humanities, art, and literature. No great attention is paid to education aimed at providing a skilled and efficient labor force. Formal education which inculcates traditional values does not contribute to development, nor does it promote growth, which always calls for innovation. Neither does it create the spirit which is proper and indispensable to development.

Even if one contests Max Weber's thesis of the influence of secular asceticism on the development of capitalism among the Protestant peoples[6]—since in recent decades rapid economic growth has come about in nations with different religious values, such as Italy, France, and Japan, or even in nations moved by antireligious forces, as in the case of the Soviet Union and China—it would be wrong to deny the

[5] Law No. 4504, of November 30, 1964, governing "rights and obligations relating to rural real estate, for the purpose of carrying out agrarian reform and promoting agricultural policy," is a timid step toward revision, very favorable to the latifundium. It is a mere bit of patchwork, not a reform, obtained from the same antireform-minded Congress by a military government that is exercising tutelage over the nation. It enjoys no support from those who work the land, since they were not heard on the matter, their unions being shut down, dissolved, or under military intervention. The statute is an act of paternalism—a very modest concession, intended more to salve the conscience of those in places of power than to meet the social needs of the country and its rural population.

[6] José Honório Rodrigues, "Capitalismo e Protestantismo," reprinted from *Digesto Econômico* (novembro, 1946); reproduced in his *Notícia de Vária História*, pp. 9–42.

complexness of the psychological factors affecting development. Between capitalism and the capitalistic spirit, between socialism and the socialistic spirit there are relations of as complex and intimate a nature as there are between development and the spirit of development. In Juscelino Kubitschek's five-year term, the mistake was made of not correlating noneconomic factors with development. No stimulus was given to saving; on the contrary, in the circles surrounding the president the spirit of conspicuous consumption prevailed.

Education directed toward consumption rather than production has its roots in colonial society, with its aversion to business, its love of idleness, its rejection of manual labor—all of which characterized the slave system. This type of education, conditioned by an outmoded society, is still encountered today. More evident in Portugal than in Brazil, it persists in the latter despite the current process of economic development. The result is that professions are ranked according to their social standing, and that schooling is directed toward the preservation and perpetuation of the existing order. This academic-type education acts then as an obstacle to economic growth, since the majority of available economic resources are directed toward satisfaction of the interests of the leisure class and not toward vocational training and other programs for providing elementary and advanced instruction aimed at producing skilled laborers at the intermediate and upper levels.

But how can Brazil think of all this if, in 1950, it held tenth place in literacy in Latin America? The population of Brazil was only 42.7 percent literate, whereas Argentina was 86.1 percent literate, Costa Rica 78.8 percent, Cuba 76.4 percent, Chile 74.8 percent, Panama 71.7 percent, Paraguay 68.2 percent, Colombia 57.5 percent, Ecuador 56.3 percent, and Mexico 55.9 percent. After Brazil came El Salvador, which was 39.1 percent literate, Honduras 35.2 percent, Nicaragua 34.5 percent, Bolivia 31.1 percent, Guatemala 28.1 percent, and Haiti 8.4 percent.[7]

In the light of the multitude of social, cultural, and economic aspirations and their mutual interdependence, balanced development is an essential requirement. The United Nations and its Economic and Social Council have made recommendations to this effect. They have set as a quantitative goal an annual minimum growth rate of 5 percent in the

[7] *La Estructura Demográfica de las Naciones Americanas: Vol. 4 Analfabetismo y Nivel de Educación*, p. 5. According to the 1960 census, the literacy rate has reached 60.52 percent (*VII Recenseamento Geral do Brasil, 1960. Censo Demográfico. Resultados Preliminares*, Série Especial, Vol. 2, pp. v and 7).

national product.[8] Brazil's annual growth rate has been 4.9 percent over the last twenty years.[9] The growth rate of Latin America from 1950 to 1958 has exceeded that of the rest of the Western world as a whole. Brazil, along with Venezuela, Nicaragua, Mexico, Ecuador, and El Salvador, was one of the countries showing most rapid development, gross domestic product as a whole growing by more than 5 percent per annum.

An examination of growth in the last twenty years shows that the cultivated area of the country increased by 32 percent from 1939 to 1959,[10] and that between 1945 and 1958 physical production grew 45 percent, or at an annual rate of 3.9 percent. New areas turned over to agriculture between 1945 and 1958 total about 19,768,000 acres, almost all in the central and southern areas of the country,[11] but in the last twenty years the total cultivated area has grown from 46,454,800 acres to 61,527,900 acres in 1959.[12]

From the industrial viewpoint, figures are even more revealing, since Brazil took first place among Latin American nations, growing at the rate of 9.2 percent per annum. The share of industry in national income leaped from 17.9 percent in 1939 to 30 percent in 1958.[13]

If the opening of new agricultural frontiers represents not only effective occupation of the land but also profitable use thereof, it is nonetheless true that the ratio of cultivated terrain to the total area of agricultural establishments is still quite low (about 10%), as compared with the United States, Canada, and Argentina (about 30%).[14]

Development has proceeded in disorganized, rather than integrated, fashion; social and economic elements have not supported or comple-

---

[8] *The United Nations Development Decade*, p. 8.

[9] "Retrospecto Parcial da Economia Brasileira nos Últimos Vinte Anos," *Desenvolvimento e Conjuntura*, 5, No. 7 (julho 1961). The rate of development has tended to decline since 1962. In that year it stood at 3.7 percent; in 1963 it was 1.4 percent; in 1964, less than 3 percent. Data for 1965 are not yet final, but they show a rate of less than 3.5 percent, which is the rate of population growth. See "Alguns Retrospectos de 1964" *Desenvolvimento e Conjuntura*, 9, No. 2 (fevereiro 1965), 7; and "Panorama do Ano," 10, No. 2 (fevereiro 1966), 3–4.

[10] "Retrospecto Parcial da Economia Brasileira nos Últimos Vinte Anos," pp. 4–11.

[11] Jorge Ahumada, "Economic Development and Problems of Social Change in Latin America." This study, prepared by a working group of experts on social aspects of economic development in Latin America, was summarized and analyzed in *Desenvolvimento e Conjuntura*, 5, No. 8 (agôsto 1961), 70.

[12] "Retrospecto Parcial da Economia Brasileira nos Últimos Vinte Anos," p. 15.

[13] *Ibid.*, pp. 5, 27–28. See also Ahumada, "Economic Development and Problems of Social Change in Latin America," pp. 70–71.

[14] "Retrospecto Parcial da Economia Brasileira nos Últimos Vinte Anos," p. 15.

mented one another, with the result that Brazilian economic growth, which attained one of the highest rates in the years previously mentioned—falling off in 1960[15]—even then showed certain negative aspects. Thus, for example, 17 percent of the population received 63 percent of the national income.[16] In national income per capita in 1956–1958, Brazil was on a level with Albania, Portugal, and Romania, the most backward countries in Europe; with Colombia, the Dominican Republic, Ecuador, Honduras, Nicaragua, Paraguay, and Peru in the Americas; with Ghana in Africa; and with Ceylon and the Philippines in Asia. In per capita electrical consumption from 1956 to 1958 Brazil was on a level with the same countries, save that Turkey is to be substituted for Romania, and India for Ceylon. As regards infant mortality, Brazil sank to a lower level, and it dropped further still—to the level of Burma, India, Indonesia, Laos, and Pakistan—with respect to numbers of children in school (see Fig. 2).[17]

The vast extent of the nation's territory, the backwardness of its population, the complexity of its problems may explain, together with other factors, these low levels, which retard development and hinder the achievement of national aspirations. In the development plans of President Juscelino Kubitschek education was assigned lowest priority and no priority whatever was given to health matters.

Many economists doubt the value of measurements per capita, fearing the distortions which are latent within them. If Brazilian economic activity had increased more rapidly than population, the people's standard of living would also have improved. Average per capita income continues at the level of $230, and forecasts for 1970 are for but $300. The truth is that not only have regional imbalances grown, with the concentration of progress in certain zones, but also certain sectors of activity, such as coffee production, have received more favorable treatment than others.

Lack of coordination, then, has produced grave threats to national unity. Attention has not been given to social goals. Worse still, wealth has continued to be concentrated in the hands of a few representatives of the economic power structure. São Paulo, which has played the role of Martha rather than that of Mary in Brazilian history, outdistances the rest of Brazil more and more, day by day. The formation of a more

[15] *Estudio Económico de América Latina, 1960*, p. 16.

[16] Ahumada, "Economic Development and Problems of Social Change in Latin America," p. 74.

[17] *Report on the World Social Situation*, pp. 48–49.

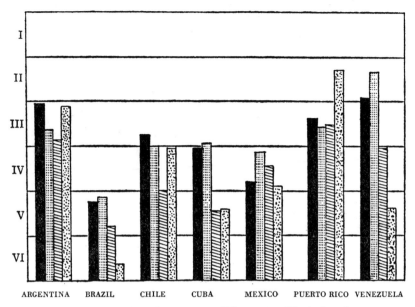

FIGURE 2. Selected Countries and Territories of Latin America

■ Per capita national income   ▨ Children in school
▨ Per capita electrical consumption   ▨ Infant mortality rate

perfect union is an aspiration which has not been realized, though the present path, despite obstacles, seems more likely to lead thereto than that previously taken, when the nation was represented by one or two state parties. The business of the country is not merely business, as the representatives of private enterprise would have one believe in their eagerness for self-enrichment.

Economic programs with social ends and social programs with economic ends produce balanced economic growth, which has as its aim the satisfaction of all aspirations taken together—satisfaction of the interests and principles of the nation and of the interests and objectives of the people. Lack of balance in planning and lethargy in the achievement of aspirations result from the fact that the structure of the nation, which is still agrarian, represents an obstacle to development; from struggles in the area of decision between traditionalistic oligarchies— the forces of private enterprise, more concerned with its own interests than those of the nation—and the forces of economic progress; and, finally, from the fact that the people are only semisovereign. "Who shall judge between you and us? Who shall be the judge between conservatives and progressives? My answer is: the nation. The nation is not a party." So said Zacarias de Góis e Vasconcelos in the Chamber of Deputies in 1864.[18]

Only with true popular sovereignty will the government become national and will priority be given to national interests, for the benefit of the common people rather than that of powerful economic groups. The freeing of the government from the alienated minorities and their henchmen the *caiados*—who as early as 1817 took sides against independence—is merely beginning. The evils in Brazilian history derive from the oligarchy, from the dominant minorities, who wish to avoid a choice in favor of progress and the liberation of the people and of the nation from all forms of servitude. It seeks to impede the cessation of its privileges and the immediate beginning of the history of the future. The dominant minorities are alienated; they detest Brazilian reality; they live in the European or Euro-American world, according to foreign patterns. They never recognize, as did the poet Carlos Drummond de Andrade, that:

> It was my people and my land that made me the way I am
> And I am glad to have been born with this failing.
> For me, the greatest of all follies is sighing for Europe.[19]

Because they sigh for Europe and worship all the major powers, Brazilian minorities aspire to maintain the *status quo*, avoiding urgent reform.

Incapable of distinguishing clearly the permanent national interests, seeking temporary and transitory solutions, via legal formulas, they persist in coexisting with the populace in fear and error. Brazilian history, slow in evolution until recently, is made up of small successes, the fruit more of the patience, persistence, optimism, and stoicism of the common people than of the adroitness or ability of the dominant minority. The latter finds in political compromise a means of deceiving the populace and of turning aside the historic course of progress and social justice.

For this reason, the victories of the common people are slow in coming, small in scope, and achieved with difficulty. The result is that

---

[18] Speech delivered on January 26, 1864, and recorded in *Anais do Parlamento Brasileiro* (1864), p. 404.

[19] Carlos Drummond de Andrade, "Explicação," *Alguma Poesia*.

genuine Brazilian radicalism threatens to adopt another form of alienation, namely Marxism, to the peril of the country's democratic processes.

The legitimate aspirations of the Brazilian populace are also the legitimate aspirations of Brazil. Their interpretation should be inspired, not in the interests of the few privileged partisans of the *status quo,* who seek to turn aside the course of history; not in those of demagogic reformers who, under the pressure of events, sell out for concessions; not in those of the antinationalists; not in those of the alienated, whether they be those who never see Brazil at all or those who see it only through borrowed glasses of foreign manufacture. Such glasses can and should be of aid to the Brazilians as an instrument for analysis, but the final word should be spoken by the people of the country, inspired in nationalism, in national interests, and in the common good.

Bibliography

INTRODUCTION: POLITICAL PSYCHOLOGY AND THE BRAZILIANS

Aranha. *See* Graça Aranha [i.e., José Pereira da Graça Aranha].
Assunção, Herculano [i.e., Herculano Teixeira de Assunção]. *A Campanha do Contestado*. Belo Horizonte: Imprensa Oficial de Minas Gerais, 1917.

Conselho Nacional de Estatística. *Flagrantes Brasileiros*. Rio de Janeiro: Serviço Gráfico do Instituto Brasileiro de Geografia e Estatística, 1958.

Dias, Gomes. *See* Gomes, Dias [i.e., Alfredo Dias Gomes].

Farber, Maurice L. "The Problem of National Character: A Methodological Analysis," *The Study of Personality*, edited by Howard Brand. New York: John Wiley & Sons, 1954.
Faure, J. L. *O que é e o que será o Brasil*, translated and edited by Oscar Rodarte. Rio de Janeiro: n.p., 1936.
Ferguson, J. Halcro. *Latin America: The Balance of Race Redressed*. London: Institute of Race Relations, 1961.
Free, Lloyd A., and Hadley Cantril. *Some International Implications of the Political Psychology of Brazilians*. Princeton, N. J.: Institute for International Social Research, 1961.
Fyfe, Hamilton. *The Illusion of National Character*. London: Watts & Co., 1940.

Gomes, Dias [i.e., Alfredo Dias Gomes]. *Journey to Bahia*, adapted from *O Pagador de Promessas* and translated by Stanley Richards. Washington, D. C.: Brazilian-American Cultural Institute, 1964.
Gorer, Geoffrey. *The American People: A Study in National Character*. New York: W. W. Norton & Co., 1948.
Graça Aranha [i.e., José Pereira da Graça Aranha]. *Canaan*, translated by Mariano Joaquim Llorente. Boston: Four Seas Co., 1920.

Lins, Álvaro [i.e., Álvaro de Barros Lins]. "Sugestão para uma História Literária do Brasil," *Diário de Notícias* (Rio de Janeiro), 22 abril 1962.
Lipset, Seymour M., and Leo Lowenthal (eds.). *Culture and Social Character*. Glencoe, Illinois: The Free Press, 1961.

Mead, Margaret. "The Study of National Character," *The Policy Sciences*, edited by D. Lerner and H. D. Lasswell. Stanford: Stanford University Press, 1951.

Moog, Viana [i.e., Clodomir Viana Moog]. *Bandeirantes e Pioneiros.* Pôrto Alegre: Globo, 1954. Published in English as *Bandeirantes and Pioneers,* translated by L. L. Barrett. New York: George Braziller, 1964.

Proença, M. Cavalcanti. *Literatura Popular em Verso, Antologia.* Vol. 1. Rio de Janeiro: Ministério da Educação e Cultura, Casa de Rui Barbosa, 1964.

Riesman, David. *The Lonely Crowd: A Study of Changing American Character.* 3d printing. New Haven: Yale University Press, 1952.

Rodrigues, José Honório. *Conciliação e Reforma no Brasil: Um Desafio Histórico-Político.* Rio de Janeiro: Civilização Brasileira, 1965.

————. *O Continente do Rio Grande.* Rio de Janeiro: Edições São José, 1954.

————. "The Foundations of Brazil's Foreign Policy," *International Affairs,* 38, No. 3 (July 1962), 338.

————. "Personalismo e Caráter Nacional," *Jornal do Brasil* (23 abril 1957).

Troeltsch, Ernst. *Der Historismus und Seine Probleme.* Tübingen: Mohr, 1922.

UNESCO. *How Nations See Each Other,* by William Buchanan and Hadley Cantril. Urbana: University of Illinois Press, 1953.

Viana, Moog. *See* Moog, Viana [i.e., Clodomir Viana Moog].

PART I: NATIONAL CHARACTERISTICS

Brazilian Writers

Abreu, João Capistrano de. *Capítulos de História Colonial.* Rio de Janeiro: M. Orosco & Co., 1907. 4th ed. Rio de Janeiro: Sociedade Capistrano de Abreu, 1954.

————. "O Caráter Nacional e as Origens do Povo Brasileiro," *O Globo* (Rio de Janeiro), 9 março 1876, 29 julho 1876.

————. *Ensaios e Estudos. 1.ª Série.* Rio de Janeiro: Sociedade Capistrano de Abreu, 1931.

————. *Ensaios e Estudos. 3.ª Série.* Rio de Janeiro: Sociedade Capistrano de Abreu, 1938.

Afonso Celso [pseud. for Afonso Celso de Assis Figueiredo Júnior]. *Porque me Ufano do meu País.* Rio de Janeiro: Laemmert & Co., 1901. 12th ed. Rio de Janeiro: Briguiet, 1943.

Afonso Rui. *A Primeira Revolução Social Brasileira, 1798.* São Paulo: Companhia Editôra Nacional, 1942.

Alcântara Machado [i.e., José de Alcântara Machado de Oliveira]. *Vida e Morte do Bandeirante.* São Paulo: 1929. 2d ed. São Paulo: Revista dos Tribunais, 1930.

Amado, Gilberto. *A Chave de Salomão.* Rio de Janeiro: Livraria Francisco Alves, 1914. 2d ed. Rio de Janeiro: José Olímpio, 1947. Articles dating from 1910 to 1913. See especially "Psicologia Brasileira do Caráter" and "O Espírito Brasileiro."

———. *Grão de Areia*. Rio de Janeiro: J. R. dos Santos, 1919. 2d ed. Rio de Janeiro: José Olímpio, 1948. See especially "As Instituições Políticas e o Meio Social no Brasil."

Andrada. *See* José Bonifácio [pseud for José Bonifácio de Andrada e Silva].

Andrade. *See* Drummond de Andrade, Carlos.

Araújo. *See* Nabuco, Joaquim [i.e., Joaquim Aurélio Barreto Nabuco de Araújo].

Bomfim, Manuel [i.e., Manuel José do Bomfim]. *O Brasil na Hisória*. Rio de Janeiro: Livraria Francisco Alves, 1931.

Carvalho, Alfredo de. *Frases e Palavras*. Recife: J. W. Medeiros e C., Livraria Francesa, 1906.

Carvalho, Ronald de [i.e., Artur Acióli Ronald de Carvalho]. *Pequena História da Literatura Brasileira*. Rio de Janeiro: Briguiet, 1919. 2d ed. Rio de Janeiro: Briguiet, 1922.

———. "A Psique Brasileira," *Estudos Brasileiros*. 1.ª Série. Rio de Janeiro: Anuário do Brasil, Briguiet, 1924.

Drummond de Andrade, Carlos. *Confissões de Minas*. Rio de Janeiro: Americ. Edit., 1944.

Fernandes. *See* Ribeiro, João [i.e., João Batista Ribeiro de Andrade Fernandes].

Figueiredo. *See* Afonso Celso [pseud. for Afonso Celso de Assis Figueiredo Júnior].

Franco. *See* Melo Franco, Afonso Arinos de.

Freyre, Gilberto [i.e., Gilberto de Melo Freyre]. *Aventura e Rotina*. Rio de Janeiro: José Olímpio, 1953.

———. *Brazil: An Interpretation*. New York: Knopf, 1945. Published in Portuguese as *Interpretação do Brasil*. Rio de Janeiro: José Olímpio, 1947.

———. *Casa Grande e Senzala*. Rio de Janeiro: Schmidt, 1945. 9th ed. Rio de Janeiro: José Olímpio, 1958. Published in English as *The Masters and the Slaves*, Translated by Samuel Putnam. New York: Knopf, 1946.

———. *O Mundo que o Português Criou*. Rio de Janeiro: José Olímpio, 1940.

———. *Nordeste*. Rio de Janeiro: José Olímpio, 1937 (Documentos Brasileiros Vol. 4).

———. *Região e Tradição*. Rio de Janeiro: José Olímpio, 1941.

———. *Sobrados e Mucambos*. São Paulo: Companhia Editôra Nacional, 1936 (Brasiliana Vol. 64). Published in English as *The Mansions and the Shanties: The Making of Modern Brazil*, translated by Harriet de Onís. New York: Knopf, 1963.

———. *Uma Cultura Ameaçada, a Luso-Brasileira*. Recife: Oficina do Diário da Manhã, 1940. 2d ed. Rio de Janeiro: Casa do Estudante do Brasil, 1942.

———. *Um Brasileiro em Terras Portuguêsas*. Rio de Janeiro: José Olímpio, 1953.

Frieiro, Eduardo. *O Brasileiro não é Triste*. Belo Horizonte: Os Amigos do Livro, 1931. 2d ed. Rio de Janeiro: Instituto Nacional do Livro, 1957.

Holanda, Sérgio Buarque de. "Le Brésil dans la Vie américaine," *Le Nouveau Monde*, (1955), pp. 55–76; discussion pp. 333–355.
——. *Raízes do Brasil.* Rio de Janeiro: José Olímpio, 1936. 2d ed. Rio de Janeiro: José Olímpio, 1948 (Documentos Brasileiros Vol. 1).
——. *Visão do Paraíso.* Rio de Janeiro: José Olímpio, 1959.

José Bonifácio [pseud. for José Bonifácio de Andrada e Silva]. "Caráter Geral dos Brasileiros." Manuscript in the possession of the Brazilian Historical and Geographical Institute, published by Alberto [do Rêgo] Rangel. *No Rolar do Tempo.* Rio de Janeiro: José Olímpio, 1937 (Documentos Brasileiros Vol. 6).

Leite, Dante Moreira. *Caráter Nacional Brasileiro.* São Paulo: Universidade de São Paulo, Faculdade de Filosofia, Ciências e Letras, 1954.
Lima, Alceu Amoroso. *Voz de Minas.* 2d ed. Rio de Janeiro: AGIR, 1946.
Lima, Cláudio de Araújo. *Imperialismo e Angústia.* Rio de Janeiro: Editôra Civilização Brasileira, 1960.
Lobato, Monteiro [i.e., José Bento Monteiro Lobato]. *Urupês.* São Paulo: Edição da Revista do Brasil, 1918.

Martins, Luís. *O Patriarca e o Bacharel.* São Paulo: Livraria Martins, 1953.
Melo Franco, Afonso Arinos de. *Conceito de Civilização Brasileira.* São Paulo: Companhia Editôra Nacional, 1936 (Brasiliana Vol. 70).
Monteiro Lobato. See Lobato, Monteiro [i.e., José Bento Monteiro Lobato].
Moog, Viana [i.e., Clodomir Viana Moog]. *Bandeirantes e Pioneiros.* Pôrto Alegre: Globo, 1954. Published in English as *Bandeirantes and Pioneers*, translated by L. L. Barrett. New York: George Braziller, 1964.
Mota, Otoniel [i.e., Otoniel de Campos Mota]. *Do Rancho ao Palácio.* São Paulo: Companhia Editôra Nacional, 1941.

Nabuco, Joaquim [i.e., Joaquim Aurélio Barreto Nabuco de Araújo]. *Discursos e Conferências.* Rio de Janeiro: Benjamim Aguila. See in particular "O Espírito da Nacionalidade na História do Brasil."

Oliveira Viana [i.e., Francisco José Oliveira Viana]. *Evolução do Povo Brasileiro.* São Paulo: Monteiro Lobato e C., 1923. 2d ed. São Paulo: Companhia Editôra Nacional, 1933 (Brasiliana Vol. 10).
——. *Pequenos Estudos de Psicologia Social.* São Paulo: Revista do Brasil, 1921. 3d ed. São Paulo: Companhia Editôra Nacional, 1942 (Brasiliana).
——. *Populações Meridionais do Brasil.* 1918. 3d ed. São Paulo: Companhia Editôra Nacional, 1933 (Brasiliana Vol. 8).
——. "O Tipo Brasileiro: Seus Elementos Formadores." *Dicionário Histórico e Geográfico Brasileiro.* Rio de Janeiro: Imprensa Nacional, 1922, pp. 277–290.

Prado, Paulo [i.e., Paulo da Silva Prado]. *Paulística. História de São Paulo.* 2d ed. Rio de Janeiro: Ariel, 1934.
——. *Retrato do Brasil.* São Paulo: Duprat-Mayença, 1928. 6th ed. Rio de Janeiro: José Olímpio, 1962.

Ribeiro, João [i.e., João Batista Ribeiro de Andrade Fernandes]. *História do Brasil.* Rio de Janeiro: Livraria Cruz Coutinho, 1900. 16th ed. Rio de Janeiro: Livraria São José, 1957.

Rodrigues, José Honório. *O Continente do Rio Grande.* Rio de Janeiro: Edições São José, 1954.

————. *Teoria da História do Brasil.* 2d ed. São Paulo: Companhia Editôra Nacional, 1957.

Romero, Sílvio [i.e., Sílvio Vasconcelos da Silveira Ramos Romero]. "O Caráter Nacional e as Origens do Povo Brasileiro," *Etnologia Selvagem.* Recife: n.p., 1875.

————. "Psicologia Nacional," *História da Literatura Brasileira.* Rio de Janeiro: Garnier, 1888. 4th ed. Rio de Janeiro: José Olímpio, 1949. Vol. 1, pp. 128–136.

Silva. *See* José Bonifácio [pseud. for José Bonifácio de Andrada e Silva].

Timandro [pseud.]. *See* Tôrres Homem, Francisco de Sales.

Tollens, Paulo. *Fundamentos do Espírito Brasileiro.* Pôrto Alegre: Livraria Tabajara, 1943.

Tôrres, João Camilo de Oliveira. *O Homem e a Montanha.* Belo Horizonte: Livraria Cultura Brasileira, 1944.

Tôrres Homem, Francisco de Sales. *Libelo do Povo.* Rio de Janeiro: Tip. do Correio Mercantil, 1849. Reproduced by Raimundo Magalhães Júnior in *Três Panfletários do Segundo Reinado.* São Paulo: Companhia Editôra Nacional, 1956 (Brasiliana Vol. 286).

Varnhagen, Francisco Adolfo de. *História Geral do Brasil.* 1st ed., Madrid: (vol. 1) Imprensa de V. Domínguez, 1854; (vol. 2) Imprensa de J. del Río, 1857. 3d ed., São Paulo Edição Melhoramentos, n.d. 4th ed., São Paulo: Melhoramentos, 1948.

Viana, Moog. *See* Moog, Viana [i.e., Clodomir Viana Moog].

Viana. *See* Oliveira Viana [i.e., Francisco José Oliveira Viana].

Foreign Travelers

Agassiz, Louis, and Elizabeth Cary Agassiz. *Viagem ao Brasil* (1865). São Paulo: Companhia Editôra Nacional, 1938 (Brasiliana Vol. 95). Originally published in English as *A Journey to Brazil.* Boston: Ticknor and Fields, 1868.

Antonil, André João [pseud. for Giovanni Antonio Andreoni]. *Cultura e Opulência do Brasil por suas Drogas e Minas.* Lisbon: Ofic. Deslandesiana, 1711.

Bryce, James. *South America: Observations and Impressions.* London: Macmillan, 1912.

Burnichon, Joseph. *Le Brésil d'aujourd'hui* (1907–1908). Paris: Perrin et Cie., 1910.

Camacho, J——— A———. *Brazil: An Interim Assessment.* London: Royal Institute of International Affairs, 1952. 2d ed. London: Royal Institute of International Affairs, 1954.

Canstatt, Oscar. *Brasil: Terra e Gente* (1868). Rio de Janeiro: Pongetti, 1954.

Originally published in German as *Brasilien: Land und Leute*. Berlin: Ernst Siegfried Müller und Sohn, 1877.

Cooper, Clayton Sedgwick. *The Brazilians and Their Country*. New York: Stokes, 1917.

Denis, Pierre. *Le Brésil au XXe Siècle*. Paris: 1908. 6th ed. Paris: Armand Colin, 1921. English translation by Bernard Miall. London: T. Fisher Unwin, 1911.

Gardner, George. *Viagens no Brasil* (1837–1841). São Paulo. Companhia Editôra Nacional, 1942. (Brasiliana). Originally published in English as *Travels in the Interior of Brazil, Principally through the Northern Provinces and the Gold and Diamond Districts, during the Years 1836–1841*. London: Reeve Bros., 1846.

Grubb, Kenneth G. "Brazil, Land and People," *Portugal and Brazil: An Introduction*, edited by H. V. Livermore. Oxford: Clarendon Press, 1953.

Isabelle, Arsène. *Viagem ao Rio da Prata e ao Rio Grande do Sul* (1830–1834). Rio de Janeiro: Zélio Valverde, 1949. Originally published in French as *Voyage à Buenos-Ayres et à Porto-Alegre par la Banda-Oriental, les Missions d'Uruguay et la Province de Rio-Grande-do-Sul (de 1830 à 1834)*. Havre: Imprimerie de J. Morlent, 1835.

Kelsey, Vera. *Seven Keys to Brazil*. New York: Funk & Wagnalls, 1940.

Kidder, Daniel Parish, and J. C. Fletcher. *O Brasil e os Brasileiros. Esbôço Histórico e Descritivo* (1835–1865). 2 vols. São Paulo: Companhia Editôra Nacional, 1941 (Brasiliana). Originally published in English as *Brazil and the Brazilians*. Philadelphia: Childs & Peterson, 1857.

Koseritz, Carl von. *Imagens do Brasil* (1851–1883). São Paulo: Livraria Martins, 1943. First published in book form in German as *Bilder aus Brasilien*. Leipzig and Berlin: 1885.

Lambert, Jacques. *Le Brésil: Structure sociale et Institutions politiques*. Paris: Armand Colin, 1953. Published in Portuguese as *Os Dois Brasis*. Rio de Janeiro: Ministério da Educação e Cultura, 1959.

Le Lannou, Maurice. *Le Brésil*. Paris: Armand Colin, 1955.

Mawe, John. *Viagens no Interior do Brasil* (1809–1810). Rio de Janeiro: Zélio Valverde, 1944. Originally published in English as *Travels in the Interior of Brazil, Particularly in the Gold and Diamond Districts of That Country*. London: Longman, Hurst, Rees, Orme & Brown, 1812.

Monbeig, Pierre. *Le Brésil*. Paris: Presses Universitaires, 1954.

———. *Pionniers et Planteurs de São Paulo*. Paris: Armand Colin, 1952.

Morazé, Charles. *Les Trois Ages du Brésil*. Paris: Armand Colin, 1954.

Ribeyrolles, Charles. *Brasil Pitoresco* (1858). 2 vols. Livraria Martins, 1941. The original French text, *Brésil pittoresque*, was published in a bilingual edition issued as *Brazil Pittoresco: História—Descripções—Viagens—Instituições—Colonisação*. Rio de Janeiro: Tipografia Nacional, 1859.

Rugendas, Johann Moritz. *Viagem Pitoresca através do Brasil* (1823–1825). São Paulo: Livraria Martins, 1940. Originally published in German as *Malerische Reise in Brasilien.* Paris: Engelmann et Cie., 1835.

Saint-Hilaire, Auguste de. *Segunda Viagem ao Interior do Brasil e Espírito Santo* (1820). São Paulo: Companhia Editôra Nacional, 1936 (Brasiliana). Originally published in French as *Deuxième Voyage à l'Intérieur du Brésil.* 1850 (Brasiliana Vol. 72).

————. *Segunda Viagem do Rio de Janeiro a Minas Gerais e a São Paulo* (1822). São Paulo: Companhia Editôra Nacional, 1938 (Brasiliana Vol. 5). Originally published in French.

————. *Viagem ao Rio Grande do Sul* (1820–1821). São Paulo: Companhia Editôra Nacional, 1939 (Brasiliana Vol. 167). Originally published in French as *Voyage à Rio Grande do Sul (Brésil).* Orléans: H. Herluison, 1887.

————. *Viagem à Província de São Paulo* (1819). São Paulo: Livraria Martins, 1940. Originally published in French as part of *Voyage dans les Provinces de Saint-Paul et de Sainte Catherine.* 2 vols. Paris: Arthur Bertrand, 1851.

————. *Viagem às Nascentes do Rio São Francisco e pela Província de Goiás* (1819). 2 vols. São Paulo: Companhia Editôra Nacional, 1944. Originally published in French as *Voyage aux Sources du Rio de São Francisco et dans le Province de Goiaz.* 2 vols. Paris: Arthur Bertrand, 1847–1848.

————. *Viagem pelas Províncias do Rio de Janeiro e Minas Gerais* (1816–1817). 2 vols. São Paulo: Companhia Editôra Nacional, 1938 (Brasiliana Vol. 126). Originally published in French as *Voyage dans les Provinces de Rio de Janeiro et Minas Geraes.* 2 vols. Paris: Grimbert et Dorez, 1830.

————. *Viagem pelo Distrito dos Diamantes e Litoral do Brasil* (1817). São Paulo: Companhia Editôra Nacional, 1941 (Brasiliana Vol. 126-A). Originally published in French as *Voyage dans le District des Diamants et sur le Littoral du Brésil.* 2 vols. Paris: Gide, 1833.

Smith, Herbert Huntington. *Do Rio de Janeiro a Cuiabá* (1870–1877). São Paulo: Mclhoramentos, 1922. (Written in Portuguese in 1866.)

Wagley, Charles. *Amazon Town: A Study of Man in the Tropics.* New York: Macmillan, 1953. Published in Portuguese as *Uma Comunidade Amazônica.* São Paulo: Companhia Editôra Nacional, 1957.

Wetherell, James. *Brazil: Stray Notes from Bahia.* Liverpool: Webb & Hunt, 1860.

Other Works Cited

A Arte de Furtar, edited by João Ribeiro. Rio de Janeiro: Garnier, 1928.

Potter, David M. *People of Plenty: Economic Abundance and the American Character.* Chicago: University of Chicago Press, 1954.

Riesman, David. *The Lonely Crowd: A Study of Changing American Character.* 3d printing. New Haven: Yale University Press, 1952.

Weber, Max. *The Protestant Ethic and the Spirit of Capitalism.* London: George Allen & Unwin, 1930.

PART II: NATIONAL ASPIRATIONS

Abreu, João Capistrano de. *Caminhos Antigos e Povoamento do Brasil.* Rio de Janeiro: Sociedade Capistrano de Abreu, 1930.
———. *Capítulos de História Colonial.* 4th ed. preparada por José Honório Rodrigues. Rio de Janeiro: Sociedade Capistrano de Abreu, 1954.
———. *Ensaios e Estudos.* 1 Série. Rio de Janeiro: Sociedade Capistrano de Abreu, 1931.
Accioly, Hildebrando. *O Reconhecimento da Independência do Brasil.* Rio de Janeiro: Imprensa Nacional, 1927.
"Agricultura no Nordeste," *Flagrantes Brasileiros,* No. 16 (1960), 28.
"A Alfabetização no Brasil Segundo o Censo de 1950," *Contribuições para o Estudo da Demografia no Brasil.* Rio de Janeiro: Instituto Brasileiro de Geografia e Estatística, Conselho Nacional de Estatística, 1961.
Amazonas, Ceçary. "Navegação Fluvial do Brasil," *Revista Brasileira de Geografia,* 21, No. 4 (outubro–dezembro 1959), 499–515.
Anais da Câmara dos Deputados. Rio de Janeiro: Imprensa Nacional, 1891–1930, 1934–1936. Rio de Janeiro and Brasília: Imprensa Nacional, 1946–1966.
Anais do Parlamento Brasileiro, 1826–1889. 253 vols. Rio de Janeiro: Imprensa Nacional, 1874–1889. (Title varies.)
Análise Estrutural da Economia Nordestina. Fortaleza: Banco do Nordeste do Brasil, 1956.
Anuário Estatístico do Brasil. ano 1, 1908–1912 (current). Published since 1938 by the Instituto Brasileiro de Geografia e Estatística.
"Aspectos da Lavra do Petróleo no Brasil," *Desenvolvimento e Conjuntura,* 16, No. 144 (dezembro 1959), 37–50.
Azevedo, Tales de. *Problemas Sociais da Exploração do Petróleo na Bahia.* Salvador: Imprensa Oficial, 1959.

Barbosa, Francisco de Assis. *J. K.: Uma Revisão na Política Brasileira.* Rio de Janeiro: José Olímpio, 1960.
Barbosa, Rui. *Reforma do Ensino Primário.* Rio de Janeiro: Imprensa Nacional, 1883. Republished as Vol. X, 1883, tome 1, *Obras Completas de Rui Barbosa.* Rio de Janeiro: Ministério da Educação e Saúde, 1947.
Bastos. *See* Tavares Bastos [i.e., Aureliano Cândido Tavares Bastos].
Benham, F. "Education and Economic Development in the Underdeveloped Countries," *International Affairs,* 35, No. 2 (April 1959), 180–187.
Bittencourt, Agnello. *Navegação da Amazônia & Portos da Amazônia.* SPVEA No. 8. Rio de Janeiro: Superintendência do Plano para a Valorização Econômica da Amazônia, 1959.
Bonfim, Sócrates. *Valorização da Amazônia e sua Comissão de Planejamento.* SPVEA No. 6. Rio de Janeiro: Superintendência do Plano para a Valorização Econômica da Amazônia, 1958.
Bouhid, Waldir. *Amazônia & Desenvolvimento.* Rio de Janeiro: Superintendência do Plano para a Valorização Econômica da Amazônia, 1959.
Bryce, James. *South America: Observations and Impressions.* London: Macmillan, 1912.

Câmara, Aristóteles de Lima, and Artur Hehl Neiva, "Colonização Nipônica e Germânica no Sul do Brasil," *Revista de Imigração e Colonização,* 2, No. 1 (janeiro 1941), 39–119.

Carneiro, José Fernandes. *Imigração e Colonização no Brasil.* Rio de Janeiro: Universidade do Brasil, 1950.

Carvalho, Orlando M. "Os Partidos Políticos em Minas Gerais," *Segundo Seminário de Estudos Mineiros.* Belo Horizonte: 1956.

Castro, Josué de. *Geografia da Fome: A Fome no Brasil.* Rio de Janeiro: Emprêsa Gráfica "O Cruzeiro," 1946. Published in English as *The Geography of Hunger.* Boston: Little, Brown, 1952.

Coleção das Leis do Brasil. Rio de Janeiro and Brasília: Imprensa Régia and Imprensa Nacional, 1808————.

Comentários. Rio de Janeiro: Ministério da Educação e Cultura, 1961.

Conjuntura Econômica, 15, No. 12 (dezembro 1961); 16, No. 3 (março 1962).

"A Correspondência do Barão de Wenzel de Mareschal," *Revista do Instituto Histórico e Geográfico Brasileiro.* Rio de Janeiro.

Couto. *See* Loreto Couto, Domingos do.

Couto. *See* Ribeiro Couto [i.e., Rui Ribeiro Couto].

Cunha, Euclides da [i.e., Euclides Rodrigues Pimenta da]. *Os Sertões.* Rio de Janeiro: Laemmert & Cia., 1902. Published in English as *Rebellion in the Backlands,* translated by Samuel Putnam. Chicago: University of Chicago Press, 1944.

Development of Information Media in Underdeveloped Countries: Report by the Director-General of the United Nations Educational, Scientific and Cultural Organization. New York: United Nations Economic and Social Council, 31st Session, January 19, 1961.

Diálogos das Grandezas do Brasil. Rio de Janeiro: Publicações da Academia Brasileira, 1930.

Diário do Congresso Nacional, 17 janeiro 1961.

Dias. *See* Gonçalves Dias, Antônio.

Diegues Júnior, Manuel. *Etnias e Culturas no Brasil.* Rio de Janeiro: Ministério da Educação e Saúde, 1956.

Documents on German Foreign Policy, 1918–1945. Washington, D.C.: United States Department of State, 1953.

La Estructura Demográfica de las Naciones Americanas: Vol. 4, Analfabetismo y Nivel de Educación. Washington, D.C.: Pan American Union, 1960.

Falas do Trono desde o Ano de 1823 até o Ano de 1889. Rio de Janeiro: Imprensa Nacional, 1889.

Faoro, Raimundo. *Os Donos do Poder: Formação do Patronato Político Brasileiro.* Pôrto Alegre: Globo, 1958.

Fernandes, Gerson. "História da Descoberta do Petróleo no Recôncavo Baiano," *Boletim Geográfico,* 16, No. 144 (maio–junho 1958), 390–393.

Freyre, Gilberto [i.e., Gilberto de Melo Freyre]. *Brazil: An Interpretation.* New York: Knopf, 1945. Published in Portuguese as *Interpretação do Brasil.* Rio de Janeiro: José Olímpio, 1947.

Furtado, Celso. *A Operação Nordeste*. Rio de Janeiro: Instituto Superior de Estudos Brasileiros, 1959.

Gauld, Charles A. *The Last Titan: Percival Farquhar, 1864–1953*. Stanford: Stanford University Press, 1964.

Gonçalves Dias, Antônio. "Relatório sôbre a Instrução Pública," *Publicações do Arquivo Nacional*, 39 (1957), 345.

Handelmann, Heinrich. *História do Brasil*, translated by Lúcia Furquim Lahmeyer. Published in *Revista do Instituto Histórico e Geográfico Brasileiro*. Vol. 162, t. 108. 1931. Originally published in German as *Geschichte von Brasilien*. Berlin: Julius Springer, 1860.

Hill, Lawrence Francis. *Diplomatic Relations between the United States and Brazil*. Durham: Duke University Press, 1932.

Hillman, Jimmye S. *O Desenvolvimento Econômico e o Nordeste Brasileiro*. Fortaleza: Banco do Nordeste do Brasil, 1956 (mimeographed).

Horta, Cid Rebêlo. *Famílias Governamentais de Minas Gerais*. Belo Horizonte: Segundo Seminário de Estudos Mineiros, 1956.

Hupé, Robert Strausz, and Harry W. Hazard. *The Idea of Colonialism*. New York: F. A. Praeger, 1958.

Huszar, G. B. de (ed.). *National Strategy in an Age of Revolutions*. New York: Praeger, 1959.

Hutchinson, Harry William. *Village and Plantation Life in Northeastern Brazil*. Seattle: University of Washington Press, 1957.

"Indústria de Petróleo," *Conjuntura Econômica*, 15, No. 10 (outubro 1961), 73–81.

Knowlton, Clark S. *Sírios e Libaneses*. São Paulo: Anhambi, 1960.

Lambert, Jacques. *Le Brésil: Structure sociale et Institutions politiques*. Paris: Armand Colin, 1953 Published in Portuguese as *Os Dois Brasis*. Rio de Janeiro: Ministério da Educação e Cultura, 1959.

Leloup, Yves. "Energia Elétrica na América do Sul," *Conjuntura Econômica*, 15, No. 12 (dezembro 1961), 83–90.

——. "A Produção de Energia Elétrica no Brasil," *Boletim Geográfico*, 19, No. 163 (julho–agôsto 1961), 469–482.

Lipson, Leslie. "Government in Contemporary Brazil," *Canadian Journal of Economics and Political Science*, 22, No. 2 (May 1956), 189.

Loreto Couto, Domingos do. "Desagravos do Brasil e Glórias de Pernambuco," *Anais da Biblioteca Nacional*. Rio de Janeiro: 1904.

Lourenco Filho, Manuel Bergström. "Educação, 1889–1941," in Ruben Borba de Morais and William Berrien, *Manual Bibliográfico de Estudos Brasileiros*. Rio de Janeiro: Gráfica Editôra Souza, 1949.

Manchester, Alan Krebs. *British Preeminence in Brazil*. Chapel Hill: University of North Carolina Press, 1933.

Manning, William Ray. *Diplomatic Correspondence of the United States con-*

cerning the Independence of the Latin American Nations. New York: Oxford University Press, 1925.

Mendonça, Salvador Menezes Drummond Furtado de. *Imigração Chinesa.* Rio de Janeiro: n.p., 1882.

———. *Trabalhadores Asiáticos,* New York: Tip. do Novo Mundo, 1879.

Menezes, Adriano. *O Problema da Colonização da Amazônia.* SPVEA No. 7. Rio de Janeiro: Superintendência do Plano para a Valorização Econômica da Amazônia, 1961.

Mensagens Presidenciais. Rio de Janeiro and Brasília: Imprensa Nacional, 1891–1931, 1933, 1935–1937, 1946–1966.

Ministério de Agricultura. *A Política Indigenista Brasileira.* Rio de Janeiro: Serviço de Informação Agrícola, 1962.

Miranda. *See* Pontes de Miranda [i.e., Francisco Cavalcanti Pontes de Miranda].

Moacyr, Primitivo. *A Instrução e as Províncias.* 3 vols. São Paulo: Companhia Editôra Nacional, 1939–1940 (Brasiliana Vols. 147. 147–A, 147–B).

———. *A Instrução e o Império.* 3 vols. São Paulo: Companhia Editôra Nacional, 1936–1938 (Brasiliana Vols. 66, 87, 121).

Monbeig, Pierre. *Quelques Traits géographiques de l'Amérique latine.* Paris: Centre de la Documentation Universitaire, 1954.

Monteiro, Tobias [i.e., Tobias do Rêgo Monteiro]. *História do Imperio: A Elaboração da Independência.* Rio de Janeiro: Briguiet, 1927.

Morais, Luciano Jacques de. "Os Recursos Naturais do Vale do Rio Doce," *Boletim da Sociedade Brasileira de Geografia,* 1, No. 3 (novembro–dezembro 1950).

Morais, Ruben Borba de, and William Berrien. *Manual Bibliográfico de Estudos Brasileiros.* Rio de Janeiro: Gráfica Editôra Souza, 1949.

Mortara, Giorgio. "A População do Brasil e seu Desenvolvimento nos Últimos 125 Anos," *Boletim Geográfico,* 19, No. 161 (março–abril 1961), 271–272.

Muller, Antônio Rubio, and Hiroshi Saito. *Memórias do I Painel Nipo-Brasileiro.* 2 vols. São Paulo: Escola de Sociologia e Política de São Paulo, 1956.

Murta, Domício de Figueiredo. "Nota Prévia sôbre a Estrutura Agrária de Minas Gerais," *Revista Brasileira de Ciências Sociais,* 1, No. 1 (novembro 1961), 62–78.

Neiva, Artur Hehl. "A Imigração e Colonização no Govêrno Vargas," *Cultura Política,* No. 21 (novembro 1942).

Nery, Frederico José Sant'Anna. "Instruction publique," *Le Brésil en 1889.* Paris: Lib. Charles Delagrave, 1889.

"Nota sôbre a Vida Média Brasileira nos Diversos Estados do Brasil," *Contribuições para o Estudo da Demografia do Brasil.* Rio de Janeiro: Instituto Brasileiro de Geografia e Estatística, Conselho Nacional de Estatística, 1961.

Oliveira, Franklin de. *Rio Grande do Sul: Um Nôvo Nordeste.* Rio de Janeiro: Civilização Brasileira, 1960.

Oliveira, José Manuel Cardoso de. *Atos Diplomáticos do Brasil.* 2 vols. Rio de Janeiro: Jornal do Commercio, 1912.

Oliveira Viana [i.e., Francisco José Oliveira Viana]. *Evolução do Povo Brasileiro.* 2d ed. São Paulo: Companhia Editôra Nacional, 1933 (Brasiliana Vol. 10).

———. *O Ocaso do Império.* 2d ed. São Paulo: Melhoramentos, n.d.

————. *Populações Meridionais do Brasil.* 3d ed. São Paulo: Companhia Editôra Nacional, 1933 (Basiliana Vol. 8).
Organizações e Programas Ministeriais. Rio de Janeiro: Imprensa Nacional, 1899. 2d ed. Rio de Janeiro: Arquivo Nacional, 1962.
[Pinheiro, José Pedro Xavier]. *Importação de Trabalhadores Chins.* Rio de Janeiro: n.p., 1869.
Pinotti, Mário. *Vida e Morte do Brasileiro.* Rio de Janeiro: Civilização Brasileira, 1959.
Pinto, Antônio Pereira. *Apontamentos para o Direito Internacional.* 4 vols. Rio de Janeiro: F. L. Pinto & Cia., 1864–1869.
Pontes de Miranda [i.e., Francisco Cavalcanti Pontes de Miranda]. "Preliminares para a Revisão Constitucional," *À Margem da História da República.* Rio de Janeiro: Anuário do Brasil, 1924.

Rebouças, André. *Garantia de Juros: Estudo para sua Aplicação às Emprêsas de Utilidade Pública no Brasil.* Rio de Janeiro: Tipografia Nacional, 1874.
Recuperação de um Vale. Documentário No. 3. Rio de Janeiro: Comissão do Vale do São Francisco.
"A Recuperação de um Vale," *Observador Econômico,* No. 170 (março 1950), and No. 240/241 (fevereiro-março 1956).
Rêgo, Luís Flôres de Morais. *O Vale do São Francisco.* Rio de Janeiro: Sociedade Capistrano de Abreu, 1936.
Reis, Artur César Ferreira. *A Amazônia e a Cobiça Internacional.* São Paulo: Companhia Editôra Nacional, 1960.
Relatório do Ministério . . . (Reports have been published by various of the ministries headed by cabinet members since 1831.) Rio de Janeiro and Brasília: Imprensa Nacional.
Represamento do São Francisco, Dois Irmãos e Pirapora. Rio de Janeiro: Comissão do Vale do São Francisco, 1958.
"Retrospecto Parcial da Economia Brasileira nos Últimos Vinte Anos," *Desenvolvimento e Conjuntura,* 5, No. 7 (julho 1961).
Ribeiro, Darcy. *Língua e Culturas Indígenas do Brasil.* Rio de Janeiro: Centro de Pesquisas Educacionais, n.d.
Ribeiro Couto [i.e., Rui Ribeiro Couto]. "O Problema da Nacionalização," *Revista de Imigração e Colonização,* 2, No. 1 (janeiro 1941), 18–34.
Robock, Stephan H. *Projeto de Planejamento Global para o Nordeste do Brasil.* Fortaleza: Banco do Nordeste do Brasil, 1955.
Rodrigues, José Honório. *Brasil e África: Outro Horizonte.* 2 vols. Rio de Janeiro: Civilização Brasileira, 1961. 2d ed. Rio de Janeiro: Civilização Brasileira, 1964. Published in English as *Brazil and Africa.* Berkeley: University of California Press, 1965.
————. "Civilização, Palavra e Conceito," *Diário de Notícias* (Rio de Janeiro), 24 maio 1953.
————. *Conciliação e Reforma no Brasil: Um Desafio Histórico-Político.* Rio de Janeiro: Civilização Brasileira, 1965.
Rogers, Edward J. "Brazil's Rio Doce Valley Project," *Journal of Inter-American Studies,* 1, No. 2 (April 1959), 123–140.
Romero, Sílvio [i.e., Sílvio Vasconcelos de Silveira Ramos Romero]. *O Alema-*

nismo no Sul do Brasil: Seus Perigos e Meios de os Conjurar. Rio de Janeiro: Heitor Ribeiro & Cia., 1908.

Saito, Hiroshi. *O Japonês no Brasil.* São Paulo: Editôra Sociologia e Política, 1961.

Sampaio, Teodoro. *O Rio São Francisco e a Chapada Diamantina* (originally published in the *Revista Santa Cruz* [São Paulo], 1906). Bahia: Editôra Cruzeiro, 1938 (Col. Estudos Brasileiros).

Santos, Clemente José dos [Baron São Clemente]. *Documentos para a História das Côrtes Gerais da Nação Portuguêsa.* Lisbon: Imprensa Nacional, 1833–1899.

Santos, José Maria dos. *A Política Geral do Brasil.* São Paulo: J. Magalhães, 1930.

São Clemente. *See* Santos, Clemente José dos [Baron São Clemente].

Schurz, William Lyttle. *This New World: The Civilization of Latin America.* New York: Dutton, 1954.

Sinopse Estatística do Ensino Médio. Rio de Janeiro: Ministério da Educação e Cultura, Serviço de Estatística da Educação e Cultura, 1961.

Sinopse Estatística do Ensino Superior, 1960. Rio de Janeiro: Ministério da Educação e Cultura, Serviço de Estatística da Educação e Cultura, 1961.

Sinopse Estatística do Ensino Superior, 1962. Rio de Janeiro: Ministério da Educação e Cultura, Serviço de Estatística da Educação e Cultura, 1963.

Soares, Armando. "Da Pequena para a Grande Siderurgia," *Correio da Manhã* (Rio de Janeiro), 15 junho 1951.

Sousa, Otávio Tarqüínio de. *José Bonifácio, 1763–1838.* Rio de Janeiro. José Olímpio, 1945.

Strauch, Lourdes Magalhães de Matos. "Atividades Econômicas da Região Sul," *Boletim Geográfico,* No. 145 (1958), 507–515.

Strauch, Ney. *Zona Metalúrgica de Minas Gerais e Vale do Rio Doce.* Rio de Janeiro: Conselho Nacional de Geografia, 1958.

Tavares Bastos [i.e., Aureliano Cândido Tavares Bastos]. *Os Males do Presente e as Esperanças do Futuro.* Rio de Janeiro: Tip. de Quirino e Irmão, 1861. 2d ed. São Paulo: Companhia Editôra Nacional, 1939 (Brasiliana Vol. 151).

———. *A Província: Estudo sôbre a Descentralização no Brasil.* Rio de Janeiro: Garnier, 1870. 2d ed. São Paulo: Companhia Editôra Nacional, 1937 (Brasiliana Vol. 105).

———. *O Vale do Amazonas.* Rio de Janeiro: Garnier, 1866. 2d ed. São Paulo: Companhia Editôra Nacional, 1937 (Brasiliana Vol. 106).

Teixeira, Anísio. "Inquérito sôbre Diretrizes e Bases," *Diário de Notícias* (Rio de Janeiro), May 13, 1962.

Tigner, James L. "Shindō Remmei, Japanese Nationalism in Brazil," *Hispanic American Historical Review,* 41, No. 4 (November 1961), 515–532.

Toynbee, Arnold. *A Study of History.* 12 vols. Oxford University Press, 1943–1954.

Valverde, Orlando. *A Velha Imigração Italiana e sua Influência na Agricultura e na Economia do Brasil.* Rio de Janeiro: Serviço Social da Indústria, 1959.

Vargas, Getúlio [i.e., Getúlio Dorneles Vargas]. *A Nova Política do Brasil.* Vol. 1. Rio de Janeiro: José Olímpio, 1941.

Viana. *See* Oliveira Viana [i.e., Francisco José Oliveira Viana].

Vieira, Antônio. "Sermão da Visitação de Nossa Senhora," *Padre Antônio Vieira:*

Sermões Pregados no Brasil, edited by Hernani Cidade. Lisbon: Agência Geral das Colónias, 1940.

Wagley, Charles (ed.). *Race and Culture in Brazil.* Paris: UNESCO, 1952.
Waibel, Leo. *Capítulos de Geografia Tropical e do Brasil.* Rio de Janeiro: Instituto Brasileiro de Geografia e Estatística, 1958.
Webb, Walter Prescott. *The Great Frontier.* Boston: Houghton Mifflin, 1952.
Webster, Charles. *Britain and the Independence of Latin America, 1812–1830.* 2 vols. Oxford: Oxford University Press, 1938.
Willems, Emílio. *Aculturação dos Alemães no Brasil.* Rio de Janeiro: Companhia Editôra Nacional, 1946.
———. *Assimilação e Populações Marginais no Brasil.* São Paulo: Companhia Editôra Nacional, 1940.

PART III: THE PERMANENT AND THE TRANSITORY:
A SUMMING UP

Ahumada, Jorge. "Economic Development and Problems of Social Change in Latin America." Paris: UNESCO, 1961. Summarized and analyzed in *Desenvolvimento e Conjuntura,* 5, No. 8 (agôsto 1961), 70.
"Alguns Retrospectos de 1964," *Desenvolvimento e Conjuntura,* 9, No. 2 (fevereiro 1965), 7.
Anais do Parlamento Brasileiro, 1826–1889. 253 vols. Rio de Janeiro: Imprensa Nacional, 1874–1889. (Title varies.)
Andrade. *See* Drummond de Andrade, Carlos.

Drummond de Andrade, Carlos. "Explicação," *Alguma Poesia.* Belo Horizonte: Edições Pindorama, 1930.

La Estructura Demográfica de las Naciones Americanas: Vol. 4, Analfabetismo y Nivel de Educación. Washington, D.C.: Pan American Union, 1960.
Estudio Económico de América Latina, 1960. Santiago, Chile: Comisión Económica para la América Latina, 1961 (mimeographed).

Mortara, Giorgio. *Contribuições para o Estudo da Demografia do Brasil.* Rio de Janeiro: Instituto Brasileiro de Geografia e Estatística, Conselho Nacional de Estatística, 1961.

"Panorama do Ano," *Desenvolvimento e Conjuntura,* 10, No. 2 (fevereiro 1966), 3–4.
The Population of South America. New York: United Nations, 1955.

Report on the World Social Situation. New York: United Nations, 1961.
"Retrospecto Parcial da Economia Brasileira nos Últimos Vinte Anos," *Desenvolvimento e Conjuntura,* 5, No. 7 (julho 1961).
Rodrigues, José Honório. *Notícia de Vária História.* Rio de Janeiro: Livraria São José, 1951.
VII Recenseamento Geral do Brasil, 1960. Censo Demográfico. Resultados Preliminares. Rio de Janeiro: Instituto Brasileiro de Geografia e Estatística, Serviço Nacional de Recenseamento, n.d.

The United Nations Development Decade. New York: United Nations, 1962.

INDEX

Abreu, João Capistrano de: on influence of Brazilian interior, xiv–xv; historiography of, xvii–xviii and n.; on Luís Alves de Lima e Silva, xxiii; on Brazilian revolts, 14; on "castrated" Brazilians, 24; compared with José Bonifácio, 35; on colonial Brazil, 37, 38, 42, 71; on Indian indolence, 41; on evolution of national characteristics, 56; on Brazilian independence, 72, 129; on Rio de Janeiro, 82; on regional dominances, 83–84; mentioned, 36
"Accusation by the People": 64
Acesita (company): 122
Acre (state): Brazil incorporates, 76 and n.; economic development of, 87
Afonso Arinos Law: 99
Afonso Celso (Afonso Celso de Assis Figueiredo Júnior): boastful attitude of, viii, ix, 57 n.; mentioned, 36
Agassiz, Louis: on Brazilian provincial administration, 45; on emancipation, 48; on Amazon region, 52
Alagoas (state): fugitive slaves in, 11 n.; uncultivated land in, 113; literacy in, 135. SEE ALSO Palmares
Albania: national income in, 154
Alcântara Machado: 37
Alemanismo no Sul do Brasil: Seus Perigos e Meios de os Conjurar, 0: 96
"Alfaiates," revolt of the: 13 n., 42 n.
Algeria: French immigrants to Brazil from, 99
All Saints Bay: 128
Álvares, Diogo. SEE "Caramuru"
Alves, Landulfo: refinery named for, 127
Alves Branco Tariff: 120 n.
Amado, Gilberto: on Brazilian voting, 63
Amapá (territory): economic development of, 87; malaria in, 150
Amazonas (state): population of, 78; economic development of, 86–87; language in, 91, 100; Indians in, 99
Amazon River: navigation of, 89

————, region of: backwardness of, 51–52; settlement of, 75, 77, 89, 98; rubber in, 76 n.; development of, 78, 79, 86–87; danger represented by, 79; income in, 88
American and Foreign Power Company: 125
American and Foreign Power Corporation: 125 n.
AMFORP: 125 n.
Andes Mountains: x
Andrada, Antônio Carlos Ribeiro de: on Brazilian government, 106; realism of, 109
Andrada, Martim Francisco Ribeiro de. SEE Ribeiro de Andrada, Martim Francisco
Andrade, Carlos Drummond de. SEE Drummond de Andrade, Carlos
Andreoni, Giovanni Antonio. SEE Antonil, André João
Angostura: Bolívar at, 11
Ankarloo, M. de: xxii–xxiii
Antonil, André João (Giovanni Antonio Andreoni): nativism of, vii; on Brazilian hierarchy, 39; book by, confiscated, 39 n.; on Brazilian riches, 56
Araguaia River: navigation of, 89
Aranha, José Pereira da Graça. SEE Graça Aranha, José Pereira da
Argentina: comparisons of, to Brazil, 54, 94, 137, 152, 153, 155 (Fig. 2); natives of, expelled from Brazil, 75
Aristotle: on middle class, 104
Armitage, John: on the Lima e Silvas, xxiii
Arte de Furtar, A: 47, 62
"Art of Stealing, The". SEE *Arte de Furtar, A*
Araújo Lima, Pedro de (Marquis of Olinda): conspiracy against, xxiii; backs emperor's right to choose ministers, 107
Assis, Machado de. SEE Machado de Assis, Joaquim Maria
Assis Chateaubriand, Francisco de. SEE

ways to, 89; settlers from, in pioneer
zones, 95–96; agrarian structure of,
113; special interests of, 118; Iron and
Steel Company of, 122; hydroelectric
plants in, 126
Ministry of Education: 139
Ministry of Education and Health, 134,
141
Ministry of Finance: 106
Ministry of Health: 141
Ministry of the Empire: 106, 107
Miranda, Francisco Pontes de. SEE Pontes
de Miranda, Francisco
miscegenation. SEE *caiados*; Indians; Ne-
groes; slavery
Monbeig, Pierre: on Brazilian dynamism,
51; repeats Lambert's thesis, 52; on
Brazilian need for history, 55
Monteiro, Tobias: on Brazilian monarchy,
72
Moog, Clodomir Viana: contrasted with
Dias Gomes, 11–12; mentioned, 37
Morais, José Manuel de: arrests José Boni-
fácio, xxii
Morais [Barros], Prudente [José] de:
election of, 114; composure of regime of,
118
Morazé, Charles: repeats Lambert's thesis,
52
mulattoes. SEE Negroes
Muller, Filinto: 99 n.
Murtinho, Joaquim: financial consolida-
tion by, 90 n.
mutirão: 60 n.

Nabuco de Araújo, José Tomás: on Bra-
zilian oligarchy, 110
Napoleon. SEE Bonaparte, Napoleon
National Democratic Union (UDN): error
of, xxii; conservatism of, 16, 18–19, 20;
disbanded, 17 n.; fear by, of Commun-
ism, 23
National Department of Public Health:
141
National Institute for Immigration and
Settlement: 98
National Iron and Steel Company: 122
National Nutrition Commission: 150
Nazis: use of moral indignation by, 104
Negroes: contribution of, to Brazilian cul-
ture, viii, xviii, 9, 12, 37, 38, 40, 54;
brought to Brazil, x; decay of culture
of, 10; settle Palmares, 11 n.; insurrec-

tions by, 13, 42; skill in controlling, 15;
social status of, 39, 48, 91, 93, 94, 101;
miscegenation with, 39, 48, 50, 91, 92,
93; bring up children, 45; skill of, in
agriculture, 96; in Minas Gerais, 111
Negro River: navigation of, 89
Netherlands, The: Brazil's war against, 39
and n., 71, 75; subjects of, leave Indonesia for Brazil, 98
Neutral Municipality: education in, 134 n.
Neves, Tancredo: 124 n.
newspapers. SEE press
New York City: financial resources of, 119
New Zealand: electric power production
by, 127
Nicaragua: literacy in, 152; economic development of, 153; national income in,
154
Northeast, the: sugar planters of, xi; revolt in, 14 n.; bandit activity in, 14 and
n.; improved standard of living sought
in, 21; Dutch control of, 39 n.; lack of
immigration to, 48–49; ruralism of, 55;
drought in, 76 n., 87; development of,
79, 85–86, 87, 119 n.; colonial predominance of, 84; poverty of, 88, 150; settlers from, in Brazilian pioneer zones,
95–96; regionalism of, 100; political influence of, 111; uncultivated land in,
113; famines in, 140–141; population of,
148–149

oil. SEE petroleum
Olinda, Marquis of. SEE Araújo Lima,
Pedro de
Olinda, Pernambuco: education in, 131
and n.
Oliveira Viana, Francisco José: on Rio de
Janeiro's unifying force, 82; on Bra-
zilian Aryanization, 93; on Brazil's lack
of class struggle, 101: mentioned, 37
Otaviano [de Almeida Rosa], Francisco:
on changeability of politicians, 109
Ouro Prêto, Minas Gerais: education in,
130
Overseas, Council for: 82

Pacaá-novo Indians: 92
Pakistan: heterogeneity of, 100; education
in, 154
Palmares: fugitive slave colony at, 11 n.,
40 n.
Palmares War: 11 and n., 13

72, 76, 81–82, 111, 129–130, 131, 133, 140; royal family of, takes refuge in Brazil, x–xi, 81; influence of, on Brazilian culture, xviii, 9, 37, 46, 53, 62, 66, 116; constitutional assembly criticizes, xxii n.; influence of, on Brazilian retail trade, 44; Brazilian independence from, 53 and n., 56, 72, 73 and n., 110; immigration to Brazil from, 54, 94, 99; deportation of loyalists to, 74; significance of birth in, 90, 91; preference in, for dark-skinned women, 92; Brazil assumes debt of, 120; university in, 130 and n.; education efforts by, 152; national income in, 154

Portuguese (language): 41, 91, 96, 100
Potter, David: on economic abundance, 58
Prado, Paulo: viii, ix, 37
"Praieira" Rebellion: 14 and n.
Prata, Rio da. SEE River Plate
press: as source of history, 7; lack of, 40, 41 and n.; immaturity of Brazilian, 47; freedom of, 49, 129; glorification of business and industrial leaders by, 58; tax system criticized in, 114
Prieto, César: criticizes tax bill, 114
PRM. SEE Republican Party of Minas
Proença, M. Cavalcanti: bibliography by, 7
Progresso, O: 114
PSB. SEE Socialist Party, Brazilian
PSD. SEE Social Democratic Party
PSP. SEE Social Progressive Party
PTB. SEE Brazilian Labor Party
Puerto Rico: comparisons of, with Brazil, 155 (Fig. 2)
puxirão: 60 n.

Quadros, Jânio: described, 28–29 and n.; election of, 114; on Doce River Valley Company, 124 n.
Queiroz, Eusébio de: called "permanent Governor General of Brazil," 120

race. SEE Afanso Arinos Law; *caiado*; Indians; Negroes; slavery
radio: 17, 55, 58, 138
Rafael, Abel: calls for land grants to Indians, 99
Ragamuffin Rebellion. SEE Farrapos Rebellion
Rangel, Alberto: xxiii
Rebellion in the Backlands: 86

Rebouças, André: on São Paulo, 84; race of, 94
Recife, Pernambuco: revolt in, 13–14 and n.
"Recollections and Notes": 130
Reis, Artur César Ferreira: on Amazon region, 79
religion: disestablishment of, xi; voodoo, 9, 11; in colonial Brazil, 38 and n.; as related to social class, 44, 48 and n., 91; toleration of, 49; homogeneity of Brazilian, 60; as related to democracy, 60–61; holidays of, 64; of Japanese immigrants, 97; in Asia, 100; education controlled by, 129; as related to economic growth, 151
Republican Manifesto of 1870: 117 and n.
Republican Party of Minas: oligarchic rule of, 112
Revolt of the Alfaiates: 13 n., 42 n.
Ribeiro (de Andrade), João (Batista): historiography of, xvii–xviii; studies regions, 83; term coined by, 147; mentioned, 36
Ribeiro de Andrada, Antônio Carlos. SEE Andrada, Antônio Carlos Ribeiro de
Ribeiro de Andrada, Martim Francisco: on education, 131
Ribeyrolles, Charles: on Parliament, 49
Riesman, David: concept by, of national character, 5–6, 36; on basic personality, 9; on traditional societies, 46
Rio Branco, Baron (José Maria da Silva Paranhos): integrates Brazilian territory, 77 and n.
Rio Branco, Viscount (José Maria da Silva Paranhos): cabinet headed by, 107; on political parties, 109
Rio de Janeiro (city): Portuguese royal family in, x–xi; Bay of, 14; Pedro I remains in, 53; notaries of, 61 n.; *caiados* of, 63; independence movement in, 72; as settlement nucleus, 75, 79; becomes capital, 76, 117 n.; improvements in 80–81; as unifying force, 81–82, 83, 117 and n.; railways from, 89; distance of Furnas from, 126; electric power consumption in, 127; education in, 129, 130, 131; population of, 149, 150
Rio de Janeiro (state): political influence of, xi, 84, 111, 112
Río de la Plata. SEE River Plate